THE CITY, THE DUKE AND THEIR BANKER

SEUH

VII

Studies in European Urban History (1100-1800)

Series Editor

Marc BOONE

(Ghent University)

The City, the Duke and their Banker

The Rapondi Family and the Formation of the Burgundian State (1384–1430)

Bart Lambert

BREPOLS

Under the auspices of the 'Interuniversity Attraction Poles Programme (Phase V nr. 10) - Belgian State - Federal Office for Scientific, Technical and Cultural Affairs' Programme

The author is a Research Assistant of the Research Foundation-Flanders

The master's thesis on which this book is based was awarded with the Dexia Prize for History 2005

Cover illustration: The Rapondi brothers worshipping the *Volto Santo* of Lucca. Frontpage *Leggenda del Volto Santo in Francese* (Vatican City, Biblioteca Apostolica Vaticana, Cod. Pal. Lat. 1988, f° 1 v°)

D/2006/0095/94

ISBN 2-503-52025-1

Printed in the E.U. on acid-free paper

TABLE OF CONTENTS

PREFACE

The years between 1300 and 1460 are commonly known as a period of economic crisis. Despite constant disagreement among historians about the causes and the gravity of the depression,[1] it is generally accepted that periodic famine, endemic warfare and the first outbreaks of what was to be called the Black Death halted or even reversed the steady growth that the European economy had known during the two previous centuries. The background against which economic activities were conducted changed drastically, dominated by serious disruptions and severe depopulation.[2] The world of international trade and finance suffered particularly hard from the crisis. War, disease and the many impediments they brought along, such as blockades and embargoes, gravely affected the work of medieval businessmen, the 'certainty of uncertainty' often being the only thing left for them to rely on.[3]

One of the activities that a growing number of these merchants had engaged in throughout previous decades was lending money to princes. Italians in particular had considered the courts, to whom they supplied luxury goods, as attractive outlets for their idle capital. Their funds had been welcomed by rulers in France, England and the Low Countries, whose political ambitions required larger and larger amounts of money. However, when fortune went against them, as it did increasingly from the beginning of the fourteenth century, the guarantees that the money-lenders had been given as an assurance of getting their capital back proved very conditional. Although the princes' involvement in the failure of some firms has been overestimated, investments in government finance were disastrous for innumerable fourteenth- and fifteenth-century businesses, whether they were one-man enterprises or colossal companies. Contemporaries, such as the Orlandini of Bruges, were convinced that "no-one ever becomes embroiled with great lords without losing his feathers in the end".[4] Similar views were held by later historians such as Richard Kaeuper, author of a study on the Riccardi, bankers to Edward II, who stated that "looking at the fate of merchant-bankers who entered government service between the fourteenth and the sixteenth centuries it is logical to conclude that, however seductive the profits and privileges awaiting the king's bankers, the relationship was inevitably fatal to them".[5]

Not all money-lenders to the crown in this period lost their feathers though. Among those who did not were the Rapondi, the subject of this book. This family, active in Bruges but originating from the Italian city of Lucca, achieved a career of more than thirty years in the money-lending business, ending with encomiums of princely praise instead of banktruptcy. Their success, and especially its continuity, has drawn the attention of more than one historian. The first of these, and so far the only one to devote an entire study to the

[1] For a bibliographical survey, see G. BOIS, *La grande dépression médiévale: XIV-XVe siècles. Le précédent d'une crise systémique*, Paris, Presses Universitaires de France, 2000, 211 p.
[2] E.S. HUNT and J.M. MURRAY, *A history of business in Medieval Europe, 1200-1550*, Cambridge, Cambridge University Press, 1999, pp. 125-128.
[3] E.S. HUNT and J.M. MURRAY, *A history of business*, p. 149.
[4] R. DE ROOVER, *Money, banking and credit in medieval Bruges. Italian Merchant-Bankers, Lombards and Money-Changers. A Study in the Origins of Banking*, Cambridge (Massachusetts), The Medieval Academy of America, 1948, p. 88.
[5] R. W. KAEUPER, *Bankers to the Crown. The Riccardi of Lucca and Edward I*, Princeton (New Jersey), Princeton University Press, 1973, pp. 248-249.

Rapondi, was Léon Mirot, in 1928. In an issue of his *Études Lucquoises*, he published a very detailed story of the family, based on an enormous amount of material, published and unpublished.[6]

Although not always that accurate, Mirot's work has remained the main source on the activities of this Lucchese company up until today. The prominent bank historian Raymond De Roover used his findings to emphasize the Rapondis' contribution to the Bruges money market.[7] The family's importance for the reigns of Philip the Bold and John the Fearless was demonstrated by Richard Vaughan, the biographer of the four Burgundian dukes.[8] Andrée van Nieuwenhuysen shed light on the Rapondis' role in Philip the Bold's finances.[9] Each of these historians, a few among many, provided very valuable insights into the family's history and each was aware of its remarkable achievement. De Roover, for example, stressed that "Dino", the most famous Rapondi, "did not share the fate of a great many others who went banktrupt because of their loans to princes".[10] None of these authors, however, was able to say exactly why this merchant company had succeeded and so many others had failed. It is the aim of this book to do so.

As the Rapondi company was most successful when it maintained simultaneous relations with the city of Bruges and the duke of Burgundy, these bonds are the main subject of the book. Relations with Bruges were reconstructed from material from the Bruges City Archives, including the city accounts and the charter collection for the period 1360 to 1470. As for the family's bonds with the duke, the findings are based on research in the accounts of the *Recette Générale de Flandres* and the *Recette Générale de Toutes les Finances* for the period 1405 to 1415, complementing Van Nieuwenhuysen's work on the reign of Philip the Bold and the published accounts for the last three years of John the Fearless' rule.[11] These documents were consulted in the *Archives Départementales du Nord* in Lille and in the Ghent University Library, where microfilms of the accounts from the *Archives Départementales du Côte d'Or* are kept. Additional data was provided by sources preserved in the Episcopal Archives in Bruges, the *Archivio di Stato* in Florence and the Borromei Family Archives on Isola Bella.

The result of this research is a mainly chronological story, for the most part taking place in Bruges but dealing with the Rapondis' activities elsewhere in Europe as well. It runs from 1360 until 1470, the first twenty-five years of which are told in the first part, illustrating how the bonds with the city and the duke were established. A second part covers the next forty-five years, in which these bonds ensured the family's success. How the relations with the city and the duke were abandoned and the Rapondi disappeared from the foreground during the final forty years, is shown in the third part. Preceded by an introduction to the economic and political context in late medieval Bruges and followed by a

[6] L. MIROT, "La société des Raponde. Dine Raponde" in : *Bibliothèque de l'Ecole des Chartes*, Paris, 1928, 89, pp. 299-389.

[7] R. DE ROOVER, *Money, banking and credit*, passim.

[8] R. VAUGHAN, *John the Fearless. The growth of Burgundian power*, London, Longmans, 1966, 320 p. R. VAUGHAN, *Philip the Bold. The Formation of the Burgundian State*, London, Longmans, 1962, 278 p.

[9] A. VAN NIEUWENHUYSEN, *Les finances du duc de Bourgogne Philippe le Hardi (1384-1404). Economie et Politique*, Bruxelles, ULB, 1984, 551 p.

[10] R. DE ROOVER, *Money, banking and credit*, p. 86.

[11] M. MOLLAT (ed.), *Comptes généraux de l'Etat bourguignon entre 1416 et 1420*, Paris, Imprimerie Nationale, 1965-1969, 3 vol.

conclusion, these three parts explain how an Italian merchant family was able to become a successful enterprise while so many of its contemporaries did not.

ACKNOWLEDGEMENTS

In 1389, the city of Bruges presented Dino Rapondi, one of the main characters of this book, with 100 francs. Rapondi, an Italian merchant-banker, was given the money for "the several involvements and good services" he had rendered to the city in times of financial need.[12] Although I will omit the 100 francs, this book would not be complete without my thanks to the many people whose involvements and good services were indispensable in my times of writing need.

I owe a deep debt to Professor Marc Boone, who suggested that I work on the Italian financiers of the Burgundian dukes when I was looking for a thesis subject. This book would not have become what it is now without his endless patience and diligence. The numerous comments provided by Professor Peter Stabel and by Tim Soens were also very valuable in the establishment of this work.

Professor Walter Prevenier and David Kusman made the effort of reading the text. Their many suggestions and interesting insights were much appreciated. The same goes for the criticism supplied by the Historical Committee of the Dexia Bank, consisting of Professor Raymond Van Uytven, Professor Claire Billen and Professor Jean-Pierre Sosson, whom I wish to thank for awarding this study with the Dexia Prize for History 2005.

I am very grateful to Professor James Bolton and Dr Francesco Bruscoli for making available their work on the Milanese Borromei bank. The third part of this book is to a large extent based on their findings. I must also mention Professor John F. Padgett, who let me use his writings on partnership systems.

This book would have been quite unreadable without the help of Dr Susie Sutch and Dr Kate McDonald. They undertook the Herculean task of introducing me to the secrets of correct English.

Archival research was facilitated by the friendly staff of the Bruges City Archives, the Archives Départementales du Nord in Lille, the Bruges Episcopal Archives and the Ghent University Library, who were always willing to satisfy my sometimes far-fetched requests.

Thanks to the financial support granted by the IUAP-V/10-project 'Urban Society in the Low Countries (Late Middle Ages-XVIth century)', which included this study in its series, and my appointment as a Research Assistant by the Research Foundation-Flanders, revision and translation of the text took place within the Department of Medieval History at Ghent University. The amicable contacts with my colleagues there made the process of writing and rewriting considerably easier.

My greatest obligation is to my parents, who gave me the chance to study medieval history, and to Barbara, who has helped me in so many ways.

[12] SAB, Stadsrekening 02/09/1388-02/09/1389, f° 107 v°.

List of Illustrations and Maps

LIST OF ABBREVIATIONS

ABIB : Archivio Borromei, Isola Bella

ACO: Archives Départementales du Côte d'Or, Dijon

ADN : Archives Départementales du Nord, Lille

ARAB : Algemeen Rijksarchief, Brussels

ASF : Archivio di Stato, Florence

BAB: Bisschoppelijk Archief, Bruges

BBr: Bruges Ledger

BLon: London Ledger

d.: pennies

gr.: groot

lb.: pounds

MAP: Mediceo avanti il Principato

par.: parisis

s.: shillings

SAB: Stadsarchief, Bruges

t.: tournois

INTRODUCTION

1. 'Mercatori Oriundi de Lucca'

On September 3, 1328, the dictator of the Tuscan city of Lucca and the surrounding regions, Castruccio Castracani, died. Although Castracani had appointed his brother as his successor, his death caused a power vacuum. Lucca fell in the hands of German mercenaries who sold the city to the highest bidder, the Genoese Gherardo Spinola. However, when the latter was unable to defend his latest acquisition properly, the Lucchese, afraid of the expansionist tendencies of their Florentine neighbours, asked for the protection of John of Luxemburg, king of Bohemia, who had taken possession of a part of Tuscany.[1] He and his son, the future emperor Charles IV, were willing to rule Lucca, on the condition that the inhabitants swore an oath of fealty to them. The Lucchese agreed and complied with John's request.

The merchant Guido Rapondi had been absent when the oath was taken. He had given a proxy to his uncle Giovanni (also known as Vanetto).[2] Guido belonged to one of the oldest families in the city, whose forebears could be traced back to the twelfth century. At that time the family members Bonuccio, Alessandro and Simone had been active, the latter described in 1194 as a merchant. Having grown rich from trade by the beginning of the thirteenth century, the Rapondi had climbed so high up the social ladder that they had earned the title of *nuovi nobili di torre* (this term infers a recently obtained noble status, although its precise meaning is not totally clear). At the end of the same century, the family was headed by Guido the elder, the father of Puccio, Giovanni and Rapondo and grandfather of Piero and the aforementioned Guido.[3] In 1308, they were part of the *potentes et casatici*, the city's economically and politically powerful class.[4]

When Vanetto Rapondi swore the oath to John of Bohemia in the name of Guido on August 23, 1331, the latter was in Paris.[5] This absence is one of the first indications of the Rapondis' activities abroad. Notwithstanding the fact that Guido would spend most of his future life in Lucca, where, with his family, he would devote himself to trade and local politics (during the first half of the fourteenth century, the Rapondi regularly sat in the college of *anziani*, who dealt with the daily governance of the city), his foreign adventure inspired most of his nine children to explore the world beyond the city's walls. Only one of them, Bartolomeo, who could not resist the call of the Lord, stayed in his home town. In 1383, the Lucchese city council proposed him as candidate bishop to Urban VI, though without success. In 1387, he rose to the ranks of Master of the *Ospidale de San Jacopo de Altopascio*, in the neighbourhood of Lucca. He fulfilled this function with so much zeal that when he died in 1394, he was commemorated with encomiums of praise.[6] Guido Rapondi's other sons, however, chose to seek their fortunes outside the Italian peninsula, in fourteenth-century Bruges.

---

[1] C. MEEK, *Lucca 1369-1400 Politics and Society in an Early Renaissance City-State*, Oxford, Oxford University Press, 1978, pp. 2-3.
[2] L. MIROT, "Les Cename" in : *Bibliothèque de l'Ecole des Chartes*, Paris, 1930, 91, pp. 142-143.
[3] L. MIROT, *La société des Raponde*, pp. 300-301.
[4] C. MEEK, *Lucca 1369-1400*, p. 190.
[5] L. MIROT, *Les Cename*, p. 143.
[6] G. SERCAMBI, *Le croniche di Giovanni Sercambi Lucchese pubblicate sui manoscritti originale*, Lucca, Ed. S. Bongi, 1892, dl. 1, pp. 316-317.

2. Bruges in the First Half of the Fourteenth Century

2.1 An Age of Tensions

As for most industrially highly developed and urbanised regions in western Europe, the fourteenth century was a period of continuous political and social tension for Bruges and the county of Flanders in general. Economic decline and dynastic troubles, together with epidemics and crop failures, caused latent unrest, which erupted time and again. The explosive situation dated from the thirteenth century, when an exclusive clique of well-to-do patrician families played a dominant role in the political environment of most Flemish cities, Bruges included. They had amassed wealth in trade, especially in cloth and wool, and exercised control over the textile industry, of crucial economic interest for the county. Nevertheless, their position of power provoked more and more resistance by a growing group of artisans who had worked to become small entrepreneurs, benefiting from economic success in previous years, and who wanted to participate in the government of their city. They were supported by the mass of the people, who were living in relative poverty and politically powerless.

About 1280, resistance deteriorated into revolt; in Bruges this was called the 'Moerlemaaie'. Instigated by discontented patricians, the masses protested vigorously against the fraud and mismanagement by certain city authorities and set houses on fire.[7] The Flemish count Guy of Dampierre, already keen on reducing municipal autonomy, took control. He took the victims of the revolt under his protection, fined the city and granted it a new charter, replacing the previous one lost in a fire in the belfry (unconnected with the Moerlemaaie). With the 1280 charter, the count restricted the power of the city's aldermen and forced the city council to keep its accounts, which enabled greater control of its financial affairs.[8] A year later, a further wave of discontent, brought about by Guy's manoeuvre, resulted in renewed riots, causing serious damage. Again the count intervened and punished the rebels, executing some of them.[9]

The attempts by Guy of Dampierre to suppress the autonomy of the Flemish patricians resulted in a coalition between the latter and the French king Philip IV, Guy's feudal lord. Philip continually tried to curtail his vassal's power and incorporate Flanders into his royal domain.[10] The artisans, seeing a chance to achieve participation in government, took the side of the count against the king and his patrician allies in Flanders (the 'leliaards').[11] After Guy had gained

---

[7] C. WYFFELS, "Nieuwe gegevens betreffende een XIIIde eeuwse «democratische» stedelijke opstand: de Brugse «Moerlemaye» (1280-1281)" in: *Handelingen van de Koninklijke Commissie voor Geschiedenis*, Brussel, 1966, 132, pp. 58-66. A. A. BARDOEL, "The urban uprising in Bruges, 1280-81. Some new findings about the rebels and the partisans" in: *Revue Belge de Philologie et d'Histoire*, Bruxelles, 1994, 72, pp. 761-791.

[8] C. WYFFELS, *de Brugse «Moerlemaye» (1280-1281)*, pp. 74-78.

[9] C. WYFFELS, *de Brugse «Moerlemaye» (1280-1281)*, pp. 78-83.

[10] M. BOONE, "Een verstedelijkte samenleving onder spanning. Het graafschap Vlaanderen omstreeks 1302" in: R.C. VAN CAENEGEM, *Feiten en mythen van de Guldensporenslag*, Anwerpen, Mercatorfonds, 2002, pp. 54-56.

[11] A. VANDEWALLE, "De Brugse stadsmagistraat en de deelname van de ambachten aan het bestuur, 14de-15de eeuw" in: W. PREVENIER and B. AUGUSTYN (reds.), *De Vlaamse instellingen tijdens het Ancien Régime: recent onderzoek in nieuw perspectief. Symposium georganiseerd te Brugge op 18 mei 1998*, Brussel, Algemeen Rijksarchief, 1999, p. 28. (Miscellanea Archivistica Studia, 111).

support in England and resigned his feudal ties, Philip annexed and occupied the whole county and imprisoned his vassal.[12]

In the subsequent clash against the king and the leliaards, Bruges played a remarkable role. On May 18, 1302, it was the scene of what modern historians have called the Brugse Metten, with most of the Frenchmen present in the city being slaughtered and the royal party being expelled. Two months later, the Flemish militia, with a considerable Bruges contingent, defeated the cream of French nobility in the Battle of the Golden Spurs. As a result, the French threat was repelled for the time being and Flanders' autonomy was saved.[13] Bruges was rewarded for its efforts with several comital concessions. Henceforth, its inhabitants were free to exercise a profession and to trade. Bruges' merchants were exempt from all tolls in the county. However, the biggest gains were made by the artisans, who had chosen the right side in the confrontation between Guy of Dampierre and the king. They obtained more independence to settle their own affairs and were to play a bigger role in the city council. It was they, and not the count, who appointed their representatives, enabling them to outnumber the patricians.[14]

The first dampener of the joy was the peace of Athis-sur-Orge, in 1305. This treaty ended hostilities between France and Flanders but turned out to be very disadvantageous to the Flemings. They had to pull down the fortifications of their biggest cities and make good the damages sustained by the 'leliaards'. Above all, the agreement forced them to pay a fine of 400 000 lb. and an annual annuity of 20 000 lb. In this context, discussion arose concerning the currency in which payments were to be made, something the Flemish negotiators had neglected to find out. In the end, the annuity had to be paid in light tournois, the fine in heavy parisis coins. Lille, Douai and Béthune, the castellanies of Walloon Flanders, served as a pledge. Bruges, accused of being the main culprit because of the Brugse Metten, had to assume the largest part in the payments and was obliged to send 3000 of its inhabitants on a pilgrimage. In 1312 at Pontoise, Philip IV conceded 10 000 lb. of the annuity, receiving instead a lump sum of 600 000 lb. The remaining 10 000 lb. was to be cancelled in exchange for Lille, Douai and Orchies (replacing Béthune). From then on, this 10 000 lb., the 'Transport Tax', had to be paid by the Flemings to their count. The 'Treaty of Injustice' caused much discontent in Bruges and in the rest of Flanders and completely superceded the 1302 agreement between the count and his subjects.[15]

The city had not yet recovered from their obligations from Athis when a new trial emerged. Heavy rains during the summer of 1315 had caused a crop failure, forcing grain prices to rise considerably in the last months of the year. The result was a general famine, starving thousands all over Europe. In Bruges, an estimated 5 to 10% of the population perished.[16] In the following years, unrest persisted because of renewed hostilities between the French king and Guy of Dampierre's successor Robert of Béthune, who refused to accept some of the Athis conditions (especially those concerning Walloon Flanders). In

---

[12] M. BOONE, *Een verstedelijkte samenleving onder spanning*, pp. 62-65.
[13] M. BOONE, *Een verstedelijkte samenleving onder spanning*, pp. 68-69.
[14] A. VANDEWALLE, *De Brugse stadsmagistraat en de deelname van de ambachten*, pp. 28-30.
[15] M. BOONE, *Een verstedelijkte samenleving onder spanning*, pp. 73-75.
[16] W.C. JORDAN, *The great famine. Northern Europe in the early fourteenth century*, Princeton, Princeton University Press, 1996, 317 p.

Bruges this led to an encounter between partisans and opponents of the count's war politics, with the former forced to leave the city. The confrontation between the king and the count ended in 1322, when Robert of Béthune died. His grandson, the pro-French Louis of Nevers, became his successor, in spite of the claims of his uncle Robert of Kassel.[17]

Immediately, the new count had to deal with one of the most important areas of tension in the late medieval Southern Netherlands, between the cities and their hinterland.[18] Bruges had fallen foul of its outport Sluis, where Louis' great-uncle John of Namur tried to take control of the strategically important Zwin estuary. Bruges feared a threat to its commercial dominance and decided to burn Sluis down.[19] A more serious conflict followed some months later. Riots broke out among the farmers on the coastal plains, where economic recession and the rigorous tax collection for the hated French reparations, together with the corruption of local authorities, proved disastrous.[20] The revolt turned against the nobility and the urban patriciate and spread to the 'smalle steden', next to the Bruges common people.[21] By the middle of 1325, the rebels were in power in the whole western part of the county[22] and had imprisoned Louis of Nevers.[23] Once he had been set free, the count was forced to conclude the prejudicial Peace of Arques. The most radical revolutionaries, however, thought the conditions of this treaty were not far-reaching enough and refused to accept it.[24] This left Louis with only one option, to summon his suzerain, the French king Philip VI of Valois, to his aid.[25] Philip dealt the rebels a decisive blow in Kassel.[26]

The Flemish count used the suppression of the uprising to issue the *mauvais privilèges*, aiming to strengthen his hold on his subjects. For that purpose, he extended the jurisdiction of the comital counsel. Originally a feudal assembly of vassals, it had developed into an institution with juridical and financial competences, consisting of professional officers. Because of the considerable increase in its tasks, even before 1329, several members had started to deal exclusively with financial matters. Another part of the personnel concentrated on juridical affairs, holding sessions called 'audiencies'.[27] The count also generalized the auditing of the city accounts, which in Bruges had to be fulfilled within a month after the renewal of the magistrates' bench.[28] Moreover, the city had to empty its pockets once more, still obliged to pay its arrears to the French Crown, and was forced to supply hundreds of hostages. Louis and the French

---

[17] J. A. VAN HOUTTE, *De geschiedenis van Brugge*, Tielt, Lannoo, 1982, p. 111.
[18] For this, see D. M. NICHOLAS, *Town and countryside. Social, economic and political tensions in fourteenth-century Flanders*, Bruges, De Tempel, 1971, 372 p.
[19] J. SABBE, *Vlaanderen in opstand 1323-1328 Nikolaas Zannekin, Zeger Janszone en Willem de Deken*, Brugge, Uitgeverij Marc Van de Wiele, 1992, pp. 18-20. (Vlaamse Historische Studies, 7).
[20] W. H. TEBRAKE, *A plague of insurrection. Popular Politics and Peasant Revolt in Flanders, 1323-1328*, Philadelphia, University of Pennsylvania Press, 1993, pp. 52-57.
[21] W. H. TEBRAKE, *A plague of insurrection*, pp. 71-75.
[22] W. H. TEBRAKE, *A plague of insurrection*, pp. 86-87.
[23] J. SABBE, *Vlaanderen in opstand*, p. 44.
[24] J. SABBE, *Vlaanderen in opstand*, pp. 51-55.
[25] W. H. TEBRAKE, *A plague of insurrection*, p. 111.
[26] J. SABBE, *Vlaanderen in opstand*, pp. 67-72.
[27] W. BUNTINX, "Audiëntie van de graven van Vlaanderen (ca. 1330-ca. 1409)" in: B. AUGUSTYN and W. PREVENIER (eds.), *De gewestelijke en lokale overheidsinstellingen in Vlaanderen tot 1795*, Brussel, Algemeen Rijksarchief, 1997, p. 125.
[28] F. BLOCKMANS, "Le controle par le Prince des comptes urbains en Flandre et en Brabant au Moyen Âge" in: *Finances et comptabilité urbaines du XIIIe au XVIe siècle, Colloque international, Blankenberge (1962)*, Bruxelles, Pro Civitate, 1964, pp. 318-319.

king ordered the execution of the leaders of the rebellion and the confiscation of their belongings. Finally, the count reversed the decisions of 1304, monopolizing again the appointment of aldermen.[29] Consequently, the pro-comital burghers were in charge again, evidently fostering the relations between Bruges and its sovereign lord.[30]

It did not take long for the perrennial opposition between the cities and comital authority to recur. This time it formed the prelude to what is known as the Hundred Years War, which began when Edward III of England disputed the rights of Philip VI, who had ascended the French throne after the death of the last direct heir of the Capetian dynasty. In 1336, reacting to the detention of English merchants by Louis of Nevers, who had sided with France since Kassel in 1328, Edward stopped the export of wool to Flanders, vital to cloth manufacture. In so doing, he hoped to force the cities to choose his side against their count. His attempts met with success in Ghent, where the embargo had resulted in a serious crisis. The popular party led by Jacob of Artevelde took control of the cloth city and obtained the resumption of the English wool import. After a revolutionary council had arisen in Bruges as well, Louis of Nevers, experiencing more and more difficulties in reconciling his pro-French attitude and the economic interests of the cities, had no other choice than to leave his county. Artevelde and his partisans then concluded an alliance with Edward III, whom they agreed to recognise as their suzerain, which brought about a strong reaction from the French king. Nevertheless, the fleet he sent to the Zwin was worsted by the English.[31] During the war, which lasted until the autumn of 1340 in Flanders, the Bruges militia were also called out regularly. The extant accounts of these expeditions show that Bruges, with its 40 to 45 000 inhabitants, had to be reckoned as one of the biggest cities in Europe at the time: outside of Italy, only Paris, London and Ghent were larger.[32]

In the absence of Louis of Nevers, Ypres, Bruges and Ghent together ruled Flanders, with the Ghentenars taking the lead. Since their first collective political action in 1127 (during the succession crisis following the murder of count Charles the Good), these cities had presented themselves as the principal representative power in the county. In exchange for their share of taxation, they wanted a voice in government and financial control. In order to discuss the state of affairs in the Flanders, Ghent, Ypres and Bruges held 'parlements'. By the end of the fourteenth century they were joined by the Franc, the rural district around Bruges, being called the Four Members.[33] From 1340 on, each of the three cities governed its own geographical area and they appointed together Simon of Mirabello, banker and brother-in-law of Louis of Nevers, as 'ruwaard' or regent of Flanders.[34]

---

[29] A. VANDEWALLE, *De Brugse stadsmagistraat en de deelname van de ambachten*, p. 30.

[30] J. SABBE, *Vlaanderen in opstand*, pp. 79-84.

[31] D. M. NICHOLAS, *The van Arteveldes of Ghent. The varieties of vendetta and the hero in history*, New York, E.J. Brill, 1988, pp. 19-38.

[32] J. A. VAN HOUTTE, *De geschiedenis van Brugge*, p. 116.

[33] W.P. BLOCKMANS, "De volksvertegenwoordiging in Vlaanderen in de overgang van Middeleeuwen naar Nieuwe Tijden (1384-1506)" in: *Verhandelingen van de Koninklijke Academie voor Wetenschappen, Letteren en Schone Kunsten van België*, Brussel, 1978, 40, nr. 90, p. 129.

[34] D. KUSMAN, "Jean de Mirabello dit van Haelen (ca. 1280-1333). Haute finance et Lombards en Brabant dans le premier tiers du XIVe siècle" in: *Revue Belge de Philologie et d'Histoire*, Bruxelles, 1999, 77, 4, pp. 843-931. P. ROGGHÉ, "Simon de Mirabello in Vlaanderen" in: *Appeltjes van het Meetjesland*, Maldegem, 1958, 9, p. 35.

This beautiful new relationship did not last, however, and the cities' revolutionary solidarity evaporated. In 1345, Jacob of Artevelde was murdered. A year later Louis of Nevers also made his exit. As a faithful servant of Philip VI, he died on the battlefield of Crécy, where the French army suffered a crushing defeat from the English. His son, thirteen-year-old Louis of Male, succeeded him, but had trouble persuading the cities to recognise him. After he had been welcomed in Aalst, which had suffered severely under Ghent's supremacy, it was Bruges, as always the most moderate in the revolutionary camp, who lent its support to Louis. Thereupon, Ypres and Ghent gave up their resistance. The new count rewarded this service, confirming Bruges' privileges, especially those from 1304, although the Bruges fullers and weavers lost their political influence because of their more prominent role during the period of rebellion.[35]

With the accession of Louis of Male in 1345, political confrontation receded into the background. Louis used the extension of central institutions to, gradually and without much resistance, extend comital power, thus preparing the way for the Burgundians. A powerful instrument for reinforcing his authority was the Audience, the highest juridical court in the county, able to oppose the jurisdiction of the cities.[36] Moreover, the count would restrict the tasks of the receiver-general to the governance of the treasury, the collection of comital revenues (collected by the under-receivers) and the making of payments. His former juridical duties were entrusted to the new office of the sovereign-bailiff, who was to head the network of bailiffs, the local representatives of the count. As a judge and prosecution officer, he secured public order, imposed peace and ended vendettas. Exceptionally, he could call to order comital vassals, aldermen's courts and other juridical bodies. These powers, together with the right to recall exiles and grant pardons, made the souvereign-bailiff an effective weapon against urban autonomy.[37] Still, the count also met his inhabitants' wishes. That is why, unlike his predecessors, he chose mainly Flemish counsellors. He recruited his receiver-general from the three chief cities, in contrast to the former counts, starting with Guy of Dampierre, who had often charged Italians with the governance of their revenues.[38]

In the Hundred Years War, Louis, compared to his father, was less bound to France and followed a more neutral policy, enabling Bruges and the other cities to maintain their economically important relations with England.[39] Nevertheless, turbulent times persisted. Among the causes were changes in the textile industries and the suppression of their guilds, together with continuous years of scarce grain and a decline in purchasing power after fluctuations in the Flemish monetary system. As a result, riots returned in 1359, with weavers and fullers in Bruges, Ghent and Ypres trying to regain their former positions.[40] It

---

[35] D. M. NICHOLAS, *The van Arteveldes of Ghent*, pp. 39-71.
[36] W. BUNTINX, *Audiëntie*, p. 126.
[37] M. BOONE, "Soeverein-baljuw van Vlaanderen" in: B. AUGUSTYN and W. PREVENIER (eds.), *De gewestelijke en lokale overheidsinstellingen in Vlaanderen tot 1795*, Brussel, Algemeen Rijksarchief, 1997, pp. 115-117.
[38] Such as Tommaso Fini and Nicolas Guidouche. B. AUGUSTYN, "Ontvanger-generaal van Vlaanderen (1245-1795)" in: B. AUGUSTYN and W. PREVENIER (eds.), *De gewestelijke en lokale overheidsinstellingen in Vlaanderen tot 1795*, Brussel, Algemeen Rijksarchief, 1997, p. 192.
[39] M. HAEGEMAN, *De Anglofilie in het graafschap Vlaanderen tussen 1379 en 1435*, Kortrijk-Heule, UGA, 1988, p. 109. (Standen en Landen, 90).
[40] J. MERTENS, "De woelingen te Brugge tussen 1359 en 1361" in: H. COPPEJANS and G. HANSOTTE (reds.), *Album Carlos Wyffels*, Brussel, Algemeen Rijksarchief, 1987, pp. 325-330.

took Louis two years to restore his authority, after which he concluded a new agreement with Bruges concerning the composition of its governement. This settlement of 1361 was one of the few in which all Bruges craft guilds had a direct political voice. In the future, they were all to be represented on the city council in accordance with their mutual hierarchy, their numbers and their importance.[41] Even this participation would not prevent riots from erupting again.

2. 2 The Formation of a European Business Centre

During the end of the twelfth and most of the thirteenth century, the fairs of Champagne were the most frequented meeting places in the European business world. At a fixed place and time, merchants from the Mediterranean world met their colleagues from the northern regions. Most southern Europeans were Italian businessmen, who brought spices, expensive fabrics and other luxury goods from more distant parts of the world. Using the most sophisticated financial techniques, they sold their merchandise and bought cloth from the Low Countries.[42]

Most of the northern merchants came from Flanders, where Ghent, Ypres and the other cloth towns produced textiles of all kinds on a large scale, following strict rules of production[43]. Flemish merchant entrepreneurs sold the sought-after poducts in foreign markets. From the end of the twelfth century on, this so-called active trade was conducted more and more by way of Champagne. To promote contact with this region, Flemish businessmen founded the Hanse of the Seventeen Cities. Flemings also travelled to other parts of Western Europe to market their wares, often passing through Bruges, which was more of a commercial centre than a textile town. Bruges was also part of a cycle of fairs itself, with Lille, Ypres, Torhout and Mesen.

The raw material needed by the Flemish cloth manufacturers came largely from England, whose finer grades of wool were more suited for the more expensive articles in the range of cloths than home-grown varieties. This trading relationship also gave rise to a mercantile alliance. After having acted in smaller groups for a while, from 1275 onwards merchants joined forces as the Flemish Hanse of London. Bruges was to take a leading part in this league. Thanks to its geographical position, the city had succeeded in capturing a large part of the wool trade from the British Isles. In so doing, it had become the biggest wool market in the county, distributing raw material to the Flemish textile-producing cities.[44]

At the end of the thirteenth and the beginning of the fourteenth centuries, a fundamental evolution in the western European trade system took place. Most important was the change from predominantly transport by land to sea, initiated by the Italian cities. More and more they preferred the maritime route that brought them to the North Sea via the Mediterranean and the Atlantic Ocean. In that way, they could circumvent political instability and

---

[41] A. VANDEWALLE, *De Brugse stadsmagistraat en de deelname van de ambachten*, pp. 31-32.

[42] R.H. BAUTIER, "Les foires de Champagne" in: *La foire*, Bruxelles, Librairie Encyclopédique, 1953, pp. 97-147.

[43] P. CHORLEY, "The cloth exports of Flanders and Northern France during the thirteenth century: a luxury trade?" in: *Economic History Review*, Cambridge, 1987, 40, pp. 349-379.

[44] See C. WYFFELS, "De Vlaamse hanzen opnieuw belicht" in: *Academiae analecta*, Brussel, 1991, 53, pp. 8-13.

growing insecurity on the overland European routes, which had forced up transaction costs,[45] and could benefit from the bigger capacity and faster speed ships could offer. As a consequence of the change, the attraction of the Champagne fairs declined and new international trading centres became prominent.

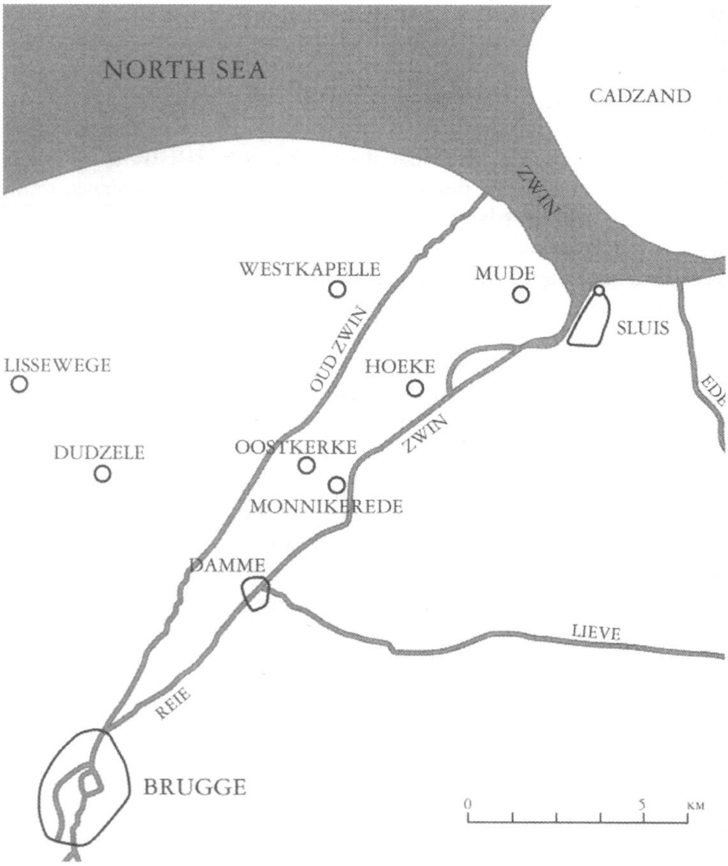

Bruges and the Zwin towns (after J. MURRAY, *Bruges, Cradle of Capitalism*, p. 30)

Bruges had perfect qualifications for this role. First, it was centrally located between the two leading European commercial entities, the Hanseatic League in north-eastern Europe and the Italian cities in the south. Moreover, the city had an exit to the sea by the Zwin. There it could maintain it supremacy over the outports of Damme and Sluis by its staple privileges, by stating that apart from some goods, it was forbidden to unload or sell any goods entering the Zwin except in Bruges. In view of its function as a distribution centre for the Flemish cloth industry, the city had no lack of infrastructure. And with 40 000 comparatively wealthy inhabitants, it offered an attractive home market and a vast hinterland. The combination of these assets ensured that Bruges could develop into one of the foremost gateway cities in the European economy and maintain this position for almost two centuries, from 1280 until 1480.[46]

[45] All costs involved when concluding a commercial transaction.

[46] H. VAN DER WEE, "Industrial dynamics and the process of urbanization and de-urbanization from the late middle ages to the eighteenth century" in: H. VAN DER WEE (ed.), *The Rise and Decline of Urban Industries*

During this commercial flowering, cloth still was the export article most traded on the Bruges market. Nevertheless, traditional Flemish drapery had had its day. Because of the unsettled conditions caused by war, transaction costs in the textile industry had risen considerably in the fourteenth century. Therefore, the cities concentrated on producing the more expensive, luxurious varieties of cloth, where these costs constituted a smaller proportion of the whole. However, by so doing, their dependence on English wool, and their vulnerability to the competition of other mercantile centres, increased. Competition came from the neighbouring regions first, such as Brabant, Holland and the smaller cities in the county itself, where the 'New Draperies'[47] caused much conflict with the nearest traditional cloth city. Yet the biggest threat to the Flemish cloth industry came from the other side of the English Channel, where a large-scale textile industry had developed in the countryside, producing and exporting more and more of its own cloth. It had the undeniable advantage that the English crown, embroiled in the Hundred Years War, had time after time raised wool taxes or even stopped wool exports, over which the Flemings had lost control in the last three decades of the thirteenth century. Protectionist measures in Flanders could not prevent these changing conditions from bringing about the end of Flemish high quality cloth.[48]

Bruges suffered relatively little from these developments in the cloth industry, mainly because the city, with its diversified production, was less dependent on textiles than were Ghent or Ypres. Only a quarter of the Bruggelings worked in this sector (compared to more than half of the Ghentenars). Most people earned their living by serving local needs, in building or food production for example, or in the production of luxury goods, very well represented in Bruges. Glove, cap- and hatmakers, furriers and tailors, just like other producers of highly finished and valuable goods, could do good business in the city. Works of art such as tapestries, jewellery, paternosters and copper funeral plates also found ready sales.

Another part of the population, about one fifth, was active in international trade.[49] Only a small minority of them visited foreign markets with their merchandise. From 1320 on, the Flemings, and the people of Bruges in particular, increasingly changed their occupations from active businessmen to more passive activities. Some of them made a living as a brokers, the go-betweens who were present at every transaction between foreign merchants. Others combined this job with that of hosteller and accomodated foreign

---

in Italy and the Low Countries (late middle ages-early modern times), Leuven, Leuven University Press, 1988, pp. 321-323.

[47] J.H. MUNRO, "The origins of the English 'New Draperies': the resurrection of an old Flemish industry, 1270-1570" in: N.B. HARTE (ed.), *The New Draperies in the Low Countries and England, 1300-1800*, Oxford, Oxford University Press, 1997, pp. 45-48.

[48] J.H. MUNRO, "Industrial transformations in the north-west European textile trades, c. 1290-c. 1340: economic progress or economic crisis?" in: B.M.S. CAMPBELL (ed.), *Before the Black Death. Studies in the 'crisis' of the early fourteenth century*, New York, Manchester University Press, 1991, pp. 110-148.

[49] J. DUMOLYN, "Population et structures professionnelles à Bruges aux XIVe et XVe siècles" in: *Revue du Nord*, Lille, 1999, 81, 329, pp. 48-58. W. PREVENIER, "Bevolkingscijfers en professionele strukturen der bevolking van Gent en Brugge in de 14de eeuw" in: *Album aangeboden aan Charles Verlinden ter gelegenheid van zijn dertig jaar professoraat*, Wetteren, Universa, 1975, pp. 292-303. For the production of luxury goods, see R. VAN UYTVEN, "Splendour or Wealth: Art and Economy in the Burgundian Netherlands" in: *Transactions of the Cambridge Bibliographical Society*, Cambridge, 1992, vol. 10, part 2, pp. 101-124.

visitors, for whom they also acted as an agent.[50] In that way, they served the foreign merchant communities, who arrived in ever-increasing numbers.

Among the first to do so were the Germans, probably first visiting the city at the end of the twelfth century. In 1252, the Flemish countess granted them a reduction in customs in Bruges and Damme, and the following year they received more legal security while they were staying in Flanders.[51] At the same time as the issuing of these privileges, merchants from northern Germany organised themselves into regional leagues or 'hanses'. In the following decades, they would fuse into the *dudesche Hanse,* an informal joint venture of cities, on the initiative of Lübeck. The *Hanzetag*, the general council that met for the first time in 1356, was its highest authority.[52] Concentrated on the southern coast of the Baltic Sea, the Hanse at its peak numbered more than two hundred cities from the east of the Netherlands to the Baltic.[53]

Bruges was not a Hanse city but hosted one of the four external outposts of the alliance, known as *Kontore*, together with London, Bergen in Norway and Novgorod in Russia. While Hanseatic merchants had a separate quarter in the other outpost cities, in Bruges they lived in hostels and houses throughout the city.[54] They performed their religious duties with the Carmelite friars.[55] On the Bruges market, the Easterlings, as they were known, supplied mainly raw materials and bulk goods from the periphery of Europe. In addition to grain, timber and other forestry goods, they delivered furs, metal and salted or dried fish.[56] More than once the Hanseatic merchants threatened to withdraw from Bruges, every time they thought their privileges were being abused. They took action in 1280, when they collectively moved to neighbouring Aardenburg. Similar actions were to be seen in 1388, 1436 and 1451, whereupon urban or comital authorities yielded and extended Hanseatic privileges.[57]

Complementary with the range of goods offered by the Easterlings was that of the Italians, suppliers of high-value objects. The latter brought dyeing stuffs, spices, paper and glass, together with expensive fabrics such as silk, brocade and velvet.[58] However, it was not until the last quarter of the thirteenth century that the Italians came to be of great importance. In 1277 the first Genoese galley entered the Zwin and a regular shipping line between Bruges and southern Europe was established.[59] Moreover, the Italians, as numerous as the Hanseatic traders, did not operate together as the Germans did, but represented

---

[50] A. GREVE, *Hansen, Hosteliers und Herbergen : Studien zum Aufenthalt hansischer Kaufleute in Brügge im 14. und 15. Jahrhundert*, Turnhout, Brepols, in preparation.

[51] P. DOLLINGER, *La Hanse (XIIe-XVIIe siècles)*, Paris, Aubier, 1964, p. 59.

[52] P. DOLLINGER, *La Hanse*, pp. 86-87.

[53] P. DOLLINGER, *La Hanse*, pp. 113-114.

[54] Their request to set up their own settlement on the banks of the Zwin was refused by the Flemish authorities.

[55] P. DOLLINGER, *La Hanse*, pp. 130-131.

[56] P. DOLLINGER, *La Hanse*, pp. 264-278.

[57] W.P. BLOCKMANS, "Konfliktregelung der Hanse in Flandern (1393-1451)" in : H. MENKE (ed.), *Die Niederlande und der europaische Nordosten : ein Jahrtausend weitraumiger Beziehungen (700-1700)*, Neumunster, Waccholtz, 1992, pp. 209-219. D.W. POECK, "Kontorverlegung als Mittel hansischer Diplomatie" in: N. JÖRN, W. PARAVICINI and H. WERNICKE (eds.), *Hansekaufleute in Brügge. Teil 4: Beiträge der Internationalen Tagung in Brügge April 1996*, Frankfurt am Main, Peter Lang, 2000, pp. 33-53. (Kieler Werkstücke, Reihe D, 13).

[58] R. VAN UYTVEN, "De overige handelsgoederen te Brugge" in: A. VANDEWALLE, *Hanzekooplui en Medicibankiers. Brugge, wisselmarkt van Europese culturen*, Oostkamp, Stichting Kunstboek, 2002, p.78.

[59] A. VANDEWALLE, "De vreemde naties in Brugge" in: A. VANDEWALLE, *Hanzekooplui en Medicibankiers. Brugge, wisselmarkt van Europese culturen*, Oostkamp, Stichting Kunstboek, 2002, p. 30.

only their city-state of origin, a reflection of the political disintegration of their peninsula.

The first Italians to travel to Bruges were mainly Venetians and Genoese. Venetian firms installed their permanent representatives in the city from the first half of the fourteenth century onwards. They were supplied by a regular convoy that was organised by the Venetian government, who took on the risks of the trip (the system of the *Muda*). The state-controlled trade system of the *Serenissima Republica* also made it unnecessary to make a long stay abroad and can partly explain why few Venetians really integrated into Bruges' social fabric. Nevertheless, Venetian businessmen had one of the first consulates in the city (they obtained the right to set one up in 1322, but it probably only started functioning in 1332), uniting for mutual moral support and the common practice of religion. Besides, members of a merchant guild also had a stronger case when bargaining for juridical protection and favourable trading conditions when acting collectively.[60] So it proved in 1358, when Louis of Male confirmed and extended the Venetian's privileges. A nation house, situated on the square of the Bourse, was erected at the end of the century.

The Venetians attended mass at the Augustinians' church,[61] where they kept the Genoese company. Merchants from Genoa were also present in Bruges from the beginning of the fourteenth century and maintained a regular maritime connection with the city. However, it was not until 1397 that they erected a consulate, following the agreement of a treaty with Philip the Bold and the establishment of their staple. Two years later, they would set up their nation house nearby the Venetians. From the middle of the fourteenth century onwards, the Genoese were known for their trade in alum, used for fixing during the dyeing process, and for maritime insurance,[62] very welcome for want of the elaborate state support that the Venetians had. The latter can also explain the stronger tendencies to integrate by the Genoese, as witnessed by the careers of the Adornes[63] and other Spinolas in the Low Countries.

The Italians were not only active in commodity trade. They also dominated in banking, flourishing in Bruges, the new clearing-house of the European economy. Lombardy, in northern Italy, gave its name to the 'Lombards' or 'Cahorsins', who also originated from neighbouring Piedmont (Asti, Chieri). They sold short-term consumer credit, keeping loan tables and demanding a pledge. Most of the time they issued small loans at exorbitantly high interest rates. In the foreign cities where they were active, Lombards usually joined together, forming corporations and paying a tax to the civic authorities, whereupon they were granted a monopoly (but many pawnbrokers ran their business illegally).[64]

---

[60] They were not subject to Bruges law but to that of their home city.

[61] P. STABEL, "Venice and the Low Countries: commercial contacts and intellectual inspirations" in: B. AIKEMA and B.L. BROWN (eds.), *Renaissance Venice and the North. Croscurrents in the time of Bellini, Dürer and Titian*, New York, Rizzoli, 1999, pp. 31-36.

[62] G. PETTI BALBI, *Mercanti e nationes nelle Fiandre: i genovesi in età bassomedievale*, Pisa, ETS, 1996, pp. 1-123. (Piccola Biblioteca Gisem, 7).

[63] See, for example, M. BOONE, M. DANNEEL and N. GEIRNAERT, "Pieter IV Adornes (1460 - ca.1496): een Brugs patricier in Gent" in: *Handelingen der Maatschappij voor Geschiedenis en Oudheidkunde te Gent*, Gent, 1985, 39, pp. 123-147. N. GEIRNAERT and A. VANDEWALLE (reds.), *Adornes en Jeruzalem. Internationaal leven in het 15de- en 16de-eeuwse Brugge*, Brugge, Gemeentebestuur, 1983, 143 p.

[64] R. DE ROOVER, *Money, banking and credit*, pp. 97-167. D. KUSMAN, "Entre noblesse, ville et clergé. Les financiers lombards dans les anciens Pays-Bas aux XIVe-XVe siècles: un état de la question" in: *Publications du Centre Européen d'Études Bourguignonnes (XIVe-XVIe s.)*, Bâle, 1999, 39, pp. 113-132. W. REICHERT, *Lombarden*

Besides the Lombards, there were the money-changers. In addition to changing coins and collecting precious metal, they received deposits. The corresponding value of the payment was deposited into the account of the customer, who was able, without the risky transport of cash, to transfer sums to others, who also had accounts. Meanwhile, the money-changer could use the deposit money for his own investments or for granting loans. Most of these money-dealers, such as Collard de Marke[65] or Willem Ruweel,[66] were native Bruggelings. Nevertheless, most foreigners, especially Hanseatic merchants, did not use them for their financial affairs but went to their hostellers, who did use the money-changers' infrastructure.[67]

Another Bruges money circuit was that of the Italian companies who used advanced techniques in banking, using bills of exchange.[68] This worked by an instruction being given by a 'taker', who had received funds from a 'deliverer' in a certain currency to a 'payer' to pay back the sum to a 'payee' at another place and another time in another currency. The bill of exchange made it possible for the Italian companies to move money from one place to another, where, for example, a payment had to be made, again without the risk of phisically moving cash. The document not only served as a means of payment, but also as a credit instrument (the 'deliverer' lending money for a certain time to the 'taker') and by gambling on the differences between the currencies, merchants could make a profit. This was not the case with the 'dry exchange', which was a pure lending transaction with the 'taker' paying back the owed sum and an extra fee to the 'deliverer' (the exchange formula only served to bypass the Church's prohibition on charging interests). Nevertheless, these advanced credit techniques were only used by a small group: the Easterlings, for example, resorted to other means of payment.[69]

During the first half of the fourteenth century, the bill of exchange was popular with the Florentines, especially with the 'super companies' such as the Bardi, the Peruzzi or the Acciaiuoli,[70] each having several agents in the city. They used their trading and banking capital to grant loans to Bruges and the Flemish counts. When these 'giants with feet of clay' folded one after the other in the 1340s, Florentine predominance in the financial sector collapsed. They were only to re-emerge in Bruges in around 1420, when they joined together as a merchant guild based at a nation house on the Bourse square and attending mass at the Franciscan monastery.[71]

---

in der Germania-Romania. Atlas und dokumentation, Trier, Porta Alba Verlag, 2003, 3 vol. (Beiträge zur Landes- und Kulturgeschichte).

[65] R. DE ROOVER, "Quelques considérations sur les livres de comptes de Collard de Marke précédées d'un aperçu sur les archives commerciales en Belgique" in: *Bulletin d'Études et d'Informations de l'École Supérieure de Commerce Saint-Ignace*, Anvers, 1930, 7, pp. 445-475. J.M. MURRAY, "Family, marriage and moneychanging in Medieval Bruges" in: *Journal of Medieval History*, Amsterdam, 1988, 14, pp. 115-125.

[66] R. DE ROOVER, "Le Livre de comptes de Guillaume Ruyelle, changeur à Bruges (1369)" in: *Handelingen van het Genootschap voor Geschiedenis*, Bruges, 1934, 77, pp. 15-95.

[67] R. DE ROOVER, *Money, banking and credit*, pp. 169-344.

[68] R. DE ROOVER, *Money, banking and credit*, pp. 7-96.

[69] R. DE ROOVER, *L'Évolution de la Lettre de Change. XIVe-XVIIIe siècles*, Paris, Librairie Armand Colin, 1953, 240 p.

[70] Called this because of their gigantic size and their centralised structure. E.S. HUNT, *The medieval super-companies: a study of the Peruzzi company of Florence*, Cambridge, Cambridge University Press, 1994, 291 p.

[71] J. MARECHAL, *Bijdrage tot de geschiedenis van het bankwezen te Brugge*, Brugge, De Anjelier, 1955, pp. 59-65.

The Florentines thus had to give way to their colleagues from Lucca, who had established a consulate by 1369 when the authorities of their republic, which had just freed itself from Pisan rule,[72] approved their statutes. The Lucchese built their nation house on the corner of the Naaldenstraat and the Grauwwerkersstraat. As did the Venetians and the Genoese, they attended the Augustijnenrei, where they made their devotion to the *Volto Santo* (the Holy Cross). From the middle of the fourteenth century on, the Lucchese took over the Florentines' lead position in banking. They were also renowed for exporting silks from the Far East finished in Lucca. In terms of integration, the Lucchese, like most of the Tuscans, were midway between the stay-at-home Venetians and the gregarious merchants from Genoa.[73] Bruges also welcomed businessmen from Milan, who united in a merchant guild, and from Piacenza,[74] Siena, Pisa, Como and Bologna[75] although these did not exercise that much influence.

The two pillars of Bruges trade, the Hanseatic League and the Italian merchant guilds, were joined by numerous merchants from many other European regions. Although France exported wine from Poitou, and later from Gascony and Burgundy, the numbers of French merchants in Bruges were comparatively insignificant.[76] English and Scots did play a bigger part, at least in the first decades of the fourteenth century, because of the wool trade. The importance of the businessmen from England would decline after the difficulties discussed above and the transfer of the staple to Calais in 1363, although Bruges was never completely ignored.[77]

As the import of English wool reduced, the supply of raw material from the Iberian peninsula became more important. The Spanish merchants acted in the name of their regional kingdoms. Most numerous on the Bruges market were the subjects of Aragon (Catalunya included), especially the Barcelonese. After 1400, the Castilians would dominate due to the boom of their merino wool. Together with the Biscayers, who would go their own way later, they would constitute the biggest merchants guild after the Hanse and the Italians. The Spaniards, also trading iron ore and southern goods such as oil and lemons, would be the last foreign community to remain in Bruges.[78] Other representatives of the Iberian world were the Portuguese, first selling mainly rural products. Following their great discoveries overseas in the course of the fifteenth century, they would enlarge their trading range and offer sugar, spices

---

[72] Pisa had kept Lucca under her thumb for 27 years, after the rule of John of Bohemia and some other short-lived governments. The originals of the statutes of the Lucchese nation have not been preserved but the text has been copied almost word for word in the confirmation of her privileges in 1478, which did survive the centuries. For this, see E. LAZZARESCHI, "Gli statuti dei Lucchesi a Bruges e ad Anversa" in: *Ad Alessandro Luzio Gli Archivi di Stato Italiani Miscellanea di studi storici volume secondo*, Firenze, Felice Le Monnier, 1933, pp. 75-88.

[73] R. DE ROOVER, "La communauté des marchands Lucquois à Bruges de 1377 à 1404" in : *Annales de la Société d'Emulation de Bruges*, Bruges, 1949, 86, pp. 23-89.

[74] G. PETTI BALBI, "I Piacentini tra Genova e i Paesi Bassi" in : *Precursori di Cristoforo Colombo : mercanti e banchieri piacentini nel mondo durante in medioevo*, Bologna, Edizioni Analisi, 1994, pp. 69-88.

[75] J. MARECHAL, *Bijdrage tot de geschiedenis van het bankwezen*, p. 57.

[76] J. PAVIOT, "Brugge en Frankrijk" in: A. VANDEWALLE, *Hanzekooplui en Medicibankiers. Brugge, wisselmarkt van Europese culturen*, Oostkamp, Stichting Kunstboek, 2002, p. 43. For the French wine trade in the Low Countries, see J. CRAEYBECKX, *Un grand commerce d'importation: les vins de France aux anciens Pays-Bas (XIIIe-XVIe siècle)*, Paris, S.E.V.P.E.N., 1958, 315 p. (Ports – Routes - Trafics, 9).

[77] J. MARECHAL, "Duizend jaar Britse aanwezigheid te Brugge" in: J. MARECHAL, *Europese aanwezigheid te Brugge*, Brugge, Genootschap voor Geschiedenis, 1985, pp. 13-40. (Vlaamse Historische Studies, 3).

[78] H. CASADO ALONSO "La nation et le quartier des Castillans de Bruges (XVe et XVIe siècles)" in: *Handelingen van het Genootschap voor Geschiedenis*, Brugge, 1996, 133, pp. 61-77. J. MARECHAL, "La colonie espagnole de Bruges, du XIVe au XVIe siècle" in: *Revue du Nord*, Lille, 1953, 35, pp. 5-40.

and ivory.[79] Francesco Balducci Pegolotti, the Florentine agent of the Bardi company and author of the *Pratica della Mercatura*, was not exaggerating, then, when he called Bruges "the place where most residing merchants live to do trade and barter".[80]

[79] J. PAVIOT, "Les Portugais à Bruges au XVe siècle" in: *Arquivos do Centro Cultural Calouste Gulbenkian*, Paris, 1999, 38, pp. 1-122.
[80] A. EVANS (ed.), *Francesco Balducci Pegolotti. La pratica della mercatura*, Cambridge (Massachusetts), the Medieval Academy of America, 1936, p. 236.

PART 1

In Search of a Privileged Relationship (1360-1384)

CHAPTER 1

From Lucca to Bruges

1.1 The Early Days

"For fourteen pieces of mixed cloth for ladies and clerks, we owe for my Lady to Henri Rasponde, cccxiii l.t." This is one of the first possible traces of the Rapondi family in the Low Countries. It is an extract from the household accounts from the counts of Hainaut from 1297 until 1299, when John II of Avesnes wielded the comital sceptre. The order of 313 lb. tourn. for fourteen pieces of mixed cloth (cloth made of different coloured wool) on behalf of his wife, Philippina of Luxemburg, was made on Easter Day 1298.[1] As to the identity of the merchant's supplier, Henri Rasponde, we are groping in the dark. We do not know how or indeed if he was related to the Rapondi, living in Lucca at the time (Guido and his sons Puccio, Rapondo and Giovanni).[2] After this single mention of Henri Rasponde, the Rapondi name or cognate took over thirty years to make its appearance again north of the Alps. This time, Guido di Rapondo was in Paris during the oath swearing by the Lucchese to John of Bohemia in 1331.[3] Nothing is known about his stay in France or other business abroad, making it difficult to determine the size and the structure of the Rapondis' foreign activities in this period.

We gain more certainty in 1345, when we meet the family for the first time in Flanders. On 25 June of that year, Alard of Os, influential counsellor-cleric and receiver of the duke of Brabant,[4] declared having received 224 gold florins from Piero Rapondi, who acted "pro se ipso et pro aliis suis sociis Societatis de Rapondis". Earlier, one Arrigo Bradiloche had given the sum to Tommaso Giganti, "fattore dei Rapondi en Bruges" to deliver them to Alard of Os.[5] This suggests that the Rapondi were operating as a company from the middle of the 1340s. In common with many other firms since the beginning of the fourteenth century, they owned an office, occupied by a factor, in Bruges, who was able to transfer funds from one person to another and whose contacts already extended to Brabant.

The company consisted of several partners ("aliis suis sociis"), including Piero, the son of Rapondo and the brother of Guido Rapondi, who must have spent most of his time in Italy, because of his busy political career (in 1345, 1347, 1348 and 1349 he was *anziano* of his city, dealing with its day-to-day management and diplomatic missions).[6] Together with eight other Lucchese residents in Bruges and with the approval of the city council, Tommaso Giganti, named as a factor in 1345, issued a 30 lb. gr. loan to the dean and the chiefs of

---

[1] M. DEHAISNES, *Documents et extraits divers concernant l'histoire de l'art dans la Flandre, l'Artois et le Hainaut avant le xve siècle Première partie : 627-1373*, Lille, L. Quarré, 1886, p. 100.

[2] L. MIROT, *La société des Raponde*, pp. 300-301.

[3] L. MIROT, *Les Cename* p. 143.

[4] See P. AVONDS, "Brabant tijdens de regering van Hertog Jan III (1312-1356). Land en Instellingen" in: *Verhandelingen van de Koninklijke Academie voor Wetenschappen, Letteren en Schone Kunsten van België*, Brussel, 1991, 53, nr. 136, pp. 72, 103.

[5] L. MIROT, *La société des Raponde*, p. 307.

[6] L. MIROT, *La société des Raponde*, p. 301, n. 3 and p. 302.

the weavers,[7] suppressed after the collapse of the Artevelde regime, two years later.[8] We do not know if Giganti was still employed by the Rapondi at this date and granted the credit in the name of the company: if he was, then we have evidence of an early example of the credit operations in which the Lucchese firm would excel later on. We lose sight of the family in Flanders in the following years (but not in Lucca, where they remained in the *anziano* college).[9]

It took Louis of Male's campaign in Brabant, once again, for the Rapondi to re-emerge. The count's wife, Margaret, was the daughter of duke John III of Brabant. When John died in 1355, the dukedom passed to Margaret's eldest sister Joan and her sisters had to content themselves with annuities. Louis would not put up with this and induced the inhabitants of the seigneury of Malines to recognise him as the lord of the city. As a consequence, a confrontation with Joan's husband Wenceslas of Luxemburg ensued, with the Flemish count trampling most of Brabant underfoot. The conflict ended with the peace of Ath, concluded in August 1357, granting Louis the seigneury of Malines and the commercial metropolis of Antwerp.[10]

The hostilities had a less beneficial effect on Faucon Lampaige, mint-master of Brabant, whose belongings were confiscated by Louis. On 3 January 1357, the count's officers paid a visit to the Bruges mansion of the Genoese Jehan Sac and that of Dino de la Chiocha, a merchant from Lucca and "companion of the Rapondi company". In the home of the latter, they took jewels, pearls and 500 ecus belonging to Lampaige. The Rapondis' debts towards the Brabant mint-master were cancelled and the count stood surety for possible actions by creditors.[11] The confiscation story shows that among the shareholders of the firm there were also non-family members, such as Dino de la Chiocha. The fact that the Bruges office was led directly by one of the partners and not by a factor could mean that the branch, compared with its position in 1345, had risen in importance and that it could claim some independence. However we do not know if there was only a factor and no partners resident in 1345, for example.

While we are restricted to momentary impressions of the Rapondis' situation abroad until 1360, the beginning of the next decade shows a more detailed picture. The change was prompted by the alternation of generations within the family which occurred in this period (the last mention of Guido was in 1362,[12] Piero had probably died some time before). With Guido's eldest son Guglielmo, a new *capo del parentado* became head of the company. He was at least 30 years old because he had fulfilled the function of *anziano* in 1355,[13] having reached the minimal age of 25 and he was married to his kinswoman Margareta, with whom he had two children, Giovanni and Filippa.[14] One of Guglielmo's first decisions was the transfer of the company's headquarters from Lucca to

[7] A. SCHOUTEET, *Regesten op de oorkonden van het Stadsarchief van Brugge 1340-1384*, Brugge, Genootschap voor Geschiedenis, 1979, pp. 38-39.
[8] See *supra*.
[9] L. MIROT, *La société des Raponde*, p. 301, n. 3.
[10] F. QUICKE, *Les Pays-Bas à la veille de la période bourguignonne (1356-1384) : contribution à l'histoire politique et diplomatique de l'Europe occidentale dans la seconde moitié du XIVe siècle*, Bruxelles, Ed. Universitaires, 1947, pp. 41-44.
[11] T. de LIMBURG-STIRUM (ed.), *Cartulaire de Louis de Male comte de Flandre. Decreten van den grave Lodewyck van Vlaenderen 1348 à 1358 Tome I*, Bruges, Louis De Plancke, 1898, pp. 559-560.
[12] C. MEEK, *Lucca 1369-1400*, p. 197.
[13] L. MIROT, *La société des Raponde*, p. 301, n. 3.
[14] L. MIROT, *La société des Raponde*, p. 307.

Bruges[15], confirming the growing importance of the Rapondis' Bruges branch of the business. This change is testified by the numbers of Rapondi family members who appeared in Flanders around the middle of the 1360s. The first to do this was probably Guglielmo himself. From 1364 on, we can find him at the Bruges market, where he seemed to be on familiar terms with the affairs of Iolanda of Bar, a member of the Flemish comital house. On August 7 of that year, for instance, she gave him 50 lb. gr.[16] Since this was a settlement of earlier debts, it would seem that Guglielmo had already had his residence in Bruges for some time, certainly since 1359, when he had served again as *anziano* in Lucca.[17] Soon he was being helped by Dino, Guido Rapondi's second son, who worked with him in concluding transactions with the countess of Bar. Guglielmo's other brothers moved to Bruges as well. On August 13, 1368, Jacopo was there to rent a house from Comtessa di Betto del Miccio, the wife of the Lucchese Nicolao de Federigo Simonetti. Dino and Guglielmo also took up their residence there, but it is not known where the house was situated and where the brothers lived before. It is possible they shared the house with Andrea Rapondi, who had lent various sums to Iolanda a couple of months before. The fifth brother, Piero, also appeared in Bruges, but only in 1370 and for a relatively short period.[18]

One of the tools of their new habitat that the Rapondi used was Bruges' advanced payment system. This is shown in the extant accounts of the Bruges money-changer Collard de Marke, active from 1366 to 1369. Guglielmo was one of 70 to 80 frequent customers, mainly Italian bankers and merchants, Lombards and Flemish merchant entrepreneurs[19] who had accounts with him. With these they could make payments by book transfer, depositing money or gold. It would seem that "Willaume Raiponde", as Guglielmo was called in the account books, enjoyed the money-changer's confidence, since on May 20, 1369 he was allowed to go into the red for more than 165 lb. gr.[20] (enjoying, in fact, a form of short-term credit).

It appears from de Marke's ledger that a large part of the Rapondis' financial and commercial contacts were with the Lucchese community in Bruges.[21] One of the foremost business partners was Forteguerra Forteguerra, the head of a firm with branches in Lucca and Bruges.[22] He figures frequently in Guglielmo's *conti*, together with compatriots with interests in the city, such as Gherardo Burlamacchi, Jakemaerd Fava and Dino Sanocci.[23] The Rapondi family may already have had contacts with Galico da Piastra, another Lucchese de Marke customer,[24] who would work for the company as a factor later on.

[15] L. MIROT, *La société des Raponde*, p. 311.
[16] J. M. FINOT, *Inventaire sommaire des archives départementales antérieures à 1790. Nord. Archives Civiles-Série B. Tome Septième*, Lille, L. Danel, 1892, p. 51.
[17] L. MIROT, *La société des Raponde*, p. 301, n. 3.
[18] L. MIROT, *La société des Raponde*, p. 310.
[19] E. AERTS, "Geld en krediet. Brugge als financieel centrum" in : V. VERMEERSCH (ed.), *Brugge en Europa*, Antwerpen, Mercatorfonds, 1992, p. 61.
[20] R. DE ROOVER, *Money, Banking and Credit*, p. 298.
[21] To some extent, this can be misleading since not all merchants, especially the non-Italians, were equally represented among the account holders as the Lucchese were and hence, they stay somewhat out of sight. R. DE ROOVER, *Money, Banking and Credit*, p. 303.
[22] L. MIROT, "Forteguerra Forteguerra et sa succession" in : *Bibliothèque de l'Ecole des Chartes*, Paris, 1935, 96, pp. 303-305.
[23] R. DE ROOVER, *Money, Banking and Credit*, p. 376.
[24] R. DE ROOVER, *Money, Banking and Credit*, p. 303.

Pieter Scandilioen, a Bruges citizen since 1360,[25] was born as Pietro Scandaleone in Lucca. Relations with him may have gone back to 1347, when he was one of the merchants with whom Tommaso Giganti issued a loan to the weavers.[26] When the Rapondi used intermediaries, who had to be present at every transaction between foreign merchants, they too seem to have originated from the Rapondis' own city: the brokers Clais Barbezaen, originally Barbagialla and having obtained Bruges' citizenship in the first half of the fourteenth century,[27] and Gilles Visolle[28] were also Lucchese natives. The names of both men appear regularly in Guglielmo's accounts.[29] This makes it clear that already there were special relationships between the Lucchese in Bruges before the Lucchese nation was set up and it was very likely that these bonds formed the foundation of the nation later on.

Guglielmo's network did not only number Lucchese. According to de Marke's books, the Rapondi also did business with other Italians, such as Lois de Robiert, Jehan de Priolle and the Venetian Marco Morosini. The English were represented by Jehan Levaie, Nicolas Halberine and William Medilton and the Spanish kingdoms by Goris Emperael. The Easterlings worked with Guglielmo as well, as indicated by the presence of Thideman Rebber,[30] alderman and messenger of the Bruges' *hanzekontor*.[31] Among these foreign names we also find Edele de Ruddervoorde,[32] which makes us believe that Rebber was not the only Hanseatic merchant committed in the plans of the Rapondi family. Until it went bankrupt in 1372, the hostel of "Mademoiselle de Ruddervoorde" was very popular with Hanse merchants,[33] who tended to use the Bruges money-changers via the accounts of the hostellers with whom they stayed. Other Flemings in contact with Guglielmo were Antonne Raimonde[34] and Pieter de Winter, a wool merchant much in business with the Lucchese.[35]

The network of the Rapondis' relationships, as revealed in these accounts, thus shows some diversity, although it is clear that the Italians, especially those from Lucca, were responsible for most of the connections in de Marke's ledgers. In these books, "sen compaignon" is frequently mentioned in Guglielmo's *conti*. The identity of this partner is not exactly clear, but it could be Dino Rapondi. Nevertheless, he figures on his own behalf in the accounts of others (for instance in those of Forteguerra Forteguerra), which might indicate a certain freedom of action from the authority of his elder brother.

Bruges had more than one money-changer. Guglielmo could make payments to individuals with accounts with de Marke's colleagues Pieter van Oudenaarde and Jacop Reups,[36] as these had accounts with each other. The

---

[25] A. JAMEES, *Brugse Poorters, opgetekend uit de stadsrekeningen en ingeleid. Deel 1: 1281-1417*, Handzame, Familia et Patria, 1980, p. 118.
[26] A. SCHOUTEET, *Regesten op de oorkonden 1340-1384*, p. 39.
[27] N. GEIRNAERT and A. VANDEWALLE, "Brugge en Italië" in: V. VERMEERSCH, *Brugge en Europa*, Antwerpen, Mercatorfonds, 1992, p. 199.
[28] A. JAMEES, *Brugse Poorters 1281-1417*, p. 19.
[29] R. DE ROOVER, *Money, Banking and Credit*, p. 376.
[30] R. DE ROOVER, *Money, Banking and Credit*, p. 376.
[31] W. PARAVICINI and H. WERNICKE (eds.), *Hansekaufleute in Brügge. Teil 3: Prosopographischer Katalog zu den Brügger Steuerlisten (1360-1390)*, Frankfurt am Main, Peter Lang, 1999, p. 329. (Kieler Werkstücke, Reihe D, 11).
[32] R. DE ROOVER, *Money, Banking and Credit*, p. 376.
[33] J. M. MURRAY, *Bruges, Cradle of Capitalism, 1280-1390*, Cambridge, Cambridge University Press, 2005, pp. 318-320.
[34] R. DE ROOVER, *Money, Banking and Credit*, p. 376.
[35] J. M. MURRAY, *Bruges, Cradle of Capitalism*, p. 325.
[36] R. DE ROOVER, *Money, Banking and Credit*, pp. 376-377.

head of the Rapondi company also did business with another money-changer, Willem Ruweel. As with van Marke, his accounts were preserved by the juridical confiscation following his bankruptcy in 1370. These documents make clear that Guglielmo concluded transactions via Ruweel only occasionally (this was also the case with Ruweel's other Italian customers, such as Forteguerra Forteguerra). Each time Rapondi opened an account with the money-changer, it was closed again after two or three operations.[37] For example a certain widow Matsenars transferred the sum of 3 lb. 10 s. gr. to his *conto*. He did not touch the money for 18 days, whereupon Francesco Totti, a Lucchese to whom he had probably given a proxy, visited Willem Ruweel to collect this amount.[38] The accounts Guglielmo kept with Ruweel were probably subordinated to those kept with Collard van Marke. However, the books of both money-changers are unlikely to show all the contacts made by the Lucchese company maintained during their early days in Bruges.

Perhaps Guglielmo Rapondi's most important contacts were never mentioned in the deposit accounts. This was the case with the sale of a golden canopy (a silk fabric with patterns, often used for the manufacture of the decoration for thrones with the same name), each worth 59 s. gr., which Guglielmo realized in 1367-68. The canopies were intended for the city, who donated the fabric to "my Lady from Brabant".[39] This may have been Joan, the wife of Wenceslas of Luxemburg and Duchess of Brabant in her own right, or her sister Margaret, the wife of Louis of Male, who bore the ducal title after he had usurpated it at Wenceslas' expense.[40] We do not know the occasion for which these gifts were given. Possibly it was at a public manifestation at which Bruges welcomed the Flemish count (which suggests the beneficiary was Margaret), Louis of Namur and the citizens of Ghent, Ypres and Sluis, all receiving prosent wines from the city.[41] For the Rapondi it would have been an event of considerable importance, since the merchants would have come into contact with the municipal authorities for the first time, one of the two factors that were to determine the development of the firm in the future. More importantly, another connection, also not to be found in the ledgers of the money-changers, would keep Guglielmo and his family in work. This was with Iolanda, countess of Bar and Lady of Kassel.

---

[37] R. DE ROOVER, *Le livre de comptes de Guillaume Ruyelle*, p. 60.
[38] R. DE ROOVER, *Le livre de comptes de Guillaume Ruyelle*, p. 32.
[39] SAB, Stadsrekening 02/02/1367-02/02/1368, f° 82 v°.
[40] See *supra*.
[41] SAB, Stadsrekening 02/02/1367-02/02/1368, f° 36 r°.

1.2 Iolanda of Kassel: a Lavish Lady

Iolanda of Kassel was the only daughter of Robert of Kassel, the second son of the Flemish count Robert of Béthune.[42] After his father's death in 1322, Robert had claimed the title of count but had had to acknowledge the superiority of the legal heir, his nephew Louis of Nevers.[43] His daughter Iolanda had married Henry IV, count of Bar in northern France, in 1340. When her husband died four years later, the countess took over the rule of the county.[44] The fearless way in which she did this has given her a bad reputation in modern historiography, not always fairly. Notwithstanding the frequent resistance to her rule, Iolanda was to reign during the minority of her eldest son Edward and, after his death, would leave her mark on the rule of her second son, duke Robert I.[45] (Robert would rid himself of his mother's interference only in 1371).[46] Despite her administrative duties in Bar, the countess often stayed in her Flemish properties, which she inherited from her father. These were in the Kassel area and the neighbouring castellanies, where Iolanda mostly lived in her castle in the Nieppe forest.[47] At times she also visited Bruges, where she owned the monumentel 'Casselberg' house in the Hoogstraat (possibly built or rebuilt by her father Robert of Kassel, who may have lent his name to the building). The presence of numerous Lombards or Cahorsins was probably one of the most important reasons for her stays in the city, since Iolanda lived in the grand style and was in permanent need of money, and thus resorted to pawnbrokers and other financiers.[48]

It may have been her contacts with the Bruges Lombards, where she had been a regular customer for some time, that brought Iolanda and the Rapondi family together. The Lucchese firm, unquestionably familiar with the Cahorsins because of its financial operations in the city, represented the pawnshop keepers in their transactions with the countess. This may have occurred for the first time on April 5, 1364, when the Lady of Kassel asked her receivers Eloi Surien and Franc de le Brique to pay Guglielmo Rapondi 1000 francs. The sum was intended for the Lombards, to whom she owed 2000 francs.[49] Seven months later, on November 3, 1364, Iolanda of Bar asked Dino to go to the Lombards and retrieve a golden crown, twelve silver drinking goblets and two golden hats. She had given these objects in pledge for a 1010 moutons d'or loan on May 11. However, the settlement, for which she had supplied Dino with 1222 moutons d'or (implying an interest rate of 23%)[50] and for which Guglielmo delivered the receipt to her, was not enough to get all of Iolanda's possessions back. She then gave the eldest of the brothers an unknown sum "to buy back the crown and other jewels belonging to Madame".

---

[42] J. SABBE, "Yolande van Vlaanderen, gravin van Bar en vrouwe van Cassel, en het huis de « Casselberg » in Brugge (1373)" in: *Handelingen van het Genootschap voor Geschiedenis*, Brugge, 2001, 138, 1-2, p. 35.
[43] See *supra*.
[44] J.M FINOT, "Le train de maison d'une grande dame au xive siècle. Étude sur les comptes de l'hotel des sires de Cassel et particulièrement sur ceux d'Yolande de Flandre, comtesse de Bar" in : *Bulletin Historique et philologique du comité des travaux historiques et scientifiques*, Paris, 1889, 1-2, p. 178.
[45] J. SABBE, *Yolande van Vlaanderen*, pp. 36-37.
[46] J.M FINOT, *Le train de maison d'une grande dame au xive siècle*, p. 184.
[47] J.M FINOT, *Le train de maison d'une grande dame au xive siècle*, pp. 177-178.
[48] J. SABBE, *Yolande van Vlaanderen*, p. 44.
[49] J. M. FINOT, *Inventaire sommaire Tome Septième*, p. 50.
[50] G. BIGWOOD, *Le régime juridique et économique du commerce de l'argent dans la Belgique du Moyen Âge Tome I*, Bruxelles, Maurice Lamertin, 1921, pp. 447-448.

At the same time, the countess had negotiated another loan for which the Rapondi served as intermediaries, probably contracted on June 10, 1364 for 6000 francs.[51] On February 15 of the following year, she still owed the Lombards 2000 francs, to be paid via Guglielmo.[52]

The Lady of Kassel also applied to the Rapondi for larger transactions. If we can believe Léon Mirot, Guglielmo was required to collect a part of the ransom needed for the release of Iolanda's son, duke Robert.[53] He had been captured in April 1369 by an ally of the inhabitants of Metz, who were involved in a conflict with the Barrois. To set Robert free, the Messins demanded 140 000 gold florins.[54] The countess was willing to contribute to the payment and asked for Guglielmo's aid, according to Mirot.[55] He induced Thomas Bonderaen and Brunet Carbon, two Lombards living in Bruges,[56] to grant a loan of 5000 francs, 3000 Hungarian and 3000 other florins, together 10 500 francs, requiring an annual interest of 30%. In exchange, five of Iolanda's knights and courtiers and two of her cities, Dunkirk and Gravelines, had to stand surety and the countess had to pawn six expensive items from her jewels. It is not clear how the repayment of the 6000 florins was made but the 5000 francs had to be redeemed in five instalments over three years.[57] At least four of these five instalments were paid to Dino Rapondi, who gave the receipts to the receivers and made over the sums to the Cahorsins.[58]

In the meantime, small loans, covering more daily expenses, continued. Dino, for instance, submitted another receipt, sealed with the company's trademark, on July 17, 1369.[59] The document also mentions two new credits, one opened with the Lombards amounting to 135 lb. 16 s. 8 d. gr. and an annual interest of 43.3% (66 lb. 15 s. 8 d. gr. for a year and seven weeks), the second with other merchants amounting to 2000 francs and 24% annual interest.[60] Similar transactions, with the Rapondi serving as a transfer point, would follow far into the 1370s. After 1380, however, such operations became much less frequent with the company's then new priorities. Still, the Lucchese were to receive important sums for the countess of Bar up until 1393, two years before her death.[61]

The Rapondi did not restrict themselves to their intermediary role but, shortly after the first known contacts, began to grant funds to the ever-indebted Lady of Kassel themselves. On August 7, 1364, four months after the receipt of the Lombards' 1000 francs, Iolanda paid Guglielmo 50 lb. gr. of what she owed him.[62] More than two months later 700 francs were paid for the same reasons. The number of loans steadily increased, although they never seem to have

---

[51] G. BIGWOOD, *Le régime juridique et économique du commerce de l'argent dans la Belgique du Moyen Âge Tome II*, Bruxelles, Maurice Lamertin, 1922, pp. 20-21.
[52] M. DEHAISNES et J.M FINOT, *Inventaire sommaire des archives départementales antérieures à 1790. Nord. Archives Civiles-Série B. Tome I*, Lille, L. Danel, 1906, p. 331.
[53] L. MIROT, *La société des Raponde*, p. 309.
[54] J.M. FINOT, *Le train de maison d'une grande dame au xive siècle*, p. 182.
[55] L. MIROT, *La société des Raponde*, p. 309.
[56] See W. REICHERT, *Lombarden in der Germania-Romania*, p. 172.
[57] G. BIGWOOD, *Le régime juridique et économique Tome II*, pp. 22-25.
[58] G. BIGWOOD, *Le régime juridique et économique Tome II*, pp. 302-305.
[59] This looks very much like the signs with which Piero and, after his return from Paris, Guido Rapondi, authenticated their oath to John of Bohemia in 1331.
[60] G. BIGWOOD, *Le régime juridique et économique Tome II*, pp. 22-23.
[61] L. MIROT, *La société des Raponde*, pp. 323-324.
[62] J. M. FINOT, *Inventaire sommaire Tome Septième*, p. 51.

assumed the proportions of the sums the Rapondi negotiated for the countess as her intermediaries. Probably their own loans mainly concerned credit to cover the daily expenses of Iolanda's lavish way of living. This must also have been why she ordered 50 lb. and 300 francs, a sum Dino had lent her, to be paid to Guglielmo on July 22, 1369.[63] They assigned her another 100 francs when she ran out of cash in Paris in August 1370. Other Rapondi brothers also granted loans to Iolanda of Bar. She borrowed several sums from Andrea in 1368, which she paid back to Dino on May 18, and 600 lb. two years later. Piero Rapondi sent her 5 francs from Bruges when she stayed in Bourget, near Paris, in 1370.[64]

The company also advanced Iolanda's payments to third parties. This was the case on April 28, 1369, when Dino passed 200 francs to Robert, Lord of Fiennes and *connétable* of France, on the countess' behalf. Eighteen months later, the Rapondi had still not received back their money and the Lady of Kassel challenged the 90 francs which Dino had charged as interest (annualized at 30%).[65] The affair must have turned out well, since the loans continued until the end of the 1370s. The Rapondi were repaid for their last known credit operation on August 20, 1377, after they had issued 100 francs in cash to Iolanda.[66] However, in a letter dated May 18, 1378, Dino still mentions "money we borrowed her [...] lately".[67] As with their activities as intermediaries, the firm granted fewer loansto the countess from this date.

The Rapondis' services for Iolanda of Kassel were rounded off nicely when they started to supply her with merchandise. The first indications of this are to be found some years after the first financial contacts and directly point to the delivery of large amounts of goods. This suggests that Iolanda first became familiar with the Rapondi through banking and only then engaged them to supply her court, although sources mentioning smaller commercial contacts from an earlier date may have been lost. The oldest document in this respect is a statement of debts addressed to Guglielmo on July 27, 1368.[68] Together with two other surveys of purchases from the company (one, very extensive, of goods bought in Bruges and delivered to Iolanda's mansion in Ypres on January 22, 1370[69] and another dated 1370-71),[70] it provides a catalogue of everything the Rapondi firm had to offer in terms of merchandise in this period. Especially striking is the sheer diversity of the stock, considering that, as with most of the Italian merchants, this was mostly luxury goods. The privileged position of expensive fabrics in this range is not surprising, given Lucca's reputation as a centre of manufacture for these (they represent more than 43% of the amount the countess of Bar paid in the three cases). Silk, painted in all possible colours figures repeatedly in the documents, as do related and derived goods, such as satin, gold brocade,[71] sendal and baldachin. To this we must add "cuevrechiés",[72] gold wire, ribbon and cords (the latter two for curtains).[73]

---

[63] J. M. FINOT, *Inventaire sommaire Tome Septième*, p. 91.
[64] M. DEHAISNES, *Documents et extraits divers concernant l'histoire de l'art*, pp. 499-500.
[65] G. BIGWOOD, *Le régime juridique et économique Tome I*, p. 75.
[66] L. MIROT, *La société des Raponde*, pp. 322-323.
[67] G. BIGWOOD, *Le régime juridique et économique Tome II*, p. 369.
[68] M. DEHAISNES, *Documents et extraits divers concernant l'histoire de l'art*, p. 485.
[69] J. M. FINOT, *Inventaire sommaire Tome Septième*, pp. 66-67.
[70] M. DEHAISNES, *Documents et extraits divers concernant l'histoire de l'art*, pp. 496-501.
[71] Silk interwoven with gold wire.
[72] A type of hat or veil.
[73] M. DEHAISNES, *Documents et extraits divers concernant l'histoire de l'art*, pp. 485 en 496-497. J. M. FINOT, *Inventaire sommaire Tome Septième*, p. 67.

Furthermore, the Rapondi obtained gold and gold leaf (from Cyprus),[74] mastic, sugar and a broad range of exotic fruit, from pomegranates, oranges, grapes and raisins to figs, almonds and preserved pineapples ("pignolat") from the Mediterranean. It is not impossible to imagine that some of these products originated from the Iberian region and had been passed trough the hands of Spanish merchants before they ended up with Guglielmo and his companions. This applies all the more to the "cibolles d'Espaigne" (peppers), hazelnut and anise, bought by Iolanda's chamberlain from the Lucchese. More exotic regions supplied spices, reaching the Italian peninsula via middlemen and probably transported by the Rapondi from there to Flanders. Many are mentioned in the sources, such as cinnamon (and cinnamon flower), clove, nutmeg, ginger and "graines de paradis".[75] Closer to home, the company laid in stocks of several highly finished products, produced by the Bruges luxury industries. Iolanda walked through her expensive life in fine shoes, of which at least twelve pairs were bought by Dino in Bruges.[76] He and his brothers also obliged Iolanda with two silver crosses, a half piece of cloth, some barrels and, another Bruges specialty, two paternosters, one in silver and one in amber,[77] probably imported from the Hanse area.

The receipt for July 1369 indicates that the Rapondi had direct contacts with the German Hanse. It not only mentions two debt settlements to the Lombards and other businessmen, but also various goods the Rapondi had sold to Iolanda. Besides 10 ells of ribbon, it concerned "une timbre de laitiche",[78] the fur of a lynx and fifty "ventres de menu vair".[79] The Rapondi probably got these from the Easterlings, who imported this kind of goods from northern and north-eastern Europe. The connections with the Hanse, which we have already noted with the appearance of Tideman Rebber in Guglielmo's van Marke accounts,[80] and possibly also with Spanish merchants, thus shade the almost exclusively Italian network of the Rapondi as can be reconstructed from the ledgers of the Bruges money-changers.

After the long debt surveys from the end of the 1360s and the beginning of the 1370s, the size and the frequency of the commercial contacts between the Rapondi and Iolanda seem to have diminished considerably. This may be explained by the fact that the Lady of Kassel was obliged to abandon her influence on the governance of the county of Bar around 1370. Due to the troubles to which this led (such as her incarceration), the countess sank even deeper into debt, which forced her to alter her purchasing policy and to search even harder for loans (these, contrary to her commercial arrangements, continued). Because of her financial difficulties, she also had to sell the

[74] M. DEHAISNES, *Documents et extraits divers concernant l'histoire de l'art*, p. 485.

[75] J. M. FINOT, *Inventaire sommaire Tome Septième*, p. 67.

[76] M. DEHAISNES, *Documents et extraits divers concernant l'histoire de l'art*, p. 497. J. M. FINOT, *Inventaire sommaire Tome Septième*, p. 67.

[77] M. DEHAISNES, *Documents et extraits divers concernant l'histoire de l'art*, p. 485. J. M. FINOT, *Inventaire sommaire Tome Septième*, p. 67.

[78] This was forty strongly white furs of an animal, related to the ermine, often used for the trimming on garments. R. DELORT , *Le commerce des fourrures en Occident à la fin du Moyen Age (vers 1300 - vers 1450)*, Rome, Ecole Française de Rome, 1978, pp. 30-32.

[79] J. M. FINOT, *Inventaire sommaire Tome Septième*, p. 65. L. MIROT, *La société des Raponde*, pp. 314-315. This is the white fur on the underside of Russian and Siberian squirrels which was manufactured into a pattern with the grey fur on their backs. R. DELORT , *Le commerce des fourrures*, pp. 42-43.

[80] See *supra*.

Casselberg house,[81] which reduced her stays in Bruges. From this time on, she retreated more to *la-Motte-au-Bois* in Nieppe, inducing her to spend less on her household.[82]

Six years would pass before we find the Rapondi concluding a commercial transaction with the countess again. On August 20, 1377, she ordered her officers to pay them 62 francs for the delivery of provisions.[83] Luxury goods were still the most popular, demonstrated by a receipt, given by Andrea Rapondi to Iolanda's receiver Tassart de la Fontaine in 1379, concerning the sale of silver plate.[84] The following year, Dino supplied her again with a paternoster and a clasp in mother-of-pearl, set with two rubies and six pearls, intended as a gift for her granddaughter and namesake, the countess of Girone. It would be Iolanda's last trade agreement with the Rapondi, if we do not consider the advance and transport of five bulls she obtained from pope Clement VII in 1385.[85] Despite the short period of intense business dealings at the beginning, as a whole the commercial relationship between Iolanda of Kassel and the company turns out to be quite modest, compared with their financial operations. The total amount it represents does not come near that of the loans, to say nothing of the capital, assembled by the Rapondi as intermediaries.

Guglielmo, Dino and the other Rapondi did not always receive the remuneration they earned with their efforts for Iolanda. Often repayments kept dragging on for years, the countess challenging certain sums or the interest charged[86] or, sometimes, she simply did not pay. Characteristic in this respect was the fuss preceding the debt settlement of 1377. This document makes clear that the loans issued by the Rapondi had run to 2504 francs, 11 s. and 3 d. gr. Dino had reminded Iolanda already a year before that according to an account extract dated July 20, 1376, they still had to receive half of her debt. Although making two payments as a result of these complaints, the countess did not just accept the claims of the Lucchese. She demanded an investigation in their presence "because there are several things that have been written unclearly, which the aforementioned Dino must explain, and things my Lady cannot remember, so Dino will have to make another final account". Consequently, Dino and his brothers had to provide a written proof of every transaction mentioned in the accounts and to show when and by whom they were concluded. We do not know which way the negotiations went, but finally an agreement was reached. The payments recommenced and on January 13, the countess was only in debt for 997 francs 12 s. gr. From then on, the two parties would be more cautious, stipulating that the account would be cancelled and a new one written should an irregularity be found. Yet, this did not happen and on August 20, 1377, Iolanda was able to declare "that my Lady is and remains quits with the aforementioned Dino and his companions".[87]

The countess's incapacity to pay was also well-known by others. When, in 1378, she asked the count of Saarbrücken, counsellor and chamberlain of the

---

[81] J. SABBE, *Yolande van Vlaanderen*, p. 43 en 45.

[82] J.M FINOT, *Le train de maison d'une grande dame au xive siècle*, p. 189.

[83] L. MIROT, *La société des Raponde*, p. 323.

[84] L. MIROT, *La société des Raponde*, p. 317, n. 2.

[85] L. MIROT, *La société des Raponde*, p. 324.

[86] See the affair with Robert of Fiennes, *supra*.

[87] L. MIROT, *La société des Raponde*, pp. 322-323.

French king Charles V, for a loan, he expected firm guarantees. For that reason Dino Rapondi, who had probably led these negotiations, required a certain Pierre du Pons to stand surety for the operation. The latter, however, demanded a security, something Dino said he could not provide. As he wrote to the Lady of Kassel on May 18, he could not offer as a security the cloth he had in stock, because he would then no longer able to sell it and it would lose its value. This took place while he was already forgoing more than 100 francs by helping others to get a warrant, and he and his brother Andrea had already been asking Iolanda for some time to repay them money they had lent her recently. They urged the countess to redeem her debts to them as soon as possible or send an advance, so that they would be able to defend her interests again.[88]

Notwithstanding these and other troubles, the Rapondi continued to work for Iolanda for a very long time, not without results. The relationship with the countess of Bar would prove very favourable for the development of the company. Nevertheless, the services of the brothers can hardly be called exceptional, being exactly the same kind of activities carried out by so many of their compatriots. The Rapondi were certainly not the only Lucchese to combine their business in banking with the trade in precious objects, such as spices, gold and silverwork and, above all, silk fabric. Less self-evident was the way they used their financial and commercial capabilities to win the confidence of Iolanda of Bar, a noblewoman with expensive tastes in constant need of capital. This ensured the company continuous orders and credit openings, in spite of the late repayments. By far the most important aspect of this relationship, however, was that Iolanda, being a member of the Flemish comital family, would be the step to the relationship that would guarantee the success of the Rapondi family for the next sixty years, beginning with the marriage of Philip the Bold and Margaret of Male, in 1369.

1.3 The Marriage of Philip the Bold and Margaret of Male

The death of the young Philip of Rouvres, the last Capetian duke of Burgundy, on November 21, 1361 was important to European politics in two ways. First, the death prompted the French king John II the Good to repossess the duchy, an important fief situated on the border with the German Empire. In 1363, he gave it in appanage to his fourth son Philip, called 'the Bold' for his courage at the battle of Poitiers (1356). One year later Philip's brother Charles V, who had succeeded John as king of France, confirmed the agreement between his late father and the new Burgundian duke.[89] The second significant political consequence of the death of Philip of Rouvres was that his widow, Margaret of Male, became reavailable on the marriage market. She was the daughter and the only heir of the Flemish count, Louis of Male, and, due to her attractive dowry, had no lack of suitors. One of the most important was the English king Edward III, who was naturally not averse to an alliance with an economically booming region on the northern border of his hereditary enemy, France. He proposed his son Edmund Langley, earl of Cambridge, as Margaret's suitor. The claims of Philip the Bold to the counties of Artois and Franche-Comté, part of the inheritance of Philip of Rouvres and also claimed by

[88] G. BIGWOOD, *Le régime juridique et économique Tome II*, pp. 369-370.
[89] R. VAUGHAN, *Philip the Bold*, pp. 2-3.

Margaret of France, Rouvres's great-aunt and the mother of Louis of Male, simplified the negotiations between the English and the Flemings, which were concluded in 1364.

This turn of events was of course unacceptable to the French, because the Anglo-Flemish alliance would tip the continental balance of power definitively in favour of England. At the request of Charles V, the pro-French pope Urban V refused to grant a dispensation for the marriage, which was necessary because Edmund and Margaret were relatives in the fourth degree. Charles V used the delay in the marriage plans to push forward his own candidate, his brother Philip the Bold.[90] Nevertheless, Louis of Male wanted to preserve the independance of his county at all costs and was very distrustful of a French rapprochement. His mother Margaret, of French origin, was more favourably disposed towards Charles V's proposition and became one of the most vigorous partisans of her grand-daughter's marriage with Philip. Still, the Flemish count would not give away his daughter for nothing. In exchange for his approval, he made high demands of the French, which prolonged the negotiations. Only in April 1369 was an agreement reached, with Louis realizing all his objectives. One was the return of Lille, Douai and Orchies, the castellanies of Walloon Flanders that Robert of Béthune had ceded to Philip the Fair with the Treaty of Pontoise (1312).[91] However, the French crown maintained the right to repurchase the castellanies should Philip the Bold die without a male heir. Moreover, Charles V had also concluded a secret agreement with his brother, that Walloon Flanders would revert to France on the death of Louis of Male. However, this arrangement was meaningless, since the Flemish count had obtained from his daughter as well as his son-in-law a written promise that Lille, Douai and Orchies would never again be separated from Flanders.[92]

In addition to the ceding of the castellanies in Walloon Flanders, Louis required the considerable sum of 200 000 francs for Margaret's hand. Half of it had to be paid by Philip the Bold before the marriage, the other half in the following two years. The Burgundian duke counted on the support of his brother, who slipped him half of the first payment. Charles V chipped in another 20 000 francs[93] but Philip the Bold still had to find 30 000 francs, which he obtained from several money-lenders. Three of them lent a considerably larger sum than the others: Barthelemi Spifame supplied 10 000 francs, Bureau de la Rivière 7000 and Guglielmo Rapondi 3000. A large number of other

---

[90] J.J.N. PALMER, "England, France, the papacy and the Flemish succession, 1361-9" in: *Journal of Medieval History*, Amsterdam, 1976, 2, pp. 339-364.

[91] See *supra*.

[92] R. VAUGHAN, *Philip the Bold*, pp. 4-6.

[93] J. RAUZIER, *Finances et gestion d'une principauté. Le duché de Bourgogne de Philippe le Hardi 1364-1384*, Paris, Ministère de l'économie et des finances, 1996, p. 668. It would not be the last time a Burgundian duke would use money from the royal treasury for his own purposes. For this, see B. A. POQUET DU HAUT JUSSÉ, "Les dons du roi aux ducs de Bourgogne Philippe le Hardi et Jean sans Peur (1363-1419). Le don des aides" in : *Annales de Bourgogne*, Dijon, 1938, 10, pp. 261-289. IDEM, "Les dons du roi aux ducs de Bourgogne Philippe le Hardi et Jean sans Peur (1363-1419). Les dons ordinaires" in : *Mémoires de la Société pour l'Histoire du droit et des institutions des anciens pays bourguignons, comtois et romands*, Dijon, 1939, 6, pp. 113-144. IDEM, "Les dons du roi aux ducs de Bourgogne Philippe le Hardi et Jean sans Peur (1363-1419). Les dons extraordinaires" in : *Mémoires de la Société pour l'Histoire du droit et des institutions des anciens pays bourguignons, comtois et romands*, Dijon, 1940-'41, 7, pp. 95-129.

persons, specifically officers and dignitaries from the ducal entourage, topped up the amount.[94]

The connections that Philip the Bold had with Spifame and de la Rivière seem evident, since the first had been a supplier and a financier to the French court for years[95] and the second was the king's right-hand man and chamberlain.[96] How Philip got in touch with Rapondi is less clear (as far as is known, the family was not yet living in Paris). However, it seems plausible that Iolanda of Bar, a close relative of Philip the Bold,[97] may have put him in the way of her preferred bankers. Another point of contact could have been Barthelemi Spifame, who, notwithstanding that he had been a naturalized Frenchman since 1342, originated from Lucca as well.[98] Other compatriots of the Rapondi, perhaps through Spifame, also took their share of the business from the marriage. In 1370, for instance, the Burgundian duke owed 17 185 francs to three merchants associated with Forteguerra Forteguerra, living in Bruges, who had been given jewels as a pledge for the redemption of the debt.[99]

Philip the Bold was not the only one dealing with money-lenders. At the end of April 1368, Louis of Male had raised a loan of 5000 lb. par. with the Lombards of Bruges, Alost, Termonde, Bergues and Malines. This has been associated by some with possible costs for the wedding, although, at this point, the negotiations were still under discussion and the outcome was far from being certain. 3000 lb. of this loan could be reclaimed by the pawnshop owners from the city of Bruges, who owed this amount every year to the count as indirect taxes, and the remaining 2000 lb. could be retrieved from the Franc of Bruges, that was still paying its share of the *aide* assigned to Louis.[100] Knowing that in this period the Rapondi acted continually as go-betweens in the transactions between Iolanda of Bar and the Lombards,[101] it is not unreasonable to assume that Guglielmo and his brothers played the same role when the same Lombards concluded a similar transaction with a relative of the Lady of Kassel.[102] This, however, is far from certain.

Once the financial arrangements were completed, the wedding festivities could go ahead. After Philip the Bold had rendered homage to Charles V on June 10, he travelled to Ghent, arriving on June 18. The next day, he was married to Margaret of Male. The ceremony and the parties that followed were a demonstration of the splendour with which Philip impressed his subjects-to-be.[103] He tried to win over the Flemish nobility, clergy and urban elites by distributing gifts and offering them sumptuous banquets.[104] A couple of days later, the new couple made their entry in Bruges. This was the occasion for the

---

[94] J. RAUZIER, *Finances et gestion d'une principauté*, p. 668.
[95] L. MIROT, "La colonie lucquoise à Paris du XIIIe au xve siècle" in: *Bibliothèque de l'Ecole des Chartes*, Paris, 1927, 88, p. 76.
[96] F. AUTRAND, *Charles V le Sage*, Paris, Librairie Arthème Fayard, 1994, pp. 699-702.
[97] Her son was married to his sister. J. SABBE, *Yolande van Vlaanderen*, p. 37.
[98] L. MIROT, *La colonie lucquoise à Paris*, p. 76.
[99] It is not known why exactly the credit had been agreed. L. MIROT, "Forteguerra Forteguerra et sa succession" in: *Bibliothèque de l'Ecole des Chartes*, Paris, 1935, 96, p. 303. J. RAUZIER, *Finances et gestion d'une principauté*, p. 614.
[100] A. SCHOUTEET, "Un emprunt de Louis de Male aux Lombards en 1368" in : *Handelingen van het Genootschap voor Geschiedenis*, Brugge, 1954, 91, pp. 160-162.
[101] See *supra*.
[102] Louis was her great-nephew.
[103] For the display of power, characteristic of the Burgundian house, see P. ARNADE, *Realms of Ritual. Burgundian ceremony and civic life in late medieval Ghent*, Ithaca, Cornell University Press, 1996, pp. 26-27.
[104] R. VAUGHAN, *Philip the Bold*, p. 6.

urban elites to win the favour of the future count by offering gifts in their turn, from wine and falcons to silk fabrics. The merchants, especially those trading in luxury goods, could thus profit handsomely from the marriage.

Among them was Guglielmo Rapondi, from whom the city council bought two "dobbele" golden baldachins, worth 12 lb. 16 s. gr., to present to the duke.[105] Interestingly, four months before, on February 5, 1369, the same sum, less a shilling, was mentioned on the credit side of Guglielmo's account with Collard de Marke, unfortunately without giving the name of the debtor.[106] Apparently the company had already made a reputation in these kinds of fabrics, since the city had ordered exactly the same from the Rapondi to give to the Duchess of Brabant, although it was not specified if the baldachin had also been a "dobbele" or lined one.[107] Again, Rapondi was not the only Lucchese doing good business on this occasion, for the city also presented a baldachin, bought from Davino Tedaldini, to Philip the Bold.[108]

The duke would stay in Flanders until the end of the month. After that he returned to France on the orders of his brother, who had resumed war with the English.[109] It did not prevent the Rapondi from converting their first contacts with the duke into cash. In the course of 1369 (on July 7 and December 16) and at the beginning of 1370 (January 15), they supplied gold and silk worth 2457 lb. 14 s. 9 d. to Philip,[110] who must have ordered these while staying in Flanders.

In view of the later history of the Low Countries, the importance of the marriage between Philip and Margaret cannot be overestimated. When Louis of Male died, the county of Flanders, with Antwerp and Malines (in Flemish hands since 1357) would pass to the new house of the Burgundian dukes. Philip, however, not only had the prospect of ruling Flanders, he would be able to expand his territories with the principality of Rethel, also part of the inheritance from Louis of Male, as well as with Artois, Franche-Comté and Nevers, three counties belonging to Louis' mother Margaret (with the first bordering on Flanders and the other two in Philip's Burgundian possessions). Therefore, the events of 1369 were the first but a decisive step towards the formation of an independent complex of territories, free from France, and towards the unification of the Netherlands, although both still had a long way to go.[111]

For the Rapondi brothers, the marriage was also a turning point. The commercial transactions with the duke that they could realize in the days following the ceremony dwarfed all their former operations, and their loan of 3000 francs that helped bring about the event was probably the biggest credit they had ever issued.[112] By releasing this amount they also headed the list of money-lenders who furnished the duke's 30 000 francs, which suggests they were already one of the most substantial business houses of the Bruges money

---

[105] L. GILLIODTS-VAN SEVEREN, *Inventaire des archives de la ville de Bruges. Première section: inventaire des chartes. Première série: treizième au seizième siècle Tome second*, Bruges, Louis de Plancke, 1871, pp. 171-173.
[106] R. DE ROOVER, *Money, Banking and Credit*, p. 376.
[107] See *supra*.
[108] L. GILLIODTS-VAN SEVEREN, *Inventaire des archives de la ville de Bruges Tome second*, Bruges, Louis de Plancke, 1871, p. 173.
[109] R. VAUGHAN, *Philip the Bold*, p. 8.
[110] J. RAUZIER, *Finances et gestion d'une principauté*, p. 624.
[111] W. P. BLOCKMANS and W. PREVENIER, *De Bourgondiërs: De Nederlanden op weg naar eenheid*, Amsterdam-Leuven, Meulenhoff, 1997, pp. 13-14.
[112] For example, it amounted to more than the total sum granted to Iolanda of Bar from 1370 to 1377.

market. Much more important than the size of the loans, was that they were the first contact between the Rapondi and Philip the Bold, with whom they would conclude so many lucrative transactions in subsequent years. In this way, the marriage was the first in a long series of manifestations of the Burgundian 'theatre state', in which the family would be involved. It is remarkable that it did not end with just a single transaction between the Rapondi and Philip the Bold. After they had financed one of the duke's undertakings, their return on this investment was in their relationship with the city, to whom they sold expensive fabrics. This situation would repeat itself more than once in successive years. This, however, would happen without Guglielmo, for whom the 1369 operations were his last major achievements. We meet him once more, on April 26, 1370, and not long after this date he must have died.[113] The repayment of the loan and the deliveries to Philip the Bold had already been handled by Dino Rapondi,[114] who would head the company from now on. He would follow the path established by his elder brother, and lead the firm to new heights.

[113] L. MIROT, *La société des Raponde*, p. 311.
[114] J. RAUZIER, *Finances et gestion d'une principauté*, pp. 614, 624.

CHAPTER 2

INTERNATIONAL ORIENTATION (1370-1384)

The first commercial contacts between the Rapondi and the city of Bruges took place at the end of the 1360s.[1] Onc might have expected these relations to evolve further and lead to more intensive commercial transactions. However, the agreements with the city were a false start and were not continued. The Rapondis' presence in Bruges seems even to have decreased after 1370, although they did not disappear completely from Flanders. Dino Rapondi, then probably between 30 and 35 years old, would have been responsible for this change. In 1369, his brother Guglielmo had established connections with Philip the Bold. Possibly, this made Dino realize what the Burgundian duke was capable of with his costly politics and what this could bring in for the company. Apparently the new head of the company considerd these perspectives to be more attractive than the older bonds with the city. This made him connect his firm's destiny with that of Philip the Bold, from the first day he was in charge.

Since, after his marriage, the duke limited his presence in Flanders to annual visits[2] and lived most of the time in Paris, near the king, his most important source of income, the Rapondi would move the centre of their activities to the French capital, joining a considerable Lucchese colony. The one-sided focus on Bruges would give way to a more international outlook, that would lead to the establishment of a new branch in Avignon at the end of the decade and in which their presence in Lucca would gain a new political importance. With this dynamic, Bruges would lose its status as the Rapondis' chief trading centre that it had inherited from Lucca, to the new house in Paris.

2.1 'Bourgeois de Paris'

Compared to the transfer of the Rapondi company's centre from Lucca to Bruges some ten years before, the shift of the main body of their activities to Paris, around 1370, seems quite abrupt. Much gradual development had preceded the Rapondis' decision to transfer their main branch to Flanders in around 1360. Nonetheless, signs of their presence in Paris before 1370 are impossible to find. The only antecedent is Guido Rapondi's visit to the French capital in 1331,[3] with, as far as we know, no sequel. After that, the Rapondi were not a presence in Paris again until after Dino took over the firm's leadership, although it is possible that the three orders of gold and silk cloth by Philip the Bold at the end of 1369 and at the beginning of 1370,[4] had already brought the company to the city. More reliable indications, in the debt settlement concerning these deliveries to the Burgundian duke, indicate that the new manager was

[1] See *supra*.
[2] Except in 1375-1376, when he represented Charles V in the peace negotiations with England in Bruges.
[3] See *supra*.
[4] See *supra*.

there in July 1371.[5] This is confirmed by an agreement with Iolanda of Bar, in which we can read that Dino received a sum from Richard Levesque for the countess in Paris in August 1371.[6] We cannot on the basis of this evidence conclude that the family had already settled permanently in France at this point. It is most likely that this had happened before or during 1373, since, from 1374 on, the Rapondi were qualified as *bourgeois de Paris* in the sources,[7] which implies a stay of at least a year in the capital.

Dino and his relatives were quite late in arriving in Paris compared with other Lucchese. Some of the Rapondis' compatriots, who had frequented the Champagne fairs for dozens of years and for longer than the inhabitants of most other Italian city-states,[8] had already owned a spot on the banks of the Seine from the last quarter of the thirteenth century. Among these were the Riccardi, in this period mainly known as bankers to the crown in the English wool trade,[9] the Guinigi and the Onesti.[10] Despite the wave of bankruptcies around the turn of the fourteenth century, fatal for the Riccardi and for others, the Lucchese colony in Paris increased in the following decades.[11] By 1369, when Lucca's authorities had granted the Lucchese living abroad the right to set up a nation (about which we know little) and to elect a consul,[12] most of the Lucchese banking and trading world was represented in the city. Some of these merchants, such as Barthelemi Spifame, did business with the French crown[13] and, before the Rapondi did, with Philip the Bold.[14]

One of the Lucchese who lived in Paris before the arrival of the Rapondi clan was Benedic du Gal. His name appears more than once in the August 1371 contract between the Rapondi and Iolanda of Bar, in which he provided the countess and her officers with money, gold and merchandise in the French capital several times during 1370 and 1371.[15] It is probable he helped his compatriots as a contact in the months before Dino and his brothers went to Paris themselves in the summer of 1371. The fact that there already was a very close collaboration with the Rapondi from their first appearance in Paris may even indicate that du Gal had represented them as a full partner.[16] He certainly fulfilled this function from 1371 on, working together with Dino in the name of the company, handling the contacts with Philip the Bold[17] and acting for Iolanda of Kassel,[18] who preferred to do business in Paris at this time. At the same time Benedic was still working on his own account as well.[19] The collaboration with

[5] J. RAUZIER, "Les approvisionnements de la cour de Philippe le Hardi, duc de Bourgogne (1371-1384)" in: *Annales de Bourgogne*, Dijon, 1998, 70, p. 8.

[6] M. DEHAISNES, *Documents et extraits divers concernant l'histoire de l'art*, p. 497.

[7] B. PROST and H. PROST, *Inventaires mobiliers et extraits de comptes des ducs de Bourgogne de la Maison Valois, 1363-1477 Tome I*, Paris, Leroux, 1902, p. 382.

[8] See T. BLOMQUIST, "The Early History of European Banking: Merchants, Bankers and Lombards of XIIIth-Century Lucca in the County of Champagne" in: *Journal of European Economic History*, Roma, 1985, 14, pp. 522-536.

[9] See R.W. KAEUPER, *Bankers to the Crown*.

[10] L. MIROT, *La colonie Lucquoise à Paris*, pp. 55-57.

[11] L. MIROT, *La colonie Lucquoise à Paris*, pp. 57-60.

[12] E. LAZZARESCHI, *Gli statuti dei Lucchesi a Bruges e ad Anversa*, p. 76.

[13] L. MIROT, *La colonie Lucquoise à Paris*, p. 76.

[14] J. RAUZIER, *Finances et gestion d'une principauté*, p. 407.

[15] M. DEHAISNES, *Documents et extraits divers concernant l'histoire de l'art*, pp. 407-409.

[16] L. MIROT, *La société des Raponde*, p. 317. It looks very much as if Dino chose him as chief partner after his brother Guglielmo had died.

[17] J. RAUZIER, *Finances et gestion d'une principauté*, p. 407.

[18] See for example L. MIROT, *La sociéte des Raponde*, p. 320.

[19] See for example B. PROST and H. PROST, *Inventaires mobiliers et extraits de comptes des ducs de Bourgogne*, p. 265.

du Gal, after Dino de la Chiocha in 1357[20] only the second non-Rapondi partner, probably lasted until 1377: the last mention of their collective activities is the debt settlement with the countess of Bar in that year.[21] After this Dino would continue business with his younger brother Jacopo and, until 1379, with Giovanni, the son of his second cousin Jacopo.[22] Both had already worked for the company in France in preceding years.[23]

Benedic du Gal was only one of the many compatriots with whom Dino and his family interacted every day. As in Bruges, the Lucchese community supplied the largest part of the Rapondis' network in Paris.[24] The family barely had to leave their house to keep up these contacts, living in the parish of *Saint-Jacques-de-la-Boucherie*, on the right bank of the Seine and within a stone's throw of the Châtelet prison. In accordance with the typically medieval topographical concentration of people with the same origins or profession, the Lucchese must have felt at home in this neighbourhood. Baptiste Arnolfini, for one, had his home in *Rue de la Verrerie*, opening on to the parish to the south-west. Benedic du Gal lived in the shadow of the *Saint-Opportune* church, just east of *Saint-Jacques-de-la-Boucherie*.

The centre of the Lucchese microcosm, however, was *Rue de la vieille Monnaie*, running parallel with *Rue Saint-Denis* and *Rue Marivaux* and, in the north, opening on to *Rue des Lombards* (a continuation of *Rue de la Verrerie*), and, in the south, on to *Rue des Écrivains*. On the eastern corner of *Rue de la vieille Monnaie* and *Rue des Lombards* lived the Sbarra,[25] Frenchified into Isbarre, suppliers of Philip the Bold[26] who later on would make a career as mint-masters to the French kings.[27] Their neighbours were the Spifame, also from Lucca and owning a couple of houses in *Rue des Lombards* and *Rue Marivaux* as well. Next to this was situated the house with a garden and a courtyard owned by Dino Rapondi but inhabited by his brother Jacopo, who must have joined him in Paris at the beginning and who had a mansion in nearby *Rue Michel-le-Comte* as well. In 1397, Dino would give the property in *Rue de la vieille Monnaie* definitively to Jacopo, "for the enlargement of his estate". Thus the younger Rapondi brother became a neighbour of the Cenami,[28] to whom his family was related by marriage and whose possessions also bordered those of the Isbarre and the Spifame.[29] Further along the street was *du Poids du Roi*, the residence of Colin Forteguerra, a relative of Forteguerra Forteguerra. He lived near the Burlamacchi, the last Lucchese family on the eastern side of *Rue de la vieille Monnaie*.[30]

---

[20] See *supra*.
[21] L. MIROT, *La société des Raponde*, pp. 322-323.
[22] E. LAZZARESCHI (red.), *Il libro della communitá dei mercanti Lucchesi in Bruges*, Milano, Rodolfo Malfasi, 1947, p. 40.
[23] See *supra*.
[24] See also the custody of Simone, son of Barthelemi Spifame, that Dino would take up in 1385. L. MIROT, *La société des Raponde*, p. 378.
[25] L. MIROT, *La colonie Lucquoise à Paris*, pp. 68-71.
[26] L. MIROT, "Les Isbarre monnayeurs royaux, Augustin Isbarre" in : *Bibliothèque de l'Ecole des Chartes*, Paris, 1927, 88, p. 303.
[27] L. MIROT, *Les Isbarre monnayeurs royaux, Augustin Isbarre*, passim.
[28] L. MIROT, *La colonie Lucquoise à Paris*, pp. 69-71.
[29] Filippa, daughter of Guglielmo, was the wife of Giusfredo Cenami. L. MIROT, *Les Cename*, p. 103.
[30] L. MIROT, *La colonie Lucquoise à Paris*, p. 70.

On the other side of the street were some of the few houses not belonging to Lucchese. One of these was the property of Henri Orlant,[31] one of the most important money-changers in Paris in the last quarter of the fourteenth century, from whom Philip the Bold bought most of his jewels and silver and goldwork.[32] In 1399, Pierre le Flament owned another building on this side of the street.[33] He was a member of a cloth merchant's family, also one of the main suppliers of the Burgundian court.[34] After this date, the house seems to have been inhabited by Pierre de l'Esclat,[35] originally Schiatta, a Lucchese who would rise to the rank of royal counsellor, president of the *cour des aides* and *maitre des requêtes* at the French court.[36]

Between these two houses was the impressive property of Dino Rapondi, praised by Guillebert of Metz in his *Description de Paris* (1407) as one of the most luxurious in the whole capital.[37] It consisted of four living units, each with its own gable, from north to south bearing the names of '*l'Image Sainte-Catherine*', '*Corne de cerf*', '*Image Saint-Jean*' and '*Image Saint-Jacques*', after the name-boards above their respective entrances. Each of these contained several halls and rooms, a cellar, stables and galleries. The kitchen had a separate provision cellar and there was a well and toilets, as well as a fenced garden, opening up at the back of the *l'Ane rayé* house in *Rue Saint-Denis*.[38] The history of the building dates from before the fourteenth century, having been owned by, among others, the tailor Guillaume Lucas and one Guy Scalle, before Dino added it to his possessions. This he had done by 1393, when the sisters of Saint-Magloire declared possessing an annuity on Rapondi's *Image Sainte-Catherine*.[39]

With the purchase of the property, that in terms of size and luxury overshadowed the possessions of the other Lucchese in Paris,[40] who already owned a considerable amount of real estate, Dino demonstrated the fortune that he and his brothers had already amassed. Buying the house immortalized the extent of these riches in stone to display his new status as supplier to the Burgundian dukes and later to the French kings. Remarkably, Dino made this statement in the immediate surroundings of his merchant colleagues Spifame, Isbarre, Orlant, and le Flament, who would be competing with him for the favour and the francs of Philip the Bold. In *Rue de la vieille Monnaie* he would also encounter some of the Lucchese families with whom the Rapondi already had good contacts in Bruges (Forteguerra, Burlamacchi).[41] Nevertheless, for their most important connection in Paris[42] they had to go some streets further to the *hôtel d'Artois*, the main residence of the Duke of Burgundy.[43]

---

[31] L. MIROT, *Les Cename*, p. 154. Mirot incorrectly gave him a Lucchese origin. L. MIROT, *La colonie Lucquoise à Paris*, p. 70, n. 6.
[32] J. RAUZIER, *Les approvisionnements de la cour de Philippe le Hardi, duc de Bourgogne*, p. 25. A. VAN NIEUWENHUYSEN, *Les finances du duc de Bourgogne. Economie et Politique*, p. 344.
[33] L. MIROT, *Les Cename*, p. 152.
[34] J. RAUZIER, *Les approvisionnements de la cour de Philippe le Hardi, duc de Bourgogne*, p. 25.
[35] L. MIROT, *La colonie Lucquoise à Paris*, p. 70, n. 10.
[36] L. MIROT, *La colonie Lucquoise à Paris*, p. 77.
[37] L. LE ROUX DE LINCY et L.M. TISSERAND (eds.), *Le Paris de Charles V et de Charles VI vu par des écrivains contemporains*, Caen, Paradigme, 1992, p. 199.
[38] L. MIROT, *Les Cename*, pp. 154-155.
[39] L. MIROT, *Les Cename*, p. 151.
[40] L. MIROT, *La colonie Lucquoise à Paris*, p. 70.
[41] See *supra*.
[42] But which dated from Flanders, see *supra*.
[43] W. PARAVICINI, "Die Residenzen der Herzöge von Burgund, 1363-1377" in: W. PARAVICINI, *Menschen am Hof der Herzöge von Burgund*, Stuttgart, Jan Thorbecke Verlag, 2002, pp. 459-460.

2.1.1 In the Footsteps of Philip the Bold

The possessions of the Rapondi in *Rue de la vieille Monnaie* would serve in the first place as headquarters for dealing with the family's relations with Philip the Bold. The foundations of these bonds had been laid by Guglielmo, Dino's elder brother and his predecessor on the manager's seat of the company. This is shown strikingly in the first undertakings of the firm in Paris, in the middle of 1371. The first known contact by Dino with the ducal administration concerned the repayment of the last purchases carried out under Guglielmo's direction, the three deliveries of gold and silk cloth to the duke (on July 7 and December 16, 1369 and January 15, 1370). This debt, totalling to 2457 lb. 7 s. 9 d., would only be redeemed in February 1372, more than two years and four instalments after the sales.[44] Dino and the other family members needed to extend and turn into money the fragile connection with the ducal house they had been left after the death of Guglielmo, working with new partners such as Benedic du Gal. The energy with which they did this leaves little doubt about their true reason for going to Paris.

Dino and Benedic du Gal had their first big order in 1374, when they supplied the gold and silk cloth given by the duke to his brother Charles V and to the wife of Bureau de la Rivière, a financial colleague in 1369[45] and one of the royal counsellors whom Philip tried to win over with repeated presents, attempting to acquire influence over the French government (at one point he even granted de la Rivière a pension).[46] Not long after this, the Rapondi collected 158 francs for the purchase of six pieces of damask cloth. Apparently the luxurious fabrics the Lucchese company offered were also popular with the duchess since Dino sold her a piece of baldachin in 1376 to make a corset with.[47]

The Rapondi company would soon develop into one of the main suppliers of gold and silk cloth, high quality furs, scarlet and other magnificent fabrics to the Burgundian court,[48] the duke's paramount instrument for visually expressing his power and wealth.[49] In this capacity they only had to fear competition from Barthelemi Spifame and Nicolas le Flament. Still, the heading of "achats de draps fourrures et tapisseries" in the ducal accounts is the only one under which the Rapondi figure abundantly.[50] This makes it clear that the range of goods they could sell to Philip the Bold was much more limited than the range they sold to Iolanda of Kassel.[51] This can be explained by the mercantile competition at the ducal court, more numerous than at the countess' court and that as many as four of these rival suppliers lived in the same street. Consquently, Dino and his brothers concentrated on the trade in goods they knew best and in which they had a reputation to protect. However, when the Rapondi saw an opportunity to sell jewellery, gold and silverwork (two trades

---

[44] J. RAUZIER, *Finances et gestion d'une principauté*, p. 624.
[45] B. PROST and H. PROST, *Inventaires mobiliers et extraits de comptes des ducs de Bourgogne*, pp. 382-383.
[46] R. VAUGHAN, *Philip the Bold*, p. 12.
[47] L. MIROT, *La société des Raponde*, p. 336.
[48] J. RAUZIER, *Les approvisionnements de la cour de Philippe le Hardi, duc de Bourgogne*, pp. 24-25.
[49] M. VANDERMAESEN and K. VANDEWOUDE, "het hof der graven van Vlaanderen en hertogen van Bourgondië" in: B. AUGUSTYN and W. PREVENIER (eds.), *De gewestelijke en lokale overheidsinstellingen in Vlaanderen tot 1795*, Brussel, Algemeen Rijksarchief, 1997, p. 29.
[50] J. RAUZIER, *Les approvisionnements de la cour de Philippe le Hardi, duc de Bourgogne*, pp. 24-25.
[51] See *supra*.

controlled in Paris by Henri Orlant) or other valuables to Philip and his entourage, they certainly seized it.[52] In that way, they provided the duke with 2,5 ounces of pearls with which he would decorate an outfit in 1374.[53] Ten years later, the ducal secretaries would write on Lombardian paper, supplied by the Rapondi.[54] That the firm sometimes had to wait a year or more for their repayments, as in 1375-1376 (204 lb. of cloth),[55] does not seem to have been a very big problem. The number of purchases kept increasing, representing larger and larger amounts of money.

Philip especially bought from the Rapondi the many gifts with which he overburdened others, a common way to gain friends, strengthen loyalty bonds and to maintain political relationships.[56] For instance, in 1379, he bought dozens of ells of baldachin to give to, again, Bureau de la Rivière and his counsellor Guy de la Trémoïlle, one of the main beneficiaries of Philip's generosity, and his colleagues Élien de Najac and Guillaume de Rosay. The same year he ordered some red velvet from the company for a covering for his armour and for the sheath of his dagger. This pattern of spending ensured that 354[57] of the 434 francs (82%) which the duke spent with the Lucchese for luxury fabrics in 1379,[58] disappeared into the purse of the Rapondi company. Dino could report even better results in 1380, when the firm was honoured with the order for the mourning for the entire ducal family at the funeral of king Charles V, who had died on September 16, 1380. Besides the black velvet in which Philip and his relatives were dressed, the Rapondi procured silk cloth, satin, blue alexandrian velvet, red and blue sendal embroidered with the ducal arms for a saddle-cloth, feathers and a sheath for a sword. Furthermore, Guy de la Trémoïlle once again enjoyed Philip's generosity, who made a present to him and another ducal counsellor, Guillaume de Reneval, of black velvet. When Charles VI (Charles V's son) was crowned some weeks later, his uncle Philip the Bold presented him with a sword, the sheath of which was covered with velvet from the Rapondi.[59] This was the beginning of a period in which almost every piece of luxury fabric, worn or given by the duke, came from Dino and his family.

Although the merits of the Rapondi for Philip the Bold during these years were mainly to do with the trade in fabrics, the duke also addressed his court suppliers for all kinds of other duties. In 1374, he sent Dino to Flanders to give a present to his father-in-law, Louis of Male, who rewarded the head of the company with a silver cross.[60] The choice of Rapondi, probably inspired by his long experience in Flanders, indicates the confidence that the duke already had in this Lucchese family. Two years later Giovanni, Dino's relative and assistant in Paris, negotiated the sale of six Puglian horses between Philip the Bold and

---

[52] J. RAUZIER, *Les approvisionnements de la cour de Philippe le Hardi, duc de Bourgogne*, p. 25.
[53] B. PROST and H. PROST, *Inventaires mobiliers et extraits de comptes des ducs de Bourgogne*, pp. 382-383.
[54] L. MIROT, *La société des Raponde*, p. 336.
[55] J. RAUZIER, *Finances et gestion d'une principauté*, p. 413.
[56] For this, see M. BOONE, "Dons et pots-de-vin, aspects de la sociabilité urbaine au bas Moyen Age. Le cas gantois pendant la période bourguignonne" in : *Revue du Nord*, Lille, 1988, 70, pp. 471-487. C. M. CHATTAWAY , "Looking a medieval gift horse in the mouth. The role of the giving of gift objects in the definition and maintenance of the power networks of Philip the Bold" in: *Bijdragen en mededelingen betreffende de geschiedenis der Nederlanden*, Den Haag, 1999, CXIV, 1, pp. 1-15.
[57] L. MIROT, *La sociéte des Raponde*, p. 336.
[58] J. RAUZIER, *Les approvisionnements de la cour de Philippe le Hardi, duc de Bourgogne*, p. 24.
[59] L. MIROT, *La société des Raponde*, p. 336.
[60] G. BIGWOOD, *Le régime juridique et économique Tome I*, p. 186, n. 4.

Nicolas Grenouart.[61] In January 1383, Dino bought back a collection of jewels for 5400 lb., which the duke had pledged to three Bruges merchants in order to borrow 2500 lb.[62]

Lacking financial foresight or indeed any concept of a budget,[63] Philip the Bold, like most medieval princes, ruled by the grace of credit. Since the Rapondi were a thriving business house with some capital at their disposal, the duke also resorted to them for loans. Still, in his early acquaintanceship with the Lucchese firm his borrowings did not amount to much, certainly not compared with what the company would issue him later, after 1384. This is understandable, since, before his succession in Flanders, Philip established relatively few of the expensive undertakings of which he had given a foretaste in 1369 and which he would indulge considerably after 1384. However, when he did, the Rapondi were ready. This is shown by the peace negotiations between France and England in 1375-1376, on the neutral ground of Bruges. Philip, as the king's brother and a skilful negotiator, was the leader of the French delegation, and used the opportunity to impress his future subjects and the competing rulers of Europe with exceptional splendour. To add lustre to his appearance, he ordered cartloads of tapestries and robes from Paris and Burgundian wine, and made an entrance with an elaborate suite, dressed in a costume designed especially for the occasion. In contrast with the ducal show, the negotiations, which continued from the end of March until June 27, 1375, were not successful and only resulted in a truce that would remain in effect for a year. This did not prevent Philip the Bold from treating all guests to a sumptuous banquet on the last day of the colloquy.

A second round of negotiations, with the duke of Burgundy being assisted by his brother Louis of Anjou, again took place in Bruges, in autumn 1375. Because of the implacability of the two parties, the talks only produced a prolongation of the truce, but were continued with the tournament Philip held in Ghent in the spring of 1376.[64] The spectacle was, as Richard Vaughan put it, "a gathering of the ruling houses and nobility of the Low Countries under Burgundian auspices",[65] at which the Flemish count Louis of Male, the duke of Brabant Wenceslas of Luxemburg and Albert of Bavaria, count of Hainault, Holland and Zeeland were present. Furthermore, the Ghentenars were able to gape in awe at John of Gaunt, the son of the English king, and the dukes of Brittany and Anjou.[66] When Philip the Bold returned to France in April 1376,[67] the Flemish population had again been deeply impressed by its future count.

[61] N. CHERRIER, "Les chevaux de Philippe le Hardi (1371-1404)" in: *Annales de Bourgogne*, Dijon, 1995, 67, p. 126.
[62] J. RAUZIER, *Finances et gestion d'une principauté*, p. 618.
[63] For this, see M. MOLLAT, "Recherches sur les finances des ducs Valois de Bourgogne" in: *Revue Historique*, Paris, 1958, 220, pp. 295-296.
[64] E. VAN DEN NESTE, *Tournois, joutes, pas d'armes dans les villes de Flandre à la fin du Moyen Age (1300-1486)*, Paris, École des Chartes, 1996, p. 247. (Mémoires et Documents de l'École des Chartes, 47). R. VAUGHAN, *Philip the Bold*, pp. 10-11. The former wrongly situates the event in 1375.
[65] R. VAUGHAN, *Philip the Bold*, p. 18.
[66] D. M. NICHOLAS, "In the Pit of the Burgundian Theater State. Urban Traditions and Princely Ambitions in Ghent, 1360-1420" in: B. A. HANAWALT and L. REYERSON (eds.), *City and Spectacle in Medieval Europe*, Minneapolis, University of Minnesota Press, p. 274. (Medieval Studies at Minnesota, 6).
[67] E. PETIT, *Itinéraires de Philippe le Hardi et de Jean sans Peur, ducs de Bourgogne d'après les comptes de dépenses de leur hôtel*, Paris, Imprimerie Nationale, 1888, p. 125.

Of course, all this pomp cost a lot, apparently more than the duke could pay for with his royal subsidies.[68] Therefore, he raised several loans, among others with some Bruges merchants, who agreed to lend him 12 000 lb. Nevertheless, this was not sufficient and Philip had to call in the aid of Dino Rapondi, who supplied him the considerable amounts of 6000 and 1000 lb., paid back in 1377-78 with interest of 380 and 110 lb. respectively.[69] This very much characterised the activities of the company in a period in which the Rapondi were willing to put all their energy and time at the duke's disposal in every possible way, and to concentrate fully on their relations with the Burgundian court, for which all other interests had to give way. Philip the Bold could always fall back on the family from Lucca, in whose hands he could leave the most diverse affairs, from commercial and financial transactions to diplomatic missions. Consequently, the 1370s were a decade in which a bond of mutual confidence between the duke and the Rapondi clan emerged. This bond would not only bring the company a lot of money, but it would give Dino and his partners a very comfortable position at the moment when Philip the Bold took possession of the county of Flanders, thus generating an even bigger need for financial and other resources.[70] This explains why the Rapondi would begin the post-1384 period with a certain edge over other, equally substantial, candidate-money-lenders. A good example is Forteguerra Forteguerra. When we look at the debts that Philip the Bold owed to this Lucchese and his partners in 1370 (17 185 francs), his transactions with the duke[71] must have been considerably larger than those of the Rapondi in the same period. However, as will become clear further on, in the 1370s Forteguerra would prefer Lucchese politics and his interests in Bruges.[72] This would deprive him of the privileged relations with Philip the Bold that the Rapondi would enjoy in 1384.

2.1.2 The King and the 'Princes des Fleurs de Lys'

The relations with the duke would not only be favourable in the long term, but also brought with them more immediate advantages, in addition to the pecuniary gain they produced. As the countess Iolanda had probably been the original link with the Burgundian court, the Rapondi would climb up another step thanks to their bond with Philip the Bold. Their faithful service to the duke provided them with the contact with his brother Charles V, king of France. Dino and his partners had already been doing business with Philip the Bold for some years when, in 1376, the king ordered them to supply a piece of red camelot[73] to make "aumuces".[74] To line the garment, Charles also bought a piece of blue sendal from the company.[75] Apparently the king was not discontented with his new suppliers, since twelve days later the Rapondi sold him another piece of fabric.[76] After this, the purchases succeeded each other swiftly, albeit that they remained quite modest in size and scarcely exceeded 60

[68] R. VAUGHAN, *Philip the Bold*, p. 10.
[69] J. RAUZIER, *Finances et gestion d'une principauté*, p. 617.
[70] See *infra*.
[71] L. MIROT, *Forteguerra Forteguerra et sa succession*, p. 303.
[72] See *infra*.
[73] This fabric is made of camel hair and originating from Asia Minor.
[74] An 'aumuce' is a short hooded cloak.
[75] L. DELISLE, *Mandements et Actes divers de Charles V (1364-1380)*, Paris, Imprimerie Nationale, 1874, p. 645.
[76] L. DELISLE, *Mandements et Actes divers de Charles V*, p. 649.

francs each in value. From the end of 1377, however, larger amounts passed across the counter to the royal residence[77] and in the end, Charles was to spend as much on goods supplied by the Rapondi company as Philip the Bold had done in the same period. Still the firm had a larger share in the total expenditure of the duke than in that of the king, which was much bigger.[78]

Charles the Wise devoted even more attention and money to the external depiction and the artistic embellishment of his power than Philip the Bold, for whom he served as an example,[79] and made most of his payments to the Rapondi to fill his wardrobe. This shows that the house traded in fabrics, considered luxurious enough for the garments of the king, one of his most powerful instruments to demonstrate his exceptional status and wealth. On March 3, 1377, Pierre de Soissons, the master of exchange in the royal treasury, was ordered to pay 52 francs to Dino for the supply of two baldachins with which he had lined clothes made.[80] Nine months later, the prince required a 'desseret',[81] for which the company was asked to supply alexandrian satin and three pieces of damask gold cloth.[82] On feast days, Charles wore Rapondi fabrics as well. For the lined clothes he would wear for All Saints' Day in 1376, he bought two pieces of baldachin with four layers of silk from the firm.[83] The royal orders tell us that on Easter 1378, he was dressed in a fur coat, made of three pieces of Rapondi silk.[84]

The king not only extended his own wardrobe, but also clothed his family with fabrics from the Lucchese company. When Dino provided the court with four pieces of 'imperial' in December 1377, they were for a 'desseret' for the queen, Joan of Bourbon.[85] Possibly she obtained the garment for the visit of emperor Charles IV, her husband's uncle, that would take place with much pomp some weeks later but which Joan would not be able to attend.[86] The king's two sons, Charles, the future Charles VI, and Louis, the future duke of Orléans, had their measurements taken at the end of 1376 for fur coats, for which the Rapondi had supplied several ells of blue satin.[87] Apparently the *dauphin* and his brother needed new coats 18 months later, with blue satin again provided by the company.[88] For his daughter Marie of France Charles bought a piece of satin in 1376.[89] The Rapondis' fabrics also served as royal gifts to strengthen the bonds with further relatives. The prince ordered four pieces of blue sendal from Dino in June 1376 to surprise his niece Bonne of Berry with.[90] Not coincidentally, she married the duke of Savoy one and a half years later,

---

[77] L. DELISLE, *Mandements et Actes divers de Charles V*, p. 761 e.v.
[78] R. VAUGHAN, *Philip the Bold*, p. 190.
[79] R. VAUGHAN, *Philip the Bold*, pp. 206-207.
[80] L. DELISLE, *Mandements et Actes divers de Charles V*, p. 697.
[81] A 'desseret' is a back-piece made of baldachin.
[82] L. DELISLE, *Mandements et Actes divers de Charles V*, p. 773.
[83] L. DELISLE, *Mandements et Actes divers de Charles V*, p. 658.
[84] L. DELISLE, *Mandements et Actes divers de Charles V*, p. 833.
[85] L. DELISLE, *Mandements et Actes divers de Charles V*, p. 773.
[86] She was too ill with her eighth pregnancy, which she would not survive. F. AUTRAND, *Charles V*, pp. 779-805.
[87] L. DELISLE, *Mandements et Actes divers de Charles V*, pp. 691-692.
[88] L. DELISLE, *Mandements et Actes divers de Charles V*, p. 833.
[89] L. DELISLE, *Mandements et Actes divers de Charles V*, p. 649.
[90] L. DELISLE, *Mandements et Actes divers de Charles V*, p. 645.

allying the crown with an important fief of the Empire at the south-eastern border with France.[91]

The king's love for art and outward show was not only demonstrated by his coats, 'aumuces' and 'desserets', but also by his impressive library, housed in the Louvre. Together with the duke of Milan, Giangaleazzo Visconti, Charles V was one of the assiduous book collectors of his time, owning more than 1000 manuscripts including some enchantingly beautiful illuminated ones.[92] The Rapondi made money from the prince's bibliophilia, in which he was imitated by his brothers again, although not in the same way as from the royal taste for beautiful clothes. The luxurious fabrics provided by the company suited very well as covers for the king's expensive books. This is shown by the order the Rapondi received in November 1377 for a load of baldachin, which Charles V wished to cover his four big volumes of "Vincent" with.[93] Another piece of fabric was used as a cover for the "chronicles of France and those our loved and faithful chancellor has made".[94] The books of the *dauphin*, a Seneca, the Gesta Karoli, the "enfances Pepin" and the "croniques d'oultre mer" by Godfrey of Bouillon were dressed in baldachin as well. To bind all the covers, the king bought another five pieces of red sendal, also used for the decoration of the case which held the prince's portable chapel.[95] Four months later Charles V asked Dino again for baldachin "to make book covers for us", as well as sendal "to bind these covers".[96]

The prestigious and lucrative bonds with the king brought Dino alarmingly near a difficult position, when he became involved in a trial that took him before the Parlement of Paris (the highest court in the kingdom). In 1379, he had accepted 1800 francs from Martin Paulet, a courtier of Charles II, king of Navarre, in Paris. In exchange Paulet, who wanted money at his disposal in Bruges, received a bill of exchange drawn on Andrea, Dino's brother and representative in Flanders.[97] What Rapondi had not fully realized, was that the Navarrese king was the arch-enemy of the French crown. On his mother's side, Charles II was the grandson of Louis X the Contentious, one of the last Capetian princes of France, which had driven him to claim the French royal title.[98] John II the Good (the father of Charles V) had tried to keep on good terms with the pretender by giving him the hand of his daughter Joan.[99] However, the Hundred Years War, having begun quite disastrously for France,

[91] For the details of this marriage, see F. AUTRAND, *Jean de Berry: l'art et le pouvoir*, Paris, Librairie Arthème Fayard, 2000, pp. 287-291.
[92] F. AUTRAND, *Charles V*, pp. 719-721.
[93] By this is probably meant the chronicler Vincent of Beauvais.
[94] L. DELISLE, *Mandements et Actes divers de Charles V*, p. 761. By this is probably meant the *Grandes Chroniques de France*, kept in the abbey of Saint-Denis since 1274 and dealing with the French monarchy. They were completed and reworked under Charles V by his chancellor Pierre d'Orgemont as a pointed reminder to the English king of his feudal duties in the light of the Hundred Years' War. The magnificently decorated personal copy of the king, preserved as one of the showpieces in the Bibliothèque Nationale in Paris, is the only version of the chronicle with the altered story by d'Orgemont, and thus must be the one covered with the Rapondi fabric. For this, see B. GUENEE, "Les Grandes Chroniques de France. Le Roman aux roys (1274-1518)" in: P. NORA, *Les lieux de mémoire. II. La Nation*, Paris, Gallimard, 1986, pp. 201-202.
[95] L. DELISLE, *Mandements et Actes divers de Charles V*, pp. 761-762.
[96] L. DELISLE, *Mandements et Actes divers de Charles V*, p. 822.
[97] L. MIROT, *La société des Raponde*, p. 326.
[98] F. AUTRAND, *Charles V*, pp. 101-105.
[99] F. AUTRAND, *Charles V*, pp. 114-117.

had prevented the king from giving Joan a suitable dowry, and Charles II had turned against him.[100]

In 1378, Charles the Bad was involved in a war with Castile. He called for the aid of the English, who offered him 500 soldiers and as many archers. As a compensation, the king of Navarre gave them Cherbourg in pledge, a part of his Norman territories, over which he thought he had complete authority and where he did not recognise the sovereignty of the Valois dynasty. For Charles V, the suzerain on whom the Norman seigneuries depended and who had been at war with the English since 1369, this was treason. In March 1379, he arrested two of Charles II's officers, who confessed shortly after. In April all the French possessions of the Navarrese prince were taken.[101] This broke the power of the Navarrese party and definitively expelled Charles the Bad from the French political stage.

In this respect, the money Dino had received in deposit from Martin Paulet was considered the property of the enemy and was confiscated on the order of the Parlement of Paris, before which the Lucchese was called, on March 5, 1379, only a few days after the news about Charles the Bad's treason had reached the French court. Rapondi was able to avoid the fine demanded by the king's attorney by saying that he had acted in good faith and had not known that Paulet was a Navarrese.[102] Moreover, his brother Andrea had refused to accept Dino's bill of exchange in Bruges.[103] Consequently, the trial does not seem to have had particularly bad consequences, as their supplies to the king continued. On October 1380, a month after the death of the king, the Rapondi were repaid 1962 francs for these purchases.[104]

The succession of Charles VI to the throne after the death of Charles V did not prejudice the Rapondis' position at the court either; on the contrary. When Charles VI entered Rheims cathedral on November 4, 1380 to be crowned as king of France, he was only eleven years old. His father had taken precautions concerning the rule of the kingdom, having appointed his brother Louis of Anjou as regent, and his younger brothers John of Berry and Philip the Bold as custodians for his son. At Charles V's death, however, a dispute arose over the settlement, and it was agreed that a regency council under the leadership of the duke of Anjou and consisting of the two royal princes and Louis of Bourbon, Charles VI's uncle on his mother's side, would reign over France. The influence of Philip the Bold in this council was considerable and would increase after 1382, when Louis of Anjou left for the Italian peninsula to conquer the kingdom of Naples, giving the Burgundian duke a free hand in France. Together with his brother John of Berry, who did not obstruct him, he determined the course of the government in the kingdom and the conduct of Charles VI, who could not undertake anything without his approval.[105]

The influence the patron of the Rapondi had on the king also advanced the relations of the Lucchese firm with the court, which were intensified and also arranged more and more financial transactions. In 1385, the Rapondi

---

[100] F. AUTRAND, *Charles V*, pp. 122-126.
[101] F. AUTRAND, *Charles V*, pp. 810-816.
[102] L. MIROT, *La société des Raponde*, p. 326.
[103] L. GILLIODTS-VAN SEVEREN, *Cartulaire de l'ancienne estaple à Bruges. Recueil de documents concernant le commerce intérieur et maritime, les relations internationales et l'histoire de cette ville*, Bruges, Louis de Plancke, 1906, pp. 325-326.
[104] L. MIROT, *La société des Raponde*, p. 326.
[105] R. VAUGHAN, *Philip the Bold*, pp. 40-42.

company even lent Charles VI 30 000 francs,[106] more than ten times everything his father had ever paid to the brothers (and five times the largest loan the Rapondi had granted until then, which makes it clear that the family's financial resources had increased immensely). The gigantic credit served "pour avancer le fait de l'armee de la mer", in other words to organise the military expedition to Scotland under the leadership of Jean de Vienne, the admiral of France.[107]

This operation in the north was to divert attention from a much bigger invasion, of England from the south, with which the French wished to strike a decisive blow in the Hundred Years War. Since 1376 this war had been proceeding by a succession of truces interrupted by occasional military campaigns.[108] Even though both raids, as so many others afterwards, was cancelled in the end, its preparations enabled the Rapondi to supply velvet, satin and sendal to the king, who would use it for coats of arms, horse-cloths and decorations for his army.[109] The author of the Scottish expedition as well as the southern invasion of the British Isles was, not coincidentally, the Burgundian duke, the brains behind the French-English policy under Charles V,[110] thus giving his trusted suppliers an opportunity to make enormous profits.

The first high point of the Rapondis' connections with the French crown, and probably also of the duke's patronage of his favoured bankers, took place on January 5, 1385. Charles VI granted Dino, his brothers Jacopo and Andrea and his nephew Giovanni (the son of Guglielmo) citizenship of Paris and the whole kingdom and all related privileges, as a reward for their services.[111]

The Rapondi, undoubtedly through the advocacy of Philip the Bold, not only added two successive kings to their clientele but, almost contemporaneously, the other royal princes. John of Berry, the ostentatious art patron with very luxurious tastes,[112] first gave the family his patronage, preceding Charles V by a year, when in 1375 he set his tailor Alain de Carnapin to work with Rapondi silk cloth. Several other transactions with the duke of Berry followed, although in terms of size and number they could not compete with the arrangements the Rapondi made for Philip the Bold and for the king. The same can be said for the other *prince des fleurs de lys*, Louis of Anjou, who in February 1376 ordered velvet, satin and silk cloth from Dino to make a respectable appearance with his knights and vassals at the peace negotiations with the English in Boulogne. The prince "was very pleased with the aforementioned Digne" and asked Moreau de Wissant, his chamberlain, more than once to buy pieces of velvet from the Lucchese company. Louis also procured silk cloth from the firm, who had to wait until 1391, seven years after the duke's death, before these fabrics were paid for.[113] This inconvenience did not offset the advantages the Rapondi would reap from their services to Anjou in another field.[114]

---

[106] B. PROST and H. PROST, *Inventaires mobiliers et extraits de comptes des ducs de Bourgogne*, p. 383, n. 6.
[107] B. PROST and H. PROST, *Inventaires mobiliers et extraits de comptes des ducs de Bourgogne*, p. 383, n. 6.
[108] R. VAUGHAN, *Philip the Bold*, p. 48.
[109] L. MIROT, *La société des Raponde*, p. 326.
[110] R. VAUGHAN, *Philip the Bold*, pp. 47-48.
[111] L. LE ROUX DE LINCY and L.M. TISSERAND (eds.), *Le Paris de Charles V et de Charles VI*, p. 336-337. Thus implying a confirmation of the status they already enjoyed from 1374 on, see *supra*.
[112] For this, see F. AUTRAND, *Jean de Berry*, pp. 385-389.
[113] L. MIROT, *La société des Raponde*, pp. 330-331.
[114] See *infra*.

The Rapondi had to thank Philip the Bold for the fact that such sluggish repayments did not occur more often. He was an indispensable link between the company and the rest of the royal family, not only making possible the contacts with Dino and his brothers but also intervening in their favour and guaranteeing them fast repayments.[115] With these services and the continuous chain of orders and other requests with which he gave work to the company, he was largely responsible for the fast climb of the Rapondi, who in ten years rose from fairly unexceptional merchants at the court of the countess of Bar to one of the most important suppliers of the kings of France and the whole royal family.[116] But the collaboration with the duke and the continued rise of the firm was not over yet. In fact, the best was yet to come.

western Europe's most important commercial centres during the high and late Middle Ages, including Bruges, Paris, Lucca and Avignon, where the Rapondi had branches in the 1370s. (after E.S. HUNT and J.M. MURRAY, *A history of business*, p.6)

[115] See, for example, L. MIROT, *La sociéte des Raponde*, pp. 327-328.
[116] See the 30 000 francs loan, *supra.*

2.2 Diminished Presence in Bruges

Until 1370, the Bruges branch of the Rapondi had been the headquarters of the company, to the degree that traces of other branches can hardly be found, if there were any. It is only certain that in this period the family must also have been commercially active in Lucca, since most of their merchandise was imported through the mother city. These operations may already have been led by Dino's second cousin Jacopo di Giovanni, who would take this role after 1370.[117] Otherwise, the Rapondi seem to have concentrated completely on Bruges. From 1370 onwards, when the new Rapondi office in Paris opened its doors, this changed drastically. The Paris shop soon attracted most of the business, and the Bruges branch became relegated to a secondary role. This is not to say that there is no indication of any Rapondi activity in Flanders, at least not after 1377. During the six years before, between 1371 and 1377, such indications are more difficult to find.

We do possess information about a trial, carried out in 1380 before the Lucchese nation, that refers to the Rapondi cash books from 1374. In this case Orlandino Volpelli, living in Bruges, accused Guido dal Portico, living in London. Both had concluded an agreement in 1374 involving the sale of some pieces of taffeta worth 60 lb. However, while it was being transported on the Canal, these fabrics had been seized by a Norman privateer, and both parties disagreed over who would absorb the loss. During the trial that followed, the books of the Rapondi, from whom the Volpelli had bought the goods, were consulted as well. These did not seem to concern documents from Bruges, but the diary of the Paris branch: the statement that Volpelli had paid for the merchandise had been recorded between July and September 1374 by Dino Rapondi,[118] who at this point was in the French capital, where he was supplying golden and silk cloth to the Burgundian duke.[119] The entry raises the question of why should a merchant, operating from Bruges, do business with the Paris branch of a company, instead of that company's Bruges branch?

When we look at the contacts between the Rapondi and Philip the Bold, we can surmise that Dino travelled to Flanders in 1374 to hand over a gift from the duke to Louis of Male,[120] but this does not guarantee that he still had interests in that region. Moreover, it is strange, with regard to the loans granted by the firm to Philip for the peace negotiations in 1375-76 in Bruges, that a Bruges house of the company is not mentioned.[121] If the Rapondi still had such a branch, it would be expected that they would use it as a hub in the credit operation to supply the duke with cash to avoid the dangerous transportation of ready money from France to Flanders. We only see the Rapondi doing business again with Philip the Bold in Bruges in 1378-79, when the duke acquired four pieces of satin, interwoven with Cyprian gold, from Dino's brother Andrea, sending them to the duchess in Burgundy as a gift for her illegitimate sisters.[122]

---

[117] See *infra*.

[118] E. LAZZARESCHI (red.), *Il libro della communitá*, pp. 66-67.

[119] L. MIROT, *La société des Raponde*, p. 335.

[120] G. BIGWOOD, *Le régime juridique et économique Tome I*, p. 186.

[121] J. RAUZIER, *Finances et gestion d'une principauté*, p. 617.

[122] M. DEHAISNES, *Documents et extraits divers concernant l'histoire de l'art*, p. 558. As well as Margaret, Louis of Male was the father of possibly 15 illegitimate children, of whom six were girls. For the duke and the duchess, who seems to have dealt personally with the welfare and the education of her brothers and sisters, they were important pawns who, because of their comital blood, were considered attractive marriage candidates and

In the relations between the Rapondi clan and Iolanda of Kassel, there was not much recorded activity after 1371 in Bruges either, except perhaps for the third and last instalment in the 1373 repayment of a loan from the Lombards to the countess (for the ransom of her son), for which Dino acted as intermediary (the first two instalments had been paid before 1371).[123] From then on, all the countess' business with the Rapondi went via Paris, until Dino asked Iolanda on May 18, 1378 "that she sends money to my brother in Bruges".[124] This may indicate that Rapondi activities in Bruges were on a very low scale or that that branch had even ceased to exist for a period between 1371 and 1378, now that the prominent clients in Paris were absorbing all the firm's energy. Yet, the fact that much more information is available from 1377 onwards, can also be explained by the presence of a source, lacking in the period before. It allows us to follow the Rapondis' activities in the nation of Lucchese merchants, established in 1369.

2.2.1 The Lucchese Nation in Bruges

In April 1369, Lucca had freed itself of the dominance of the Pisans, who had controlled their city since 1342.[125] The Lucchese merchants in Bruges, among whom good contacts already existed, had used this opportunity to grant their community an official character. After they had contributed very generous loans to their home city to buy its independence, they requested the authorities of the new republic to approve their statutes.[126] The rulers of Lucca agreed to this on September 27, 1369, whereupon the *università* or *communità* of Lucchese merchants in Bruges came into being.[127] The community was established to foster the worship of the *Volto Santo* (the holy cross in the cathedral of Lucca and the most important symbol of the city), and unity among Lucchese businessmen in Flanders, according to the statutes. In reality the merchants had joined together to take better care of their interests and to have a stronger case against the Flemish authorities. The Lucchese could address their nation to ask for help and support but, on the other hand, they had to respect some obligations (for example, participation in a possible boycott).[128]

At the head of the community, there was a consul, elected every year by all members older than 14 years of age[129] (in emergencies the city council of Lucca appointed someone itself).[130] He was the official representative of the Lucchese republic, vis-à-vis the Bruges and Flemish authorities, for whom he acted as spokesman for his mother city, as well as vis-à-vis the Lucchese merchants, who owed him absolute obedience. The latter were obliged to swear an oath of faith every year, declaring they would respect the statutes of the *communità*. The consul also represented the nation itself, for example in

---

could be used, for example, in order to set up networks of confidence. For this, see P. ROGGHÉ, "Gent in de XIVe en XVe eeuw" in: *Appeltjes van het Meetjesland*, Maldegem, 1968, 19, pp. 252-253.

[123] G. BIGWOOD, *Le régime juridique et économique Tome II*, p. 305.

[124] G. BIGWOOD, *Le régime juridique et économique Tome II*, p. 369.

[125] C. MEEK, *Lucca 1369-1400*, pp. 4-5.

[126] E. LAZZARESCHI, *Gli statuti dei Lucchesi a Bruges e ad Anversa*, pp. 75-76.

[127] The Lucchese magistrate immediately granted the same rights to Lucchese citizens in London, Paris and Venice. E. LAZZARESCHI, *Gli statuti dei Lucchesi a Bruges e ad Anversa*, pp. 76-77.

[128] R. DE ROOVER, *La communauté des marchands Lucquois à Bruges de 1377 à 1404*, pp. 42-43.

[129] R. DE ROOVER, *La communauté des marchands Lucquois à Bruges de 1377 à 1404*, p. 47.

[130] R. DE ROOVER, *La communauté des marchands Lucquois à Bruges de 1377 à 1404*, pp. 54-55.

negotiations with the Flemish government. As such he had to watch over the observance of the community's commercial privileges and to protect the members and their interests. Finally he also administered justice in all criminal and commercial cases between Lucchese.[131] He made most decisions together with his three councillors, among whom was an outgoing consul (having to wait another year before he could occupy the seat again). In exceptional circumstances he left the decisions to the general assembly of all nation members.[132] When the consul or one of the councillors was out of the city for more than three days, they had to appoint a replacement.[133]

The financial concerns of the nation were taken care of by the two *operari* (receivers).[134] They had to collect the fines and the *diritto di Santa Croce*, a tax of 0,1 gr. for a lb., taken on all goods coming out of Lucca (comparable to the Florentine *consolaggio* and the Genoese *denaro della nazione*). If the nation members could not fulfil these and other financial requirements, they had to appoint a *pagatore* while swearing the annual oath, the latter pledging himself for all payments by his colleagues.[135] The *operari* also took care of the maintenance of the *Volto Santo* chapel occupied by the Lucchese in the Augustinians' church. There, members were required to attend mass, or else pay a fine.[136] After a year the *operari* accounted for all revenues and expenses claimed, and one was relieved of his office. At the same time the councillors appointed two new *pacieri* (masters of ceremony). They were responsible for all ceremonial conduct and had to maintain order and peace within the nation.[137]

Most of this happened in the Lucchese nation house, on the corner of the Naaldenstraat and the Grauwwerkersstraat. The *università* certainly owned this property from 1377 on, according to the *libro della communità dei mercanti lucchesi in Bruges*, preserved from that year on.[138] The *libro della communità dei mercanti lucchesi in Bruges*, covering the period until 1404, was the consulate's register of the community and contains reports of all the meetings of the nation, the alterations of the 1369 statutes and the rulings of the consul in his capacity as judge. It recorded the fines, imposed for infractions of the rules, and annual surveys of the Lucchese firms with their marks and the names of their members in Bruges, Paris and London. The register is a treasure of information on the activities of Lucchese merchants in Bruges during the last quarter of the fourteenth century.

One of these was Andrea, brother of Dino Rapondi. As a *governatore* or manager, he oversaw the daily running of the Bruges branch of the Rapondi company in 1377.[139] A year later, he was joined by his nephew Giovanni at the head of the office.[140] Giovanni was the only son of Guglielmo and had worked under the guardianship of his uncle Dino since the death of his father in 1370.[141]

[131] As with other nations, the *communitá* was not liable to Flemish laws but to those of her city of origin.
[132] R. DE ROOVER, *La communauté des marchands Lucquois à Bruges de 1377 à 1404*, pp. 48-49.
[133] R. DE ROOVER, *La communauté des marchands Lucquois à Bruges de 1377 à 1404*, p. 53.
[134] R. DE ROOVER, *La communauté des marchands Lucquois à Bruges de 1377 à 1404*, pp. 49-50.
[135] R. DE ROOVER, *La communauté des marchands Lucquois à Bruges de 1377 à 1404*, pp. 52-53.
[136] R. DE ROOVER, *La communauté des marchands Lucquois à Bruges de 1377 à 1404*, pp. 49-51. Which were really collected, see for example E. LAZZARESCHI (red.), *Il libro della communitá*, p. 30.
[137] R. DE ROOVER, *La communauté des marchands Lucquois à Bruges de 1377 à 1404*, p. 50.
[138] E. LAZZARESCHI (red.), *Il libro della communitá*, p. 54.
[139] E. LAZZARESCHI (red.), *Il libro della communitá*, p. 10.
[140] E. LAZZARESCHI (red.), *Il libro della communitá*, p. 40.
[141] L. MIROT, *La société des Raponde*, p. 317. Not to be confused with Giovanni, that is the son of his second cousin Jacopo, who worked for the firm in Paris and Lucca during this period, see *supra*.

He may have reached the age of majority in 1378, when the Rapondi brothers made him a partner in the company. Together, Giovanni and Andrea led the Bruges branch of the firm. One year later, in 1379, Andrea is no longer on the lists of the members in the register of the Lucchese nation. In his place one of Dino's other brothers, Michele, had taken the duty of watch-dog over Giovanni, who apparently did not yet control enough credit to run the business alone.[142]

On the pay-roll of the Bruges office was also Galica da Piastra. This Lucchese already figured among the account holders of Collard de Marke[143] and had years of experience in the business world. When, on September 15, 1377, the Lucchese nation asked for the file of the firm's staff in Bruges, as it did every year, Galico seemed to be running the house on his own.[144] Since 1345, in the early days of the company, there is no evidence of the Rapondi leaving their Bruges solely branch in the hands of the factor, then Tommaso Giganti.[145] Andrea, Giovanni and Galico led the business in Bruges until 1382, when the former moved on to look for other opportunities. After this, Giovanni had to manage alone, with the experienced da Piastra at his side.[146]

Giovanni, Andrea and Galico acquitted themselves well in the Lucchese nation and participated fully in the social life of the community. Sometimes they occupied one of the honorary functions in the *communità*, although this was rare and they left most of the jobs to others. However, Galico da Piastra seems especially to have made a suitable *cursus honorum*. He served three times as consul (in 1382-83, in 1383-84 when the consul of the previous year, exceptionally, remained in office, and in 1389-90).[147] In 1379, he made it to *paciero* or master of ceremonies.[148] Giovanni too held this post in 1384, the year in which the son of Guglielmo was also appointed as a replacement councillor. Not coincidentally, he then also replaced Galico da Piastra, who was absent for some days.[149]

When the Rapondi did not hold a function within the community, they still made their voice heard in the meetings of the nation and they were consulted frequently on important affairs. In 1378, Andrea, together with twenty other Lucchese, had to judge Giovanni Scandaleone, who had not respected the *università*'s statutes.[150] Andrea's nephew Giovanni was one of the called upon nation members who, together with the consul and the council, acquitted Piero Testa in February 1380, again when his factor da Piastra acted as councillor. Testa had omitted to wear the appropriate garment on the eve of and on the feast of Santa Croce.[151] The Rapondi clan, who seem to have been one of the most respected families in the Lucchese community, was not always an example of good behaviour itself. Andrea Rapondi, for one, was convicted on July 4, 1378, because he had missed mass, sung for the *Volto Santo*.[152] Two years later

---

142 E. LAZZARESCHI (red.), *Il libro della communitá*, p. 57.

143 R. DE ROOVER, *Money, Banking and Credit*, p. 303.

144 E. LAZZARESCHI (red.), *Il libro della communitá*, p. 11. Something that was not possible two years before with Giovanni, a partner *nota bene*.

145 See *supra*. This may indicate the importance of the hub in this period.

146 See E. LAZZARESCHI (red.), *Il libro della communitá*, p. 122.

147 In 1382-83, in 1383-84 when the consul of the previous year exceptionally stayed in office and in 1389-90. R. DE ROOVER, *La communauté des marchands Lucquois à Bruges de 1377 à 1404*, pp. 87-88.

148 E. LAZZARESCHI (red.), *Il libro della communitá*, p. 53.

149 E. LAZZARESCHI (red.), *Il libro della communitá*, pp. 119-120.

150 E. LAZZARESCHI (red.), *Il libro della communitá*, pp. 41-43.

151 E. LAZZARESCHI (red.), *Il libro della communitá*, p. 70.

152 E. LAZZARESCHI (red.), *Il libro della communitá*, p. 30.

he and Giovanni each had to pay another two shillings because they had left the Holy Cross service prematurely without permission.[153]

Within the *communità dei mercanti lucchesi*, the Rapondi seem to have mainly associated with the same entourage with whom they socialised in Paris at the same time, and with which, according to the records of the Bruges money-changers, they had mixed in Flanders ten years before. To this in-group belonged Pietro Scandaleone, who had issued a loan to the weavers' guild in 1337 with Tommaso Giganti, the factor of the Rapondi company, and had figured frequently on Guglielmo's *conto* with Collard de Marke later on.[154] In a trial before the Lucchese nation in 1377, the Rapondi declared that they would pay Scandaleone's debts to Dino Malapresa,[155] also a colleague-borrower of Giganti in 1337, and in 1381, he pledged himself for Giovanni.[156] Obliging colleagues who served as *pagatori* for Andrea were Francesco Totti (1377),[157] who had withdrawn a sum from Guglielmo's account with Ruweel in 1370,[158] and Dino Sanocci (1379),[159] who was a business connection of the Rapondi, according to the books of Collard de Marke. Another old acquaintance who had regularly appeared in Guglielmo's de Marke accounts was Jacopo Fava.[160] He stood surety for Galico da Piastra and for Giovanni in 1379.[161] Finally, Giovanni himself also acted as *pagatore* in 1384 for Davino Tedaldini,[162] who had sold baldachin with Dino Rapondi to the city in 1369.[163] Andrea did the same in 1380 for Bartolomeo Sbarra,[164] whose family lived next to the Rapondi clan in Paris.[165] However, the Rapondi, who sometimes assured each others' payments as well,[166] sometimes expanded their clique. For on the list of their *pagatori*, we can see new names coming in, such as Ramoli,[167] Volpelli[168] and Sandei.[169]

On one occasion, the Lucchese nation in Bruges welcomed Dino Rapondi as well. This happened in September 1377, when he even swore loyalty to the statutes of the *communità* and Orlandino Volpelli registered as *pagatore* for him.[170] It is likely that Dino's visit was caused by the trial of Dino Malapresa four days after the oath-taking. In this case, one of only two commercial affairs in the *libro della communità*[171] in which the company was mentioned,[172] the head of the Rapondi family appeared in person before the consul and his councillors. Dino Malapresa asked him to pay 104 lb. in the name of Pietro Scandaleone.[173]

---

153 E. LAZZARESCHI (red.), *Il libro della communitá*, p. 70.
154 See *supra*.
155 E. LAZZARESCHI (red.), *Il libro della communitá*, pp. 10-11.
156 E. LAZZARESCHI (red.), *Il libro della communitá*, p. 81.
157 E. LAZZARESCHI (red.), *Il libro della communitá*, p. 10.
158 See *supra*.
159 E. LAZZARESCHI (red.), *Il libro della communitá*, p. 53.
160 See *supra*.
161 E. LAZZARESCHI (red.), *Il libro della communitá*, pp. 52-54.
162 E. LAZZARESCHI (red.), *Il libro della communitá*, p. 120.
163 See *supra*.
164 E. LAZZARESCHI (red.), *Il libro della communitá*, p. 61.
165 See *supra*.
166 Galico for Andrea in 1378 and 1380. E. LAZZARESCHI (red.), *Il libro della communitá*, pp. 39, 60.
167 E. LAZZARESCHI (red.), *Il libro della communitá*, p. 53.
168 E. LAZZARESCHI (red.), *Il libro della communitá*, pp. 8, 60.
169 E. LAZZARESCHI (red.), *Il libro della communitá*, p. 10.
170 E. LAZZARESCHI (red.), *Il libro della communitá*, p. 8.
171 The other one being the 1380 trial between Volpelli and dal Portico, see *supra*.
172 Possibly a consequence of the firm's modest activities in Bruges.
173 Why the Rapondi had to make good this debt is not known, but the cause was probably in the confidence relationships illustrated above.

This was the amount due for the purchase of goods from Malapresa, who did business for Giusfredo Cenami's account. Rapondi was willing to take on the debt and requested the plaintiff in his turn to pay the 50 lb. owed by a Nicoló Ciaura to the company. Malapresa, probably a business partner of Ciaura, accepted the debt, whereupon the case was closed.[174] After this, Dino Rapondi disappeared from the *libro della communità* for a long time, although he must have commuted between the branches in Bruges and in Paris, where, according to the personnel files in the consulate's register, he worked with his brother Jacopo.[175] Galico da Piastra often had to bridge the distance between Flanders and France as well, which caused him to leave his duties for the Lucchese nation to Giovanni.[176] All of this confirms the picture of a company whose centre was no longer situated in Bruges but in Paris.

2.3 Neglect of Rapondi Interests in Lucca

The Lucchese nation in Bruges was not the only link connecting the Rapondi with their mother city. For more than ten years they were the only Lucchese and one of the few Italian companies with their headquarters north of the Alps, but they always remained active in Lucca. It is probable that the city still supplied the family's stock of silk fabrics and other typically Lucchese goods which they sold in Bruges and Paris. Nevertheless, it was not the Rapondi brothers themselves who coordinated the activities on the home front but Jacopo, the son of Dino's great-uncle Giovanni.[177] He had a firm himself, functioning independently of that of his second cousins as a juridically separate entity. However, it is beyond doubt that there was a close collaboration between both companies, which would even use the same mark in 1397.[178]

According to the records of the *Corte de' Mercanti* (the Lucchese commercial tribunal), Jacopo di Giovanni was running his firm alone in 1370. A year later, he recruited Cionelli Volpastri as a factor, who was also to work for the Bruges branch of Dino's company (which also supports the supposition that the separation between the two businesses only existed on paper). It is possible that Jacopo continued working with Volpastri until 1379, when he took his own son Giovanni into the business.[179] In the preceding years, Giovanni di Jacopo[180] had proved his worth with Dino in Paris, where he had represented another Lucchese in the sale of horses to Philip the Bold in 1376 and, if we may believe the Bruges *libro della communità*, was admitted as a partner in the firm of the Rapondi brothers in 1378.[181] Probably Jacopo had sent him to France to learn the ins and outs of business, a practice that, looking at Pegolotti's *Pratica della mercatura*, was quite common in the Italian merchant community. The experience Giovanni had gained in Paris he could now apply in Italy, where he would join his father at the head of his firm. The activities of this house were probably,

[174] E. LAZZARESCHI (red.), *Il libro della communitá*, pp. 10-11.
[175] See E. LAZZARESCHI (red.), *Il libro della communitá*, pp. 40, 57, 65, 83, 99.
[176] E. LAZZARESCHI (red.), *Il libro della communitá*, pp. 116, 120, 123.
[177] Or Vanetto, the one whom Guido Rapondi had appointed as proxy in 1331 to swear obedience to John of Bohemia, see *supra*.
[178] E. LAZZARESCHI (red.), *Il libro della communitá*, p. 252.
[179] R. DE ROOVER, *La communauté des marchands Lucquois à Bruges*, pp. 74-75.
[180] Not to be confused with Giovanni di Guglielmo, who remained in Flanders at this time.
[181] See *supra*.

given its modest staffing, limited to trading in the surroundings of Lucca and in the supply of the firm of Dino and his partners.

Not so much the economic, as the political complications of their home city would preoccuppy the Rapondi most. Since 1369, when they had freed themselves from the Pisans and restored the republic, the Lucchese had had their political destiny in their own hands again. But one family would gain so much influence under this republican system that the achievements of 1369 would be jeopardized. The Guinigi, like the Rapondi, were one of the oldest merchant dynasties in the city, making their mark as far back as the tenth century. From the second half of the thirteenth century they had dispersed throughout Europe to try international trade, with reasonable success. By 1370, they had turned into the largest Lucchese business house,[182] on an international level only surpassed by the Florentine Alberti company. In addition to Lucca, the Guinigi had branches in Bruges, London, Paris, Rome[183] and Pisa, on the whole staffed by some 16 to 22 people.[184] The commercial drive evidently brought in a lot of money and in 1369 they were by far the economically most powerful family in the city, with an estimated capital of 200 000 florins.

With Lucchese independence Francesco, at that time the *pater familias* of the Guinigi clan, thought the time had come to turn their financial capacity into political power. He assembled a party of supporters,[185] in which his brothers, cousins and their many sons formed the core. He also engaged the loyalties via marriages and recruited from within his company, although not all of the Guinigi's relations by marriage and their employees joined his party. However, most partisans were colleague merchants who thought that joining the Guinigi was the most promising option in terms of politics.[186]

On its way to power, the Guinigi party needed to get rid of an opposing faction. It is not clear if this group emerged as a reaction to the developments in Francesco's camp or if both parties developed simultaneously. In any case, the axis of the resistance to the Guinigi was made up of two families, one of them being the Rapondi, who as the second richest Lucchese family were the natural opponents of the Guinigi.[187] However their fortune of 100 000 florins put them at a distinct distance from Francesco and his friends in terms of the power they could wield. On the occasion of the *Massa*, when burghers paid a sum to the *commune* to lighten the public debt and then received 10% of this amount every year, the Guinigi were able to spend double what the Rapondi, represented by Jacopo di Giovanni, could afford.[188]

The political interests of the Rapondi family were Jacopo's responsibility as well. He acquitted this duty very zealously and regularly made himself heard in the *anziani* college, in which he sat nine times before 1385.[189] In 1373, he even rose to the rank of *Gonfaloniere di Giustizia*,[190] the highest office in

---

[182] C. MEEK, *Lucca 1369-1400*, p. 197.
[183] Where they would do business for the pope, see *infra*.
[184] C. MEEK, *Lucca 1369-1400*, p. 197. The highest number for the Rapondi company is eight, but does not take into account all branches of the firm and thus is smaller than the real number of personnel, probably some 10 to 12 at the height of its success. See E. LAZZARESCHI (red.), *Il libro della communitá*, p. 155.
[185] C. MEEK, *Lucca 1369-1400*, pp. 204-205.
[186] C. MEEK, *Lucca 1369-1400*, pp. 207-214.
[187] C. MEEK, *Lucca 1369-1400*, pp. 217-219.
[188] C. MEEK, *Lucca 1369-1400*, p. 203.
[189] C. MEEK, *Lucca 1369-1400*, p. 220, n. 106.
[190] L. MIROT, *La société des Raponde*, p. 301.

the republic, in charge of presiding over the *anziani*, putting forward proposals with the legislative councils and summoning citizens in times of crisis.[191] In the struggle for political power, Jacopo could also rely on the support of his son Giovanni, although in the 1370s he moved to Paris for a long time. Later, certainly from 1385 onwards, both would be supported by Piero,[192] Dino's brother, who had previously stayed abroad. In 1379, for instance, he was in Venice, where he represented the Rapondi company.[193]

In their resistance against the Guinigis' craving for power, the Rapondi had an ally whom they met often in Bruges and Paris: Forteguerra Forteguerra. He and his nephew, the judge Bartolomeo Forteguerra, together with the Rapondi clan, would be the driving force of a party that intended to halt the richest family of the city and its partisans (although there was no lack of ambition and lust for power in their ranks either). This group mainly had the same social and economic composition as that of the Guinigi, but numbering far more judges.[194] Both factions were primarily composed of rich merchants and did not consist of members of the *Popolo minuto*.[195] In other respects, the composition of the two parties was similar as well. They more or less held the same view on foreign politics,[196] and the old Italian line of demarcation between the Guelfs and the Ghibellines (respectively the papal and the imperial parties) was not a politically distinguishing criterion either.[197]

Still, a number of Rapondi partisans seem to have had something in common, which has not been discussed before and which we do not find with the Guinigi. A large part of the Rapondi-Forteguerra party coincided with the same group of Lucchese merchants who had contact through the accounts of Collard de Marke and Willem Ruweel, who resided closely together on *Rue de la vieille Monnaie* in Paris and who got along in the Lucchese nation in Bruges. Besides Forteguerra Forteguerra, a familiar face for the Rapondi abroad, the faction had the Cenami family[198] in its ranks, Dino and Jacopo's neighbours in France[199], as well as the Maulini,[200] *pagatori* of Andrea and his associates in the *communità dei mercanti Lucchesi in Bruges*,[201] and the Totti,[202] also pledges in the Lucchese nation and old business relations of Guglielmo according to the Willem Ruweel books.[203]

Another pre-eminent partisan of the Rapondi clan was Gherardo Burlamacchi,[204] one of Guglielmo's foremost connections among the de Marke account holders, who also had relatives living in *Rue de la vieille Monnaie*. Orlandino Volpelli, who had stepped into the breach for Dino in 1377 when the

---

[191] C. MEEK, *Lucca 1369-1400*, p. 10.
[192] C. MEEK, *Lucca 1369-1400*, p. 252.
[193] The firm had already a partner in Venice in 1370 too, see *supra*.
[194] C. MEEK, *Lucca 1369-1400*, pp. 220-222. This probably was a consequence of the leadership of Bartolomeo Forteguerra.
[195] Artisans and other people with a rather modest income, who could not take part in the government of Lucca. C. MEEK, *Lucca 1369-1400*, pp. 224-225.
[196] This also concerned the choice between Florence and Milan, the two regional powers who influenced Lucca throughout the whole of its history. C. MEEK, *Lucca 1369-1400*, pp. 227-229.
[197] C. MEEK, *Lucca 1369-1400*, pp. 229-235.
[198] C. MEEK, *Lucca 1369-1400*, p. 222.
[199] See *supra*.
[200] C. MEEK, *Lucca 1369-1400*, p. 222.
[201] See *supra*.
[202] C. MEEK, *Lucca 1369-1400*, p. 222.
[203] See *supra*.
[204] C. MEEK, *Lucca 1369-1400*, p. 223.

latter showed up in the Lucchese nation[205] and whose brother stood surety for Andrea in 1380,[206] was also one of the most active members of the Rapondi-Forteguerra group.[207] The Sbarra, another family that shared the same street with Dino and his brothers in Paris and got them a pledge in Bruges,[208] were divided, with some family members collaborating with the Guinigi, while others - among whom was Bartolomeo,[209] he who joined the Rapondi in the Lucchese nation[210] – chose their opponents' side.[211] This is not to say that the Rapondi had not done business with someone belonging to the rival party at any time. In 1387 they would even engage Paulo di Poggio as a factor, whose relatives were among the most ardent partisans of Francesco Guinigi.[212] However, these remained exceptions and they never undertook any business dealings with the Guinigi, the Onesti or other important merchant companies who were well suited for cooperation in Paris or Bruges but adhered to the opposing side in Lucca.

Although, as Christine Meek, the author of an authoritative synthesis on Lucca in the second half of the fourteenth century has put it,[213] the economic composition of the two groups in terms of their members' professions did not really differ, the formation of the Lucchese parties had an economic dimension. It would be interesting to know whether any of the commercial affinities that the Rapondi had with some of their allies, such as Gherardo Burlamacchi and Forteguerra Forteguerra, went back to the beginning of the 1370s,[214] the period in which Meek situates the start of the political polarisation[215]. Thus, the question arises of whether the party struggles had already taken root before the beginning of the 1370s[216] and the economic coalitions abroad were a symptom of these tensions (and possibly reinforced them), or if the formation of parties built on existing understandings that had taken shape due to economic collaboration outside Italy.

It is not so clear when the rivalry between the two parties emerged for the first time. The Guinigi, who did not occupy a privileged position under the Pisans, seem to have stepped forward as the most prominent family of the city immediately after independence.[217] The first signs of dissension followed one year later, in 1371, when the Rapondi complained that they had to pay too much in the *Estimo*, a forced loan imposed on all citizens to bear the costs of the republic's defence. Dino's brother Bartolomeo, they stated, should not have to pay taxes, as he was a cleric, nor should their many relatives living abroad.[218]

The real rivalry would only break out after 1376, when, on the proposal of the Guinigi, the *conservatores libertatis* were established, a *balìa* or ad hoc

---

[205] See *supra*.
[206] E. LAZZARESCHI (red.), *Il libro della communitá*, p. 60.
[207] C. MEEK, *Lucca 1369-1400*, p. 225.
[208] See *supra*.
[209] C. MEEK, *Lucca 1369-1400*, p. 222.
[210] E. LAZZARESCHI (red.), *Il libro della communitá*, p. 64.
[211] As was the case with many Lucchese families. C. MEEK, *Lucca 1369-1400*, p. 233.
[212] E. LAZZARESCHI (red.), *Il libro della communitá*, p. 155.
[213] C. MEEK, *Lucca 1369-1400*, p. 225.
[214] See *supra*.
[215] C. MEEK, *Lucca 1369-1400*, p. 195.
[216] Which in that case cannot be explained by the rise of the Guinigi, which did start about 1370. C. MEEK, *Lucca 1369-1400*, p. 198.
[217] It is possible that they had played an important part in the liberation of Lucca, which had have given them this special status. C. MEEK, *Lucca 1369-1400*, p. 196.
[218] C. MEEK, *Lucca 1369-1400*, p. 218.

commission that had to organise the defence, the peace and the well-being of the city. This body, contrary to the former *balie*, was not limited in time and had its responsibilities very vaguely defined, which would present a fertile ground for manipulation.[219] Francesco Guinigi, who had probably called the commission into life for this purpose, would use the *conservatores* as his pre-eminent instrument for gradually expanding his power. As well as himself, he put three Lucchese in the *balìa* whom we can certainly consider as his partisans; four others probably had the same sympathies. Of the four other *conservatores libertatis*, only was a certain supporter of the Rapondi, who were conspicuous by their absence. In that way, the Guinigi were sure of a majority which they did not automatically have in the other government bodies.[220]

In the *anziani*, which dealt with daily administration, regular expenses and correspondence, in the *Consiglio dei Trentasei*, together with the *anziani* responsible for the making of the laws and the election of functionaries, and in the *Consiglio generale*, that had to decide on all important matters, such as jurisdiction, properties and the repeal of decisions,[221] the Guinigi were often more numerous than their opponents as well,[222] the latter apparently preferring their foreign activities to Lucchese political business. Meek's assertion that the Rapondi did not neglect local politics in favour of their foreign interests more than did the Guinigi[223] is difficult to endorse. Up against the Guinigi family, who despite its busy schedule outside Lucca could place four to five family members in the legislative meetings,[224] the Rapondi could only put forward Jacopo di Giovanni. The rest of the clan, temporarily also including Giovanni di Jacopo, was in north-western Europe, where they worked unstintingly for Philip the Bold. What the Rapondi gained by focusing totally on their relations with the Burgundian duke, they lost in their home city, where their position was remarkably weak. With the Forteguerra family, only two members of whom made their appearance in Lucca in this period,[225] matters hardly stood better, so that the leaders of the Guinigi party must certainly have had much more of a presence.

Taking advantage of this weakness and the indifference of many Lucchese citizens,[226] the Guinigi succeeded in transferring more and more tasks of the regular governmental bodies to the *conservatores libertatis*, who more and more behaved as the actual rulers of the city.[227] The concentration of too much power in the hands of too few people however must have provoked some protest, since the commission was expanded from 12 to 36 members in 1381. Notwithstanding the fact that the Rapondi now had their own representative on this expanded *balía*,[228] the presence of their faction in this body remained marginal and they could not rise to their opponent's challenge. Consequently, the Guinigi pressed through on the same course that they had taken before

[219] C. MEEK, *Lucca 1369-1400*, pp. 237-238.
[220] C. MEEK, *Lucca 1369-1400*, pp. 245-249.
[221] C. MEEK, *Lucca 1369-1400*, p. 10.
[222] C. MEEK, *Lucca 1369-1400*, p. 250.
[223] C. MEEK, *Lucca 1369-1400*, p. 224.
[224] C. MEEK, *Lucca 1369-1400*, pp. 207-208.
[225] C. MEEK, *Lucca 1369-1400*, p. 220.
[226] C. MEEK, *Lucca 1369-1400*, p. 249.
[227] C. MEEK, *Lucca 1369-1400*, pp. 238-243.
[228] C. MEEK, *Lucca 1369-1400*, p. 246.

1381. The responsibilities of the *Trentasei* and the *Consiglio generale* were eroded further and those of the *conservatores* reinforced.[229]

This evolution only stopped in 1385, when Francesco Guinigi died. His death encouraged the Forteguerra and the Rapondi, who now stood stronger with Giovanni di Jacopo and Piero in their ranks, to champion the removal or, as Jacopo di Giovanni proposed it, the further expansion of the *conservatores libertatis*. Their complaints were responded to surprisingly fast. On January 10, 1385, the *conservatores* were replaced by a new *balìa* with clearly limited and less excessive competences and including more sympathizers from the opposing party, among whom was Piero Rapondi. The abolition was a first blow for the Guinigi, who would fight back. Soon they would try to regain control over Lucchese politics, provoking new dissension.[230] Whereas these kinds of disputes had occurred quite peacefully before 1385 (for instance they had not prevented Lucca from unanimously proposing Bartolomeo Rapondi as candidate for the bishop's seat in 1383),[231] they would be more tumultuous after this date.

2.4 Mercatores Camere

One of the things that must have preoccupied Jacopo and Giovanni Rapondi and the other Lucchese was connected to the consequences of the *Otto Santi* war.[232] In 1375, this conflict ended the old alliance between the papacy, in exile since 1304 in Avignon on the border of France and the German Empire, and Lucca's neighbour Florence. The Florentines, provoked by the aggressive actions of the papal legates on the Italian peninsula, incited a major revolt in the Papal States. Gregory XI responded with an expedition through Tuscany, where Florence and the smaller cities formed a league against the pope together with Milan. The Holy See also launched an attack on Florence's commercial interests in his territories and severed all financial bonds with its bankers, who had conducted the transfers of papal funds to Avignon for years (particularly the Alberti Antichi).[233] Nevertheless, he still needed to get his revenues to the papal city and therefore approached the merchants of Lucca, that other Tuscan banking center. They had joined the Florentine league for fear of displeasing their powerful neighbours but had continued to act as neutrally as possible and had constantly assured Gregory of their support.[234]

At the moment the crisis broke out, however, the big Lucchese merchant houses, including the Rapondi, did not have a branch in Avignon (due to the Florentine monopoly). For that reason, Gregory used the services of some lesser lights from Lucca, such as the Interminelli, who had a residence near the papal court.[235] However, the Interminelli family did not have the financial resources necessary for the large-scale transfers of papal funds. In a letter of August 14, 1376, the pope insisted that they seek a pledge from more financially powerful Lucchese in Paris, with whom the *camera apostolica* could not

---

229 C. MEEK, *Lucca 1369-1400*, pp. 243-246.
230 C. MEEK, *Lucca 1369-1400*, pp. 252-256.
231 C. MEEK, *Lucca 1369-1400*, p. 252.
232 C. MEEK, *Lucca 1369-1400*, pp. 142-151.
233 R.C. TREXLER, *The Spiritual Power. Republican Florence under Interdict*, Leiden, E.J. Brill, 1974, pp. 29-43.
234 R.C. TREXLER, *The Spiritual Power*, pp. 77-78.
235 For a survey of them, see Y. RENOUARD, "Compagnies mercantiles lucquoises au service des papes d'Avignon" in: Y. RENOUARD, *Études d'histoire médiévale*, Paris, S.E.V.P.E.N., 1968, t. II, pp. 825-831. (Bibliothèque Générale de l'École Pratique des Hautes Études, 6).

work directly, including Betto Schiatta, Forteguerra Forteguerra and Dino Rapondi. These agreed to the pledge and were thus able to participate for the first time in the collection of papal funds.[236]

It is difficult to consider this step independently from the relations the Rapondi had with Philip the Bold. The duke, their direct patron whose wishes they fulfilled blindly, put a lot of effort into the maintenance of good contacts with Gregory XI. Moreover, in 1376, persistent rumours were circulating saying that the pope was determined to move back to Italy. These plans did not meet with the approval of king Charles V, who preferred god's representative on earth to remain in his neighbourhood and under his influence. Numerous diplomatic missions were sent from Paris to talk Gregory out of this projected removal to Rome. Philip also did his duty and travelled with a large following and his usual pomp to Avignon. The visit, with the duke making all possible efforts to convince the pope, took place in August 1376,[237] interestingly the same month in which the Rapondi participated for the first time in the collection of papal funds. It would appear that the commitment of the Rapondi and their large capital resources gave Gregory XI, who never had too much money, an extra reason for changing his mind. For Philip the Bold's point of view, the transfers of August 1376 represent another sign of the Rapondis' willingness to work for his political interests; for Dino and his brothers they meant another chance for financial gain and prestige via the duke's impeccable contacts.

However, this situation would not last very long. The *Otto de Guerra*, the Florentine war council, also known as the *Otto Santi*, kept challenging Gregory, despite Florence's excommunication. In 1377 the pope sent an army, commanded by Robert of Geneva, to the rebellious regions. He decided to return to Italy himself, to ensure his possession of Rome. By making an end to the 70-year 'Babylonian captivity' of the papacy in Avignon, Gregory XI made conciliatory moves towards a long cherished wish in the Christian world but displeased the French king Charles V.[238] With this move the fragile new contacts between the *camera* and the Rapondi also collapsed. When the pope disembarked on the Italian peninsula, he concluded a monopoly contract for the transfer of papal funds with the Guinigi,[239] who, having a branch in Rome, were more suited for the job. However, more serious problems were on the horizon.

On March 27 1378, Gregory died in Rome. Twenty-one days later, the cardinals met in conclave against a background of riots among the Roman people and unanimously elected the Neapolitan Bartolomeo Prignano as the new pope, who would begin his pontificate as Urban VI at Easter. At some point in mid June however, the French members of the college withdrew to Anagni[240] on the initiative of Cardinal de la Grange, who had been absent during the conclave, and *camerarius* Pierre de Cros (the member of the Curia watching over the papal treasury),[241] stating that the April election had taken place under

---

[236] Y.RENOUARD, *Les relations des papes d'Avignon et des compagnies commerciales et bancaires de 1316 à 1378*, Paris, Editions E. De Boccard, 1941, p. 110.
[237] R. VAUGHAN, *Philip the Bold*, pp. 11-14.
[238] R.C. TREXLER, *The Spiritual Power*, p. 92.
[239] J. FAVIER, *Les finances pontificales à l'époque du Grand Schisme d'Occident 1378-1409*, Paris, Editions E. De Boccard, 1966, p. 480.
[240] R.H. BAUTIER, "Aspects politiques du Grand Schisme" in: *Genèse et débuts du Grand Schisme d'Occident*, Paris, Éditions du Centre de la Recherche Scientifique, 1980, p. 457.
[241] R.H. BAUTIER, *Aspects politiques du Grand Schisme*, pp. 464-465.

pressure from the Roman mob. The true reason for their volte face was probably that Urban VI had planned to place more Italians in the Curia, a move that would reduce the majority and the position of authority that the French, especially the Limousins, had built up in Avignon. Moreover, the new pope was determined to recast the church in a mould of evangelical sobriety, a reform unpopular with the cardinals' college, which was reluctant to lose the luxurious way of life it had adopted during the fourteenth century.[242]

By the beginning of August, the French had been joined by the rest of the cardinals in Anagni and together they demanded the abdication of Urban VI. The pope would not give in to their demands, and appointed 28 new cardinals himself. Thereupon the rebels elected a new pope on September 18, 1378, the French Robert of Geneva, who was crowned as Clement VII on October 31 and returned to Avignon.[243] France, the Spanish principalities and Scotland recognised this antipope. England, Flanders and the main part of the German Empire remained in obedience to Urban VI.[244] In this way, the Great Western Schism came about.

Many contemporaries, as well as modern historians, pinned the responsibility for the schism on Charles V, who of course was more satisfied with a French pope at the backdoor of his kingdom than with an Italian in Rome. He would have exerted his influence on the revolt by the cardinals, led by his counsellor Jean de la Grange, in favour of the rupture and the election of Robert of Geneva, who was his cousin let it be noted.[245] More recent studies, on the other hand, point out that Charles was somewhat reticent regarding the developments in Italy and that his brother Louis of Anjou, for one, was from the outset a much more fervent partisan of Clement VII.[246] Also, Robert-Henri Bautier has demonstrated that the letters the king wrote to the cardinals to urge a decision can only have reached the council after the decisions had already been taken.[247]

Yet official correspondence does not reveal everything and the cardinals must have been aware of Charles V's preferences, who, just a few months earlier, had not really concealed his displeasure with the move of the papacy from Avignon to Rome and had used all diplomatic means at his disposal to prevent this.[248] In any event, from the moment of the election of the antipope, little remained of the king's reservations and Charles did his utmost to consolidate Clement VII's position, "at whose service he would put all diplomatic and financial resources", according to Bautier.[249] Certainly on finances work had to be done, since Clement was often out of cash. The French prince therefore advanced him 20 000 florins,[250] and other loans followed, from Louis of Anjou as well.

---

[242] R.H. BAUTIER, *Aspects politiques du Grand Schisme*, pp. 458-459.
[243] R.H. BAUTIER, *Aspects politiques du Grand Schisme*, p. 457.
[244] G. BARRACLOUGH, *The Medieval Papacy*, London, Thames and Hudson, 1968, pp. 165-166.
[245] See for example G. BARRACLOUGH, *The Medieval Papacy*, pp. 165-166.
[246] E. DELARUELLE, E.-R. LABANDE and P. OURLIAC, *L'Église au temps du Grand Schisme et de la crise conciliaire*, , Bloud & Gay, 1962, pp. 21-22.
[247] R.H. BAUTIER, *Aspects politiques du Grand Schisme*, pp. 462-464.
[248] E. DELARUELLE, E.-R. LABANDE and P. OURLIAC, *L'Église au temps du Grand Schisme*, p. 4.
[249] R.H. BAUTIER, *Aspects politiques du Grand Schisme*, p. 464.
[250] E. DELARUELLE, E.-R. LABANDE and P. OURLIAC, *L'Église au temps du Grand Schisme*, p. 22.

Since 1376, Charles V's and Anjou's financial arms also included the Rapondi.[251] From 1379 onwards they would open their purse for the Avignon papacy. At the beginning of this relationship their operations did not really differ from their first contacts with the Holy See three years earlier and they participated in the transfers of papal funds on a limited scale, by way of other Lucchese.[252] If it is already difficult to believe that the bond between the Rapondi and the papacy in 1376 had emerged independently from the existing bond between the Rapondi and the French court, then it seems even more improbable after 1379. When the Rapondi clan agreed to stand surety for the Interminelli, the position of Gregory XI, despite the war of the *Otto Santi*, was unthreatened and their involvement did not involve any risk. In 1378, on the contrary, the papacy, in Avignon as well as in Rome, was precarious and its future was very uncertain. Consequently, very few merchants were willing to put their capital at stake immediately after the establishment of the Schism by providing Clement with liquidity.[253] One of the few who were prepared to help him out was Dino Rapondi, not coincidentally the supplier and banker to the French court, which, even if it had no hand itself in the election of the antipope, was certainly not unfavourable to it, and in whose interest it was that its papal coalition partner was as strong as possible, not least financially.

The Avignonese camp also had the Burgundian duke among its members, the Rapondi's most important and most direct patron and employer,[254] who seems to have used them already to serve his relations with the Holy See.[255] Although Philip acted discreetly in the establishment of the Schism,[256] he was an active contributor to the Clementine case. If Leopold III, duke of Austria, switched from Rome to Avignon, it was only because he had been able to conclude a marriage contract between his son and Philip the Bold's eldest daughter.[257] Taking all this into consideration, it is not impossible to imagine that the duke and/or his brothers were responsible for firming up the business connection between their bankers and Clement VII, or at least that they facilitated the establishment of this bond with their support for the antipope. Another contributing factor could have been Iolanda of Bar, one of the Rapondis' most important customers and one of the most fervent supporters of the Avignon papacy, in contrast to the position of her second cousin Louis of Male.[258]

Lucca, the family's home base, remained faithful to Urban VI.[259] The latter could also rely on the Guinigi, with whom his predecessor Gregory XI had settled his affairs.[260] However, the Rapondi did not choose to provide the Avignon pope with financial services only because their Lucchese rivals transferred funds to Rome. This would neglect the complex financial interests involving the duke, and thus the Rapondi, concerning Clement's position. Their

---

[251] See *supra*.
[252] J. FAVIER, *Les finances pontificales*, p. 486.
[253] J. FAVIER, *Les finances pontificales*, p. 570.
[254] R. VAUGHAN, *Philip the Bold*, p. 185.
[255] See *supra*.
[256] This was not surprising since the majority of his future subjects, the Flemings, where pro-Urban.
[257] E. DELARUELLE, E.-R. LABANDE and P. OURLIAC, *L'Église au temps du Grand Schisme*, p. 24.
[258] R. VAUGHAN, *Philip the Bold*, p. 185. In 1385, Dino would even take with him four bulls of Clement for her. L. MIROT, *La société des Raponde*, p. 324.
[259] C. MEEK, *Lucca 1369-1400*, p. 153.
[260] J. FAVIER, *Les finances pontificales*, p. 480.

choice does illustrate that when the interests of Philip the Bold and the French royal family entered the game, those of the merchant-bankers' mother city were subordinate.

In spite of their ties with the French court, which was their most powerful factor in coming to the aid of the antipope, the Rapondi initially played a waiting game. The first two years they only used their firm's wealth and experience to receive papal funds in Paris and transfer them to Avignon. There, various correspondents made the money over to Clement's treasury, without the need for representatives of the family at the papal court itself.[261] On March 31, 1379, for example, Filippo Astareo put the *camera apostolica* into possession of the 2000 francs that Dino had received in the French capital.[262] The Rapondi only showed up in person in Avignon in 1381, when Dino visited the papal palace to hand over 600 francs changed by some *nuntii* with his brother Jacopo in Paris.[263] The manager had probably also explored the commercial possibilities and prepared for the opening of a new branch of the firm. This must have taken place in 1382 under the leadership of Dino's brother Andrea. He no longer figured on the personnel sheets of the Lucchese nation in Bruges from that date,[264] and appeared more and more in the financial documents of the Holy See.[265] He certainly had a house in Avignon from 1385 onwards. On November 6, 1384, one Catalan de la Rocca told Buoninsegna di Matteo, factor of Francesco di Marco Datini, the famous merchant of Prato,[266] that he would have to leave his shop in the city the following January, because the pope had sold the building to Andrea Rapondi.[267]

In his new home Andrea could also house his new wife, the daughter of Helena of Piacenza, whom he married on August 26, 1385 in Avignon. Being succesful bankers, the Rapondi were able to conclude "a nice money marriage", collecting 3000 florins, plus what they could expect from Helena of Piacenza. According to Buoninsegna di Matteo, like his master mainly interested in finances, more than 100 florins of this immediately disappeared into the pockets of Jacopo del Nero, a merchant who supplied the torches and candles for the wedding party.[268]

From the outset, Andrea Rapondi could rely on collaboration with some regular partners. One of these was Maffredo Frami, who would transfer 8067 florins to the papal treasury in the period from 1383 to 1390, of which 6750 came from Dino in Paris. With the Rapondi he would even send 2250 florins at once to the south of France in 1390. The Lucchese firm could also call on the services of Giovanni Caransoni, who was familiar with the papal financial system and who from 1384 to 1394 was responsible for the transfer of 21 554 florins, mainly collected by the Rapondi in Paris. However, neither Frami nor Caransoni were employees of the Rapondi company. Both worked principally

---

[261] J. FAVIER, *Les finances pontificales*, p. 486.
[262] J. FAVIER, *Les finances pontificales*, p. 483.
[263] J. FAVIER, *Les finances pontificales*, p. 486.
[264] For his last mention in Bruges, see E. LAZZARESCHI (red.), *Il libro della communitá*, p. 99.
[265] See for example J. FAVIER, *Les finances pontificales*, p. 492.
[266] See I. ORIGO, *The merchant of Prato: Francesco di Marco Datini, 1335-1410*, Boston, David R. Godine Publisher, 1986, 415 p.
[267] R. BRUN, "Annales avignonnaises de 1382 à 1410, extraits des archives de Datini" in: *Mémoires de l'institut historique de Provence*, 1935, p. 67. This may have been the house next to that of Cardinal de Thury in the parish of Saint-Agricol, where Rapondi would later live. See L. MIROT, *La société des Raponde*, p. 312.
[268] R. BRUN, *Annales avignonnaises*, pp. 84-85.

on their own account but considered it wise to get their share of the success of Dino and his companions by working with them, rather than trying to compete against their rapidly overwhelming dominance in Clementine finances.[269]

Andrea Rapondi would lead the activities of the Avignon branch until the end of 1385. He was relieved then by his younger brother Filippo, who would head the office until the beginning of 1389. The next one in line was cousin Giovanni di Guglielmo, who only stayed in Avignon for a year and a half. He was replaced in October 1390 by factor Jacopo Rongui, who would manage the next five years of the Rapondis' activities at the papal court.[270] Afterwards, probably from 1395 on, Andrea seems to have returned to the papal city,[271] where he would remain until his death in 1417.[272] Dino Rapondi himself may have visited Avignon only once after his first stay in 1381, in 1389 when he joined Charles VI on his trip through southern France.[273]

The struggle between Urban VI in Rome and Clement in Avignon depended for a large part on their financial resources. It was of the utmost importance to get these revenues quickly, efficiently and safely to where the pope needed them most. For this purpose, the Rapondi were the right men. Not only because they had a perfect knowledge of the most advanced payment techniques, but especially because they were one of the most important merchant houses in Paris, where the largest and most crucial collection points of the Clementine obedience were situated.[274] For in the French capital, not only the collector of Paris, but also those of Rheims, Tours and Bourges gathered their funds.

Thus, the biggest challenge for the Rapondi was not in Avignon, but in Paris, where they had to sell themselves to the designated collectors, who were free to use any financial channel they wanted.[275] In this respect, the participation of the Rapondi in papal finances, given the position and the resources they already had in Paris, did not require much more than the installation of a representative in Avignon. This partly explains why Dino, the head of the family and of the enterprise, always stayed in Paris and rarely visited Avignon. What mattered most was to offer the collectors the fastest and safest way to supply their superiors in the papal palace. Given the acute shortage of money, the *camera apostolica* would not appreciate revenues being late because a bill of exchange was protested, for example. It was on this level of resources and efficiency that the Rapondi had an undeniable advantage over most of their competitors. An impressive demonstration of this was given on May 19, 1385, when Andrea managed to pay three bills of exchange to the treasury on one single day, one amounting to 2000 florins and two others to 3000 florins.[276] There may have been other firms with a Paris centre and an Avignon factor from whom the collectors could choose, but few of them would have been able to instantly pay out 8000 florins.

---

[269] J. FAVIER, *Les finances pontificales*, pp. 484-485.
[270] J. FAVIER, *Les finances pontificales*, p. 486.
[271] J. FAVIER, *Les finances pontificales*, p. 488.
[272] L. MIROT, *La société des Raponde*, p. 312.
[273] L. MIROT, *La société des Raponde*, pp. 324-325.
[274] The same applies to the Guinigi, with their branches in Rome and Flanders, ideally situated to deal with the transfers for Urban VI.
[275] J. FAVIER, *Les finances pontificales*, p. 487.
[276] The first amount originated from the Paris collector, the latter two from the Rheims and Tours collectors. J. FAVIER, *Les finances pontificales*, p. 497.

For these reasons the collectors in Paris and Rheims opted to use the Rapondi from December 1381 onwards, the one in Tours from 1384.[277] Dino and his company would carry out the majority of the money transfers to the papacy in Avignon up to and including 1389.[278] This happened in two ways, depending on when the payment by the collectors to the firm took place. For instance, Dino could order his representative in Avignon to pay the sum to the *camera* owed by a collector to the papacy, after which he was reimbursed for this amount in Paris by the collector there.[279] This happened in 1382, when Marle, a nuncio from Paris, paid back to Dino the 800 francs that the company had advanced him in Avignon. An alternative was that the collectors could transfer the proceeds of their collections in advance to Dino in Paris, who then drew a bill of exchange on his factor in Avignon, who paid out the sum to the treasury.[280] In this way, the nuncios Murol, Girard and Marle provided Rapondi with 1000 francs on January 10, 1382, and the pope received this amount from Rapondi at the beginning of March.[281] Similarly, Murol and Girard would pass on another 4600 francs to Avignon from October 1381 to May 1382.[282]

All in all, by way of these two ways of payment no less than 109 428 florins intended for the papacy went through the hands of the Rapondi from 1381 to 1395, essentially the collectors' proceeds[283]. Moreover, the *communs services*, which the prelates had to give to the Holy See every year, also passed sporadically through the Rapondi headquarters in *Rue de la Vieille Monnaie*, as in September 1385 did those of the bishops of Rodez, Maurienne, Saint-Brieuc, Famagusta and Le Puy.[284] To the above have to be added the amounts the Rapondi transferred for other Lucchese, mainly Giovanni Caransoni.[285] All this activity made the Rapondi company the most important transfer point between the Parisian money market and the Avignonese papacy for almost fifteen years. Exceptionally, the firm also made payments in Avignon for Flemish clerics, probably by way of the Bruges branch. Giovanni, for one, advanced the funds to hold four religious services for Louis, the Bishop of Tournai in March 1390, one for Andre, Bishop of Cambrai in April 1391 and one for the Abbot of Cysoing, in August 1391.[286] Still, this was very modest, since the lion's share of the ecclesiastical revenues from Flanders, which had remained faithfull to Urban VI, disappeared into the treasury of the Roman pope via the Guinigi.

The Rapondis' grip on the papal cash flow would increase temporarily, though not coincidentally, at the moment when the interests of the French royal family came again to prominence. The occasion was the Neapolitan expedition by Louis of Anjou.[287] Lured by a desire to exercise power over the Italian

[277] Only the Bourges collector chose for the Solario-Ricci from Asti.
[278] J. FAVIER, *Les finances pontificales*, p. 500.
[279] In fact this concerned a loan, which resulted in the most profit for the Rapondi, given the interest that accrued.
[280] In this case, the Rapondi only took on the transportation of the funds.
[281] J. FAVIER, *Les finances pontificales*, p. 422.
[282] J. FAVIER, *Les finances pontificales*, p. 453.
[283] The Solario-Ricci were the next on the list, with 83 125 florins transferred throughout a longer period. J. FAVIER, *Les finances pontificales*, p. 487.
[284] J. FAVIER, *Les finances pontificales*, p. 472.
[285] Many people from the above-mentioned in-group, such as Carlo Spifame in 1397, benefited from the Rapondis' services as well. J. FAVIER, *Les finances pontificales*, p. 487.
[286] G. BIGWOOD, *Le régime juridique et économique Tome I*, p. 188. The Flemish bishops chose ClementVII's side, contrary to most other Flemings. R. VAUGHAN, *Philip the Bold*, pp. 184-185.
[287] J. FAVIER, *Les finances pontificales*, p. 487.

peninsula, the focal point of the confrontation between the two popes, in 1380 Clement VII had convinced Joan, the heirless queen of the papal fief Naples, to adopt Louis of Anjou, one of his closest allies, as her heir. Thereupon Urban VI had deposed Joan and given her kingdom to Charles of Durazzo, one of his partisans, who conquered the area without striking a blow.[288] In 1382, however, Louis of Anjou, who had had his hands full with the regency in France for the previous two years, chose the *voie de fait* as well and launched a campaign intended to retrieve Naples and secure his long-coveted royal title on the one hand, and to strengthen Clement's influence on the Italian peninsula on the other hand.[289]

Clement VII supported the Angevin project in every possible way, including the assignment of all papal revenues for the duration of the operation to Louis. Nevertheless, to transfer the financial resources from the treasury in Avignon to Nicolas de Mauregart, the threasurer of Anjou, a "procureur" was needed, and Andrea Rapondi was the one selected to fulfill this function.[290] The choice of the Rapondi, who were usually familiar with the papal financial system and had been for two years, probably had a lot to do with the good services the family had rendered to the duke of Anjou and the royal family in previous years, and more particularly with the fact that they had been the only ones willing to step into the financial breach and consolidate the position of the antipope, for whom Louis had been one of the most fervent advocates.[291]

For two years, Andrea would serve as the intermediary between the papal treasury in Avignon and the Angevins on the Italian peninsula, gathering all papal funds arriving in southern France, as well as the extraordinary revenues, such as the 7500 florins loan issued in June 1385 by the French *connétable* Olivier de Clisson, and get them to Mauregart one way or another. In so doing, he was responsible for the sending of the necessary capital to Venice in 1385 for the expedition of Pierre de Murles and Cavallino de Cavalli.[292] The entries concerning all other Italian operations in the Anjou accounts conclude with the formula "Recepi A. Repondi". The transfers to Naples themselves were left to others by the Rapondi, mostly Florentines,[293] probably because the former did not have a representative of their own in southern Italy.

Despite the financial support from the Rapondi and others, the Clementine-Angevin project in Naples was a fiasco. Notwithstanding some modest successes by the French forces at the beginning, Charles of Durazzo was able to hold out easily.[294] After the expedition had lost its driving force with the death of Louis of Anjou in September 1384, the papacy first of all tried to secure his few conquests in southern Italy by sending three galleys in the summer of 1385. Because of the continuous financial burden of the hostilities, however, the *camera apostolica* was in an even greater need of money and the captains' wages for the 1385 fleet had to be advanced by Andrea Rapondi[295] (in

---

[288] E. DELARUELLE, E.-R. LABANDE and P. OURLIAC, *L'Église au temps du Grand Schisme*, pp. 38-39.
[289] F. AUTRAND, *Charles VI La folie du roi*, Paris, Librairie Arthème Fayard, 1986, p. 89.
[290] J. FAVIER, *Les finances pontificales*, p. 487.
[291] See *supra*. The efforts he now made to reinforce the position of the Rapondi, again confirm the impression that he and/or his brothers had been involved in the establishment of the bond between Clement and the Lucchese firm in about 1378.
[292] The Rapondi probably had a partner in Venice, see *supra*.
[293] J. FAVIER, *Les finances pontificales*, pp. 487-488.
[294] E. DELARUELLE, E.-R. LABANDE and P. OURLIAC, *L'Église au temps du Grand Schisme*, p. 40.
[295] J. FAVIER, *Les finances pontificales*, p. 624.

whose interest it was, after all, that operations should continue). After 1385 the ambitious campaign petered out.[296] For the Rapondi, on the other hand, the balance was extremely positive. For three years they had controlled hundreds of thousands of florins, which had permitted them to earn a fortune themselves.[297] Although their collaboration did not lead to the planned reinforcement of the position of their patrons Clement VII and Louis of Anjou, their unreserved and high quality services ensured that the considerable confidence that the Angevins and the French royal family, as well as the pope, had already put in them, increased even further and that they could strengthen their hold on the financial affairs at the French and the Avignon courts.

Besides the money transfers, the Rapondi also eased the papacy's need for liquidity by making loans. In this branch of their activities, however, they were not as prominent as they were in transferring funds, and they had to yield precedence to people like Aguinolfo de Pazzi, Catalan de la Rocca,[298] dal Poggio, Caransoni and Ricci.[299] However, Dino and his family were still responsible for a total credit of 17 200 florins, granted from December 1381 up to and including May 1394.[300] To avoid the transport of currency, the repayment of these loans was made by way of an assignment on the funds of a collector in Paris,[301] which implies that, on the first occasion, a corresponding amount was subtracted from the sum he was to hand over to Avignon for the collectors.[302] Yet, it could take some time before the Rapondi saw their capital again. The collector of Paris, for example, needed eight to ten months to make a repayment which he had been ordered to do by the treasury (in addition to the two months required for the assignment to make its way from Avignon). The order to pay the 1300 francs for which Dino gave him a receipt on August 20, 1382 was received by him on February 2, 1381. For the 300 florins and 200 francs the Rapondi enter as revenue in their ledger on October 7, 1393, even two assignments had been necessary, one in February and one in August 1393.[303]

Taking into account the long time periods that loans to the papacy entailed, the Rapondi and other money-lenders were not prepared to simply part with their money. First, no merchant in Avignon would issue a credit without a pledge.[304] This served as a security for the agreement, and was normally rendered to the *camera* when the loan was redeemed. However, it happened more than once that the treasury was not able to pay at the fixed time, so that the pledge object remained the property of the creditor. Andrea Rapondi became the owner of a silver water bowl in this way, given in pledge for his account to Maffredo Frami, for a loan to the pope.[305]

---

[296] Until the next duke of Anjou, Louis' son with the same name, resumed the Neapolitan adventure at the end of the 1380s. E. DELARUELLE, E.-R. LABANDE and P. OURLIAC, *L'Église au temps du Grand Schisme*, p.71.
[297] J. FAVIER, *Les finances pontificales*, p. 488.
[298] The former owner of Andrea Rapondi's house, see *supra*.
[299] J. FAVIER, *Les finances pontificales*, pp. 571-572. However, they did not need to cover the gigantic sums loaned by the Rapondi at the same time to the Burgundian duke and the French Crown. Moreover, they were not involved to the same extent or, as with the Pazzi, at all in the transfers of papal funds, so that, in full, they have only supplied to the *camera* a small portion of the capital that the Rapondi were able to make available.
[300] J. FAVIER, *Les finances pontificales*, p. 571. This is more or less the same period as for the transfers.
[301] An order to the latter from the papal treasury to pay back the sum the Rapondi had granted it.
[302] There was no difference from the transfers for which the collectors only paid the amount afterwards, except that now, the initiative came from the *camera apostolica*.
[303] J. FAVIER, *Les finances pontificales*, p. 562.
[304] J. FAVIER, *Les finances pontificales*, p. 548.
[305] J. FAVIER, *Les finances pontificales*, p. 127.

Besides a pledge, the mainly Italian businessmen also expected financial compensation, since they were denied the use of a part of their capital. The church, the papacy first, had always condemned and resisted the practice of imposing interest on loans. In reality it had more and more tolerated the request for compensation from the twelfth century on, when the ban on usury had become untenable because of the expansion of international trade. When, from 1378, the competition with the rival pope became more important than the church's own canonical regulations, it even started borrowing on interest itself. The prohibition to cite the interest openly in the contracts was got around by, as was usual, disguising it as a gift, a present or an indemnity (which was officially permitted). In that way, on May 4, 1389, the collector of Paris was ordered to pay 1600 francs to Dino for a loan, for the delivery of a silk cloth and for the risk he had incurred. There was probably also an interest payment involved when Giovanni and Andrea Rapondi received 50 francs to buy two pieces of camelot and get themselves a jacket on January 31, 1390. After Dino had granted a credit of 1000 francs to the pope on December 2, 1381 and 100 francs on December 6, he was repaid 1000 francs to redeem the debt and 300 francs "as a special gift" on August 20, 1382.[306] The annual pension the Rapondi received from the pope for services rendered from 1383,[307] may have concealed interest payments on one or more loan transactions as well.

The loans that the Rapondi arranged with the Holy See make implausible Christine Meek's assertion that the activities of the firm in Avignon were limited to the transfer of funds, contrary to the much larger and more complicated operations undertaken by the Guinigi in service of Urban VI.[308] Moreover, besides credit operations and transfers, Dino also settled small banking transactions for the pope, such as the payment for a delivery of luxurious fabrics to Giovanni Caransoni in 1387[309] or the redemption of a loan granted by Francesco Datini to the pope in 1382.[310] Thus, Jacques Favier is correct in calling the Rapondi "Clément VII's principal bankers".[311]

Moreover, they supplied merchandise to the court in Avignon as well, although in modest amounts.[312] As far as is known, the pope only purchased from Andrea a clasp, decorated with jewels, and some cloth and other requirements for a chapel for Advent and Lent, from Filippo a cartload of fabrics which Clement presented to the *sénéchal* of the Provence[313] and from Dino an amount of silk[314] and a tapestry worth 1800 gold francs.[315] The often discussed complementarity between the capital flow from the papal treasury to the merchant world in Paris (for the Guinigi in Flanders), where the pope had the funds the merchants needed to do business because of the presence of his

---

[306] It is likely that the initial 100 francs were the warranted interest on the 1000 francs loan, which implies a high interest rate of 42.5%. J. FAVIER, *Les finances pontificales*, pp. 556-557.
[307] J. FAVIER, *Les finances pontificales*, p. 486.
[308] C. MEEK, *Lucca 1369-1400*, p. 219, n. 104.
[309] J. FAVIER, *Les finances pontificales*, p. 484.
[310] J. FAVIER, *Les finances pontificales*, p. 492.
[311] J. FAVIER, *Les finances pontificales*, p. 572.
[312] This is quite remarkable, given the firm's specialisation in high-end luxury products and the large demand for this from the sumptuous papal environment. Perhaps it was only Dino's intention to make sure that Clement had sufficient financial resources, because this was in the interest of his employers, which was far less the case for the maintenance of commercial relations.
[313] L. MIROT, *La société des Raponde*, pp. 311-313.
[314] J. FAVIER, *Les finances pontificales*, p. 556.
[315] L. MIROT, *La société des Raponde*, p. 325.

collection points and the reverse movement in Avignon (for the Guinigi in Rome), where the merchants provided the purchase-prone but cash-strapped courts with goods and loans, with the two movements partly neutralising each other and making big settlements redundant, could not be used fully by the Rapondi, because of the absence of lasting commercial ties in Avignon.

These imperfect commercial relations however did not prevent the capital movements between the Rapondi and the papacy from increasing up to and including 1389. After this, an abrupt turnabout took place. While the Rapondi company transferred seven times more than its competitors, the Solario-Ricci from Asti, to Avignon each year from 1381 on, the Astesans seem to have made over more than 17 000 florins to the *camera apostolica* in 1390, compared to only 9080 from the Rapondi. This tendency would continue in the following years, until the transfers of papal funds by the Lucchese enterprise stopped completely in 1395.[316]

The causes of this change are evident. The political context around 1390 makes us believe that the contacts between the Rapondi and the papacy ended as they had begun: as a consequence of the interests of the family's patrons. The duke of Burgundy came into possession of Flanders in 1384, which put him in a difficult position concerning his choice of the true pope. Most of the Flemish population were strong adherents of pope Urban VI, while the other parts of his possessions, as well as he himself and his interests (the French crown was one of his most important sources of income), were in the Clementine camp. For that reason the duke, more than most other European princes, benefited from a possible ending to the schism and, in the beginning, was the only one to support the university of Paris when it began to call for more energy to be invested in searching for a solution. The obvious means to do so was by the *via cessionis*, where both popes would abdicate simultaneously and the colleges in Rome and Avignon would together elect one new father of the church. Some, however, wanted a more drastic course and Philip the Bold told Clement's legate in Paris that if his superior refused to step down, France and the whole French church would withdraw from Clementine obedience.[317]

The consequences for the Rapondi of this more aggressive and initially quite isolated stance by the duke followed quickly. In May 1390, the Datinis' correspondent in Avignon knew that Giovanni Rapondi had constantly tried to collect money but could only make headway with the Lucchese and the Pisans, because of his bond with Philip the Bold. In light of the growing tensions between the prince and the pope, the factor of the cautious Datini thought it was better to halt business with Giovanni altogether.[318] The reduction in liquidity which ensued may explain why the Rapondi stopped their loans to the *camera* in May 1394.[319] This may also have taken place at the insistence of Philip the Bold, who became more and more critical, or on the initiative of Clement himself, since the pope may have begun to realise that the financial means of power which his former allies had given him through the Rapondi, could also turn against him, as a lever in the hands of those who wanted to put pressure on him.

---

[316] J. FAVIER, *Les finances pontificales*, p. 500.
[317] R. VAUGHAN, *Philip the Bold*, p. 46.
[318] R. BRUN, *Annales avignonnaises*, p. 123.
[319] J. FAVIER, *Les finances pontificales*, p. 571.

In Paris, the decisions of its patron also seriously hindered the firm. The papal collectors in the city, whose business the Lucchese company had almost completely sewn up in 1384, started to wonder if it was still a good idea to entrust their money to the Rapondi, the most faithful partisans of Philip the Bold, who might well threaten the position of their patron in Avignon. Therefore, from 1390 on, one by one they thanked Dino and his nephew Giovanni for their services and changed to the less political Solario-Ricci or another channel to get their revenues to the pope.[320] The volume of the exchanges that the Rapondi drew on in Avignon decreased proportionally, with the most spectacular dip occurring in 1391,[321] the year when the Burgundian duke openly vented his discontent with the absence of a solution for the schism for the first time.[322] As Philip's pressure on Clement VII increased, and the French royal family also were persuaded of the desirability of ending this rupture in western Christendom, mainly because of its intentions of making advances to England in the Hundred Years War again,[323] the Rapondis' transfers represented smaller and smaller amounts.

The possibility of an end to the impasse came in September 1394, when Clement VII died. The French crown requested the cardinals in Avignon to put off their election of a successor, but this request was not needed by the college, which appointed the Aragonese Pedro de Luna as pope Benedict XIII. Although he had declared before that he would abdicate when necessary, it soon became apparent that Benedict would cling to the papal tiara with as much tenacity as his predecessor had done. In an attempt to change his mind, an impressive fleet led by the dukes of Burgundy, Berry and Orléans (brother of Charles VI) and a large following sailed down the Rhone in May 1395. However, this ostentatious demonstration of power by the three royal princes could not soften the pope, and the delegation had to return with nothing achieved.[324]

Shortly after the failure of this ultimate attempt at negotiations, the Rapondi definitively ended their financial transfers. The last operation they performed for the papacy was the sending of 4000 florins to the Angevins in Pisa.[325] Thereupon, a decision by the French church made all participation in papal finances completely impossible. To urge the pope to acquiesce, at a synod in May 1396 the French prelates threatened to deprive him of the right to benefices and all ecclesiastical revenues.[326] Nevertheless, Benedict kept rejecting every appeal to abdicate, and the papacy was denied all financial resources for the future.[327] For the Rapondi, this brought down the curtain on an episode lasting fifteen very lucrative years, which must have brought them thousands of florins. However, though a very welcome bonus, their contacts with the Holy See had never been indispensable for the development of the company, which was completely determined by its relation with Philip the Bold. Since 1369, these

---

[320] J. FAVIER, *Les finances pontificales*, pp. 500-501.
[321] J. FAVIER, *Les finances pontificales*, p. 490.
[322] R. VAUGHAN, *Philip the Bold*, p. 46.
[323] F. AUTRAND, *Charles VI La folie du roi*, p. 276. Probably also because the duke was able to regain the control of the French government that he had lost in 1388, when king Charles VI started to show the first signs of madness from 1392 onwards. See R. VAUGHAN, *Philip the Bold*, p. 43.
[324] R. VAUGHAN, *Philip the Bold*, pp. 46-47.
[325] From this transaction we can conclude the presence of Andrea Rapondi for the first time since 1385. J. FAVIER, *Les finances pontificales*, pp. 487-488. Possibly he had to assist the factor Jacopo Rongui in searching a solution for the firm, now that business in the city looked alarmingly thin.
[326] E. DELARUELLE, E.-R. LABANDE and P. OURLIAC, *L'Église au temps du Grand Schisme*, p.89.
[327] E. DELARUELLE, E.-R. LABANDE and P. OURLIAC, *L'Église au temps du Grand Schisme*, p. 92.

connections with the Burgundian duke had dictated all the firm's other activities, including the operations with the pope, which were really only a sideline. In this perspective, it was only because Philip's interests made doing business with the papacy desirable, that the Rapondi entered the world of papal finance. As long as those interests ran parallel to those of the pope, the family's activities in Avignon did not cause any problems, on the contrary. However, when the two separated, Dino and his brothers unconditionally followed the duke, even though this effectively ended their work for the pope.

Although the Rapondi had no direct financial and commercial interests in Avignon after 1394-95, Andrea, who had returned in 1395,[328] seems to have remained at his post in the city after the rupture between Benedict and the Valois. Soon he would even step into the political arena himself, again concerning the problems with the papacy, which still had not disappeared. The measures of May 1396 had not been effective and Benedict stood firm. This gave Philip the Bold, who controlled a large part of the French government, the opportunity to make good the threats he had addressed to Clement VII at the beginning of the 1390s. On his instigation, a national synod convened in the summer of 1398, at which the French clergy, despite the resistance of Louis of Orléans, decided to withdraw from the obedience of Benedict XIII thus becoming subject to neither pope.

After most cardinals had dissociated themselves from Benedict as well, the French forces laid siege to the papal palace.[329] Thereupon some members of the cardinals' college insisted on the speedy incarceration or removal of the pope, in which they were joined by the citizens of Avignon. To make their grievances known, the Avignonese decided in February 1399 to send a mission, consisting of three deputies, to the French court. One of these was Andrea Rapondi, already quite well-known in Paris. It is difficult not to see in this evidence of manoeuvres by Rapondi's patron Philip the Bold, one of the most implacable adversaries of the Avignon papacy. This would confirm that, now that the interests of the duke and the pope collided, the Rapondi had indeed without any problems chosen Philip's side, even cooperating with his resistance to the Holy See, their previous employer. Notwithstanding, the Avignon delegation was received without warmth in Paris and did not yield any result, except for a drinking bowl and ewer in gilt silver presented by Charles VI to Andrea and his co-deputies.[330]

The speedy imprisonment of the pope, for which this embassy had been zealous, did not happen, as Benedict had entrenched himself in his palace, where he could hold out with his Spanish forces against the French besiegers.[331] He would stay entrapped for four years, until he was able to escape in 1403.[332] In the meantime, a formidable opponent to Philip the Bold in the struggle for power in France had arisen in the person of Louis of Orléans, the brother of the mentally disordered Charles VI.[333] He had always been much more sympathetic

---

[328] See *supra*.
[329] E. DELARUELLE, E.-R. LABANDE and P. OURLIAC, *L'Église au temps du Grand Schisme*, pp. 92-96.
[330] L. MIROT, *La société des Raponde*, p. 312.
[331] E. DELARUELLE, E.-R. LABANDE and P. OURLIAC, *L'Église au temps du Grand Schisme*, pp. 95-97.
[332] E. DELARUELLE, E.-R. LABANDE and P. OURLIAC, *L'Église au temps du Grand Schisme*, pp. 106-107.
[333] R. VAUGHAN, *Philip the Bold*, p. 47.

to the pope in Avignon and in May 1403, he succeeded in bringing France back into the obedience of Benedict XIII.[334]

Suggestively, the French return in the Benedictian obedience made Andrea Rapondi decide to re-enter the papal financial service once again. In September 1405, he was repaid 2000 francs by the Holy See, assigned on Pierre de Savoisy, Bishop of Bayeux.[335] However, it seems to have been limited to this one operation, the extensive transactions of before 1396 being a thing of the past. Moreover, it is not clear if the Rapondi still had a branch in Avignon after 1396. With Andrea, the family had a representative in the city, but he does not seem to have undertaken many commercial activities after 1405. On the political and diplomatic level, he made himself more noticed. In 1411, the Avignonese entrusted him with a diplomatic mission; a year later he was 'syndic' of the city,[336] which after all these years must have become his second home.[337] Avignon was also the place where he died, probably shortly after January 17, 1417.[338] But for a few months he missed the outcome of the Council of Basel, which obtained the abdication of the three rival popes and elected one new church father, residing in Rome. This finally made an end to the Great Western Schism,[339] which had determined the life of Andrea Rapondi and his family in Avignon for forty years.

INTERMEDIATE CONCLUSION

From its first ventures in the merchant world, the Rapondi family had looked for business relationships that would enable its company to develop in the best possible way. Upon Guglielmo assuming the direction of the enterprise, their realization that they would probably succeed better in economically prosperous Flanders caused the move of the firm from their familiar home town of Lucca to the world market of Bruges. There, the Rapondi first looked for economic success by associating with Lucchese colleagues. The first commercial activities from this were quite modest in their returns, but made contact possible with Iolanda of Bar, a member of the Flemish comital house with expensive tastes requiring ever-increasing funding, which gave the company many more attractive opportunities for growth. It was likely that contact with her enabled the Rapondi to be involved in the marriage of Iolanda's great-niece with the Burgundian duke Philip the Bold, in which they found the privileged relationship they were looking for.

Their association with the duke was the all-determining key in the rise of the Rapondi company, whose future development would completely depend on Philip the Bold's political interests. Bruges was left behind for a more international policy radiating from Paris, the ducal headquarters, where the firm under the leadership of Dino grew into one of the ambitious duke's most important suppliers and succeeded in gaining his confidence. This ensured that

[334] E. DELARUELLE, E.-R. LABANDE and P. OURLIAC, *L'Église au temps du Grand Schisme*, p. 107. After which the schism simply continued, and grew worse in 1409 when the Council of Pisa, intended to arrange the abdication of the two popes and the election of one single new pope, resulted in the appointment of a third pope. E. DELARUELLE, E.-R. LABANDE and P. OURLIAC, *L'Église au temps du Grand Schisme*, p. 155.
[335] J. FAVIER, *Les finances pontificales*, p. 350.
[336] L. MIROT, *La société des Raponde*, p. 312.
[337] As Paris would be for Dino and Bruges for Filippo.
[338] When he is mentioned for the last time. L. MIROT, *La société des Raponde*, p. 385, n. 1.
[339] E. DELARUELLE, E.-R. LABANDE and P. OURLIAC, *L'Église au temps du Grand Schisme*, p. 200.

the company was first in line, when, in 1384, Philip the Bold was to handle somewhat larger challenges, with the financial consequences this would have. Also, due to the duke, the Rapondi won access to the French royal family, which yielded vast amounts of money and prestige, particularly when Philip's influence at the court increased again when his brother Charles V was succeeded by his weak nephew Charles VI. Again, thanks to the duke, the company established themselves in Avignon, where pomp-loving popes and cardinals competed to acquire ostentatious and expensive luxuries. The Rapondi, however, paid a price for this. Their presence in Bruges was now weak, especially in the middle of the 1370s, as it was in Lucca, where they had lost the political struggle before it even started. Then, their lucrative activities in Avignon were sacrificed when they were no longer in tune with Philip's political plans.

Nevertheless, the gradual and, seen from hindsight, perfectly logical rise of the Rapondi company cannot be taken as proof that everything was destined to happen the way it did. When Guglielmo left the walls of Lucca in 1360, it was certainly not written in the stars that a quarter of a century later his brother Dino would receive the citizenship of Paris from the king of France. This was only the (provisional) outcome of a long and hard road, with the Rapondi making the right choices at every turning. Their judgements involved luck and coincidence as well, and more than once things turned out splendidly for them. When the firm decided to do business with Iolanda of Bar, for example, the later marriage of her great-niece with a member of the French royal house, leading to the company's success, was not a prospect at all. On the contrary, the expectations were that the Flemish hereditary princess would cross the Channel and marry Edmund of Langley.[340] The firm would never have transferred one penny for the Holy See without the Western Schism and with only one pope, living in Rome. That the Rapondi brothers responded so flexibly to these changing opportunities and made the most of them, however, can only be credited to the genius of Guglielmo and of Dino, already lauded by many authors. This family far-sightedness would not let them down in the future.

[340] In this perspective, the Rapondi would rather have moved to London than to Paris.

PART 2

The City, the Duke and Their Banker (1384-1430)

CHAPTER 3

The Birth of a Triangular Relationship (1384-1396)

3.1 The Ceremonial Entry of Philip the Bold and Dino Rapondi

"In the year of our Lord 1384, on the twenty-sixth day of April, Lord Philip, duke of Burgundy and Lady Margaret, duchess of Burgundy, entered the city of Bruges around midday. And our deacon, chapter and all at the choir, clad in silk robes, went out in procession to meet and join them to the gate of the Burg that opens on the market square, where they entered and dismounted". In this way, Peter van Eyck, scribe of the Bruges' Saint Donatian's chapter, described the first Ceremonial Entry of Philip the Bold in Flanders as its new count.[1] Fifteen years after his marriage to the hereditary princess Margaret, the time had finally come for the duke to take over the helm from Louis of Male, the former count, who had died some months before. The Ceremonial Entry, according to medieval custom the ritual exchange of rights and duties between a new prince and the most important cities of his territory,[2] was thus the beginning of a new period for Philip, but also for his many new subjects, thousands of whom came to greet him in Bruges that day in 1384.[3]

The Rapondi family was probably present as well on April 26. Also fifteen years earlier, not coincidentally, they had left Bruges to take their chances in Paris. In the French capital, by means of their unflagging services, they had succeeded in building a mutual and unbreakable bond of fealty with the Burgundian duke throughout the 1370s, to whose destiny they had connected theirs from then on. This bond brought them back as important men to Flanders, a Flanders that would be Burgundian from this moment on. So they ended up in new surroundings, in which their efforts of the 1370s would finally be rewarded. The Bruges municipal accounts tell us that the company's purses were already full to bursting when the new count and the Rapondi were taking their first steps into their new habitat. In 1385-86 Bruges was still paying off the debt to the company, represented by Galico da Piastra, taken on a year earlier when the city had bought a ship[4] from Dino "that was presented to our lord the duke" at the Entry.[5] The Lucchese only supplied the receipt for the full repayment of the vessel's cost of 1500 lb. in 1387.[6] This exemplifies a period in which the Rapondi could expect new and almost unlimited possibilities. Still, this situation had not come about without a hitch.

---

[1] J.M. MURRAY, "The Liturgy of the Count's Advent in Bruges, from Galbert to Van Eyck" in: B.A. HANAWALT and K.L. REYERSON (eds.), *City and Spectacle*, pp. 137-138.
[2] P. ARNADE, *Realms of Ritual*, pp. 128-129.
[3] J.M. MURRAY, *The Liturgy of the Count's Advent in Bruges*, p. 146.
[4] Without further details. It was possibly a miniature jewelled model, something for which Paris, still the head quarters of the company, had a reputation and the kind of object bought by Bruges from the Rapondi many times later.
[5] SAB, Stadsrekening 02/09/1385-02/09/1386, f° 21 r°.
[6] SAB, Stadsrekening 1387-1388, f° 21 r°.

3.1.1 A New Dynasty

When the new count took formal possession of Bruges in 1384, he was not yet in control of the biggest city in his territory, Ghent. For a long time, it had looked even worse. The Flanders succession, in which Philip had invested so much money and energy that in the spring of 1379 the transition only seemed a formality, was threatening to collapse. The main cause was the 'plague of insurrection' that rumbled on in large parts of western Europe, as it had done in 1280, 1320 and 1328. Yet again, the old Flemish powder keg, that had been kept under control during the 'silent' centralization of Louis of Male but had never been extinguished completely, took fire, and tensions, especially between comital authority and the cities but also within the municipal communities and between the cities mutually, came to the surface.

This time, two incidents sparked things off, again in Ghent, the most rebellious Flemish city in this period. At stake were the Ghentenars' privileges, starting with the staple rights they had on all goods transported via the Lys and the Scheldt. This right implied the obligation to sell a part of these wares in their city, which in this way was assured of a regular grain supply. Besides, this gave Ghent the powerful economic advantage of imposing taxes on the staple commodities.[7] In 1379 the count, always willing to undermine community autonomy, granted Bruges permission to dig a canal connecting to the Lys.[8] In that way, the city would be able to get its grain supplies directly from the granaries of Hainaut and Artois without passing the Ghent staple. The Ghentenars, with the weavers out in front, always the artisans with the most revolutionary potential, sent out the militia of the White Hoods, to change the minds of the Bruges canal-diggers. A second conflict erupted when Louis of Male ordered his bailiff to arrest one of the militia leaders. This action clashed with Ghent common law, which did not permit an arrest without the approval of the bench of aldermen. The Ghentenars would not stand for this and decided to kill the bailiff[9] and burn down the count's castle in Wondelgem. This, once again, escalated the revolt and violence over the whole of Flanders.

As in 1340, the 1379 revolt rapidly spread to the rest of Flanders and before the end of October the whole county had turned once again against its count, who could only rely on the smaller cities of Oudenaarde and Termonde. This desperate situation left Louis no choice but to negotiate with the communal coalition, the opponents who presented themselves time and again as the alternative authority when the count fell short in their opinion. Therefore, Louis called on the aid of Philip the Bold, who made his entry into Flemish politics much earlier than he had expected. The duke, worried that this large inheritance in which he had already invested so much time and effort would be lost because of an uprising, was understandably willing to secure his father-in-law's position, and, in the long term, his own, by acting as an acceptable negotiator with the cities. He started the talks with the three Members of Flanders in November and was able to conclude them at the end of the month with the classical banquet, where it became clear that the three cities had

[7] W. P. BLOCKMANS and W. PREVENIER, *De Bourgondiërs*, p. 37.
[8] R. VAUGHAN, *Philip the Bold*, p. 20.
[9] W. P. BLOCKMANS and W. PREVENIER, *De Bourgondiërs*, p. 37.

obtained a great deal at the expense of the count.[10] The former had won the right to form a commission that would control the behaviour of the count's officers, and would also ban some of them.[11] However, duke Philip had succeeded in saving Louis of Male's position, and especially his own inheritance and had again been able to present himself as a competent statesman in front of his future subjects.

However, the agreement was only a pause, and tensions soon reappeared between the count, whom it was unlikely had ever intented to respect the November 1379 agreements, and the coalition of the three big cities, as their former unity again began to give way to divisions arising from colliding interests.[12] This was seen first within the cities, where the 'Little Tradition of urban revolt', between the different social layers, began to interfere with the 'Great Tradition of urban revolt', between the comital and the communal authority[13]. In Ghent, the self-willed actions of the weavers, who were reluctant to relinquish or share their recently acquired power, provoked irritation from the fullers, the second largest guild. The upper and middle classes also demonstrated their resentment of the arrogance of all textile workers in general. The darkest days of the weavers' dictatorship of 1345-49 seemed about to return[14] and, to add to the complex of loyalties, the old rivalry among the three big cities also recurred. As a result Bruges, where the patrician element had always been better represented, and Ypres dropped out of the three cities' alliance,[15] and Louis of Male was able to win them over again. After the count had also succeeded in restoring his reign over the rest of Flanders, Ghent stood alone. Attempts to force the city to surrender did not have any effect and in May 1382, Philip of Artevelde, the leader of the Ghent weavers and the son of Jacob, who had united the Flemings against the count forty years before, was able to break out and conquer Bruges after a victory on the nearby Beverhoutsveld. This was enough to persuade the rest of Flanders to range themselves on the side of Artevelde and restart the battle with Louis of Male, who was back where he had begun in 1379.[16]

At this point, the hostilities between the count and his subjects got confused with the much broader conflict of the Hundred Years War, just as it had done in 1340. Behind the Flemish counts had always stood, more or less, the interests of the French Crown and a last resort when they were unable to resolve an internal crisis, was always to ask their French suzerain to step in, as Louis of Male's father had done in 1328.[17] This was even more an option in 1382, given the presence of Louis' future successor Philip the Bold, who, on the one hand, had been willing to come to the aid of his father-in-law before and, on the other hand, had been in complete control of the French king and government since 1380. The duke, on his side, recognised the call for aid by the

---

[10] R. VAUGHAN, *Philip the Bold*, pp. 20-22.
[11] W. P. BLOCKMANS and W. PREVENIER, *De Bourgondiërs*, p. 39.
[12] R. VAUGHAN, *Philip the Bold*, p. 22.
[13] For this, see M. BOONE and M. PRAK, "Rulers, patricians and burghers: the Great and the Little Traditions of urban revolt in the Low Countries" in: K. DAVIDS and J. LUCASSEN (eds.), *A miracle mirrored. The Dutch Republic in European Perspective*, Cambridge, Cambridge University Press, 1999, pp. 99-134.
[14] For this, see the vivid description with the revealing title "Vengeance Is Mine" in D. M. NICHOLAS, *The van Arteveldes of Ghent*, pp. 120-159.
[15] W. P. BLOCKMANS and W. PREVENIER, *De Bourgondiërs*, p. 39.
[16] R. VAUGHAN, *Philip the Bold*, pp. 22-24.
[17] See *supra*.

count as an attractive opportunity to use his influence in France to intervene once again in Flemish politics after the negotiations of 1379, in the short term to secure his father-in-law's position and thus his inheritance, and in the long term to strengthen his own status with the parties whose collaboration would be important in times to come. This he did without using his own resources but those of the French Crown,[18] not for the last time in the development of the Burgundian state.

Following Philip's involvement it did not take much effort to convince Charles VI, who would not have wanted the continuation of a revolutionary situation in one of his most important fiefs either, of the necessity to end the Flemish uprising. This led to a large-scale military campaign that advanced fast and forced Philip of Artevelde to an open confrontation. This took place on November 27 on the battlefield of Westrozebeke, where the Flemings were crushed, the rebellion against the count was broken and Louis of Male could restore his authority over Flanders. However, the conflict was not over completely. After having extorted money from several cities, including Bruges, which had to pay 120 000 francs to prevent its pillage, the French king broke off his campaign, crucially before Ghent had been forced to its knees.[19]

The Ghentenars simply continued their revolt against the count and called on the aid of another ally. While the Flemish counts were operating with French interests in the background, the interests of the Flemish cities, Ghent not the least, were aligned with those of England, a realm of vital importance for their economy.[20] Consequently, it was to England that the Ghentenars looked for help, as they had done in 1340. The English, who seized every opportunity to help an enemy of their enemy and possibly even gain influence in France's backyard, willingly sent an expedition to Flanders in May 1383, under the guise of a crusade against the supporters of pope Clement. England's support, however, was not as robust as it had once been and the campaign faded after some modest successes, without lasting results.[21] When Louis of Male died in January 1384 and Philip the Bold began the Ceremonial Entries with which we began this chapter, the duke could call himself the ruler of a singularly large territory, of which Flanders would only be part besides Artois, Burgundy, Nevers and Rethel,[22] but the biggest city in all these possessions did not recognize his authority.

In the beginning, Philip continued the struggle with Ghent and imposed a monthly tax on the other Flemish cities to pay for it. When, after prolonged hostilities, neither party had succeeded in forcing a decision and both forces had started to give out, they realized that it was both their interests to come to terms. This led to peace negotiations in Tournai, which resulted in a treaty on December 13, 1385. The duke pardoned Ghent and its allies, generously confirmed all its privileges and made sure that no one was forced to abjure their fealty to the Roman pope Urban VI against their will. In exchange the city promised to recognize the count's authority and to give up its alliance with the English.

---

[18] R. VAUGHAN, *Philip the Bold*, pp. 24-25.
[19] R. VAUGHAN, *Philip the Bold*, pp. 25-28.
[20] M. HAEGEMAN, *De anflofilie*, *passim*.
[21] R. VAUGHAN, *Philip the Bold*, pp. 28-31.
[22] W. P. BLOCKMANS and W. PREVENIER, *De Bourgondiërs*, p. 39.

Although the Peace of Tournai allowed Philip to reign over the whole of his county, it left the struggle for power between the comital and the communal authority undecided. The duke certainly had not gone down on his knees; Ghent had held out until the end and had not made any excessive concessions. Thus, the city remained a centre of resistance, and in the future would not draw back from a confrontation if in its opinion communal liberties were being threatened.[23] A general uprising of the three big cities and the whole county against the count, however, would not take place within the next few years. In that perspective, 1385 was the end of a period. The dream of the city-state, the idea that not the count but the cities would take the governance of the county upon themselves and which had inspired more than one Flemish revolt throughout the disastrous fourteenth century,[24] dropped to the background. The future lay with the Burgundian centralisation, the alpha and omega of the Rapondi company.

3.1.2 A New Administration

With Philip the Bold's accession to the comital throne, the world of ducal receivers and chancellors, of treasurers and chamberlains became the Rapondis' habitat. From the first accounts onwards of the new Burgundian lands, Dino Rapondi is described as "conseillier et maistre dostel".[25] Already joining the duke "pour le fait de ses finances" some weeks after the peace of Tournai,[26] he would act as the undisputed and most consulted advisor in all matters to do with money and one of the few who would sit regularly on the ducal council for the next thirty years. His function as *maître d'hôtel* was a rather honorary title with which Philip the Bold rewarded him for services rendered and which he gave his confidants a status he found appropriate.

Although the Rapondi were still private merchants, they also participated in the steady flow of *décharges*, assignments and other capital movements among the Burgundian receivers, a collaboration to the benefit of both parties. Ducal finance could use the Lucchese bankers' enormous, immediately available financial reserves, a blessing for every government when money was scarce and difficult to transport. Dino and his brothers were able to use the vast network of ducal receivers and functionaries, having at their disposal ways of exchanging money and merchandise that few other merchants had. The Rapondis' participation in this cash flow would even exceed that of the 'regular' officers and others involved in the organisation of ducal fundraising. For more than three decades, they would exchange *décharges* with the ducal personnel, grant them credit and act as intermediaries for their payments.

A striking example can be found in the accountancy of Joceran Frepier, *receveur général de Bourgogne* from 1394 to 1400 and treasurer in the next four years,

[23] R. VAUGHAN, *Philip the Bold*, pp. 32-38.

[24] For this, see M. BOONE and W. PREVENIER, "De 'stadstaat'-droom" in: J. DECAVELE, *Gent: apologie van een rebelse stad: geschiedenis, kunst, cultuur*, Antwerpen, Mercatorfonds, 1989, pp. 81-105. J. DUMOLYN and J. HAEMERS, "Patterns of urban rebellion in medieval Flanders" in: *Journal of Medieval History*, 2005, 31, pp. 376-380.

[25] H. BEAUNE, "État des officiers de Philippe le Hardi duc de Bourgogne d'après les comptes de ses Receveurs et Trésoriers, de 1384 à 1386" in: *Revue nobiliaire historique et biographique*, Paris, 1865, 1, p. 54.

[26] A. VAN NIEUWENHUYSEN, *Les finances du duc de Bourgogne. Economie et Politique*, p. 50.

whose written records were made available by Andrée Van Nieuwenhuysen.[27] Concerning the number of folios as well as the amounts they mention, the accounts Frepier devoted to the Rapondi are noticeable. The banker and the receiver maintained constant contact with each other and debt settlements took place very regularly. More than once Rapondi came to Joceran's aid: in 1394 he lent him 250 francs and at the beginning of the next year another 100 francs. Many *décharges* on Frepier's revenues were made by Dino as well. Consequently the Burgundian receiver general was often in the Rapondis' debt and from May 5, 1384 to February 13, 1395, his arrears even amounted to 14 629.50 francs. To redeem these debts, he usually paid the persons who were to receive money from Andrea, the firm's representative in Avignon, or he transferred the necessary sums to Dino's factor in the papal city by way of the ducal receiver in Lyons.[28]

What the Rapondi did for Joceran Frepier, they did for many other receivers and officers. In 1404, Dino was paid 2000 lb. par. for a *décharge* in favour of Jehan le Chien, receiver general in Flanders.[29] In 1387 and 1392, he advanced the revenues of the *recettes* of Biervliet and Harelbeke to the duchess. In 1386, garrison commander Pierre Varopel received 11 000 francs "by the hand of" Giovanni Rapondi in the name of the Burgundian and the Flemish receivers general and the *maître de la chambre aux deniers*. The Rapondi also received amounts owed by Philip the Bold to several Bruggelings, to Iolanda of Bar, to Antonio Porro, councillor of the Milanese duke Giangaleazzo Visconti, and to numerous Genoese and Venetian merchants,[30] all of whom had been reimbursed by Dino and his brothers before, using their offices in the northern and the southern parts of the Burgundian possessions, as well as in Paris.[31] All this time the Rapondis' capital was the mainstay of ducal finance.

The Rapondi clan not only granted money to the Burgundian administration by way of small *décharges* on the revenues of a local receiver. They also continued the work they had already done for Philip the Bold before 1384, financing his gigantic prestige projects, although the size and the rate of these services cannot be compared with what was usual in the 1370s. The Rapondi helped establish the duke's undertakings by paying for them entirely or in part, which they did in Flanders in particular. Another possibility was their contribution to Philip's search for other money-lenders, as demonstrated by the loan by Giangaleazzo Visconti. To forget the failed expedition of the previous year, Philip the Bold, the most powerful man at the French court, made plans for a new invasion of England in 1386. As the operation promised to be expensive, he approached Visconti, the duke of Milan who to a large extent was indebted to Philip for the engagement of his daughter Valentina with the French king's brother. Planning to ask his Milanese colleague for a considerable loan, the duke ordered Dino Rapondi and Amiot Arnaut to encourage Giangaleazzo to agree with the project. Having travelled to Lombardy, both negotiators returned home on September 2, 1386 with 60 000 florins, one of the largest

[27] A. VAN NIEUWENHUYSEN, "La comptabilité d'un receveur de Philippe le Hardi" in: *Hommage au Prof. P. Bonenfant (1899-1965) : études d'histoire médiévale dédiées à sa mémoire par les anciens élèves de son séminaire à l'université libre de Bruxelles*, Wetteren, Universa, 1965, pp. 409-419.

[28] A. VAN NIEUWENHUYSEN, *La comptabilité d'un receveur de Philippe le Hardi*, pp. 413-414.

[29] ADN, B 4087, n° 145856.

[30] A. VAN NIEUWENHUYSEN, *Documents relatifs à la gestion des finances*, pp. 109-110.

[31] A. VAN NIEUWENHUYSEN "Le transport et le change des espèces dans la recette générale de toutes les finances de Philippe le Hardi" in : *Revue Belge de Philologie et d'Histoire*, Bruxelles, 1957, 35, p. 60.

sums raised during Philip the Bold's reign. Rapondi and Arnaut made up a separate account for the loan, which was apparently not expected to be repaid. 4000 francs of this money reached the receiver general of Flanders and 1468 francs ended up with the *Recette Générale de Toutes les Finances*. Still, we do not know for which purpose the largest part of the funds was used,[32] bearing in mind that the invasion in England was cancelled once again. Wherever the florins went to, Dino's trip to Milan exemplified the Rapondis' work after 1384, which was intended to keep all wheels of the Burgundian financial machinery going, whether by gargantuan loans or by modest *décharges*.

3.1.3 Bruges, again the Place to Be

"These are the ones who tapped in the Brugghemaerct of the year eighty and three... Willem Csrockeel, living with Dijn Raponde, Lucchese, in the Cuperstrate, at the Cross of Lucca". This passage in the Bruges bailiff's accounts suggests that the Rapondi had a house in Bruges, known as the Cross of Lucca, in 1383. Not only the name of the building commemorated the origin of the family: the mansion was situated in the Kuiperstraat, in the middle of the Bruges commercial centre where numerous compatriots such as Paulo Domaschi, Bartolomeo Bettini and Gentile Gasconi lived[33] and which, together with the neighbouring Naaldenstraat, where the Lucchese nation house was, formed the core of the Lucchese neighbourhood in the city. This mention in the accounts of 1383-84 is not the only indication of a permanent Rapondi residence in Bruges. In the *libro della communità dei mercanti lucchesi* we read that the meeting of the nation on April 3, 1381 happened exceptionally "in la casa de' Rapondi".[34]

Bruges' commercial centre with the Genoese, the Florentine and the Venetian nation house surrounding the Bourse Square, and the Kuiper- and the Naaldenstraat, where the Lucchese nation house and the Rapondi house were situated. Detail Map Marcus Gerards (1562) (after edition Koninklijke Brugse Gidsenbond)

[32] A. VAN NIEUWENHUYSEN, *Les finances du duc de Bourgogne. Economie et Politique*, pp. 340-341.
[33] J. MARECHAL, *Bijdrage tot de geschiedenis van het bankwezen*, p. 69.
[34] E. LAZZARESCHI (red.), *Il libro della communitá*, p. 78.

These indications that Dino and the company owned a permanent base of operations in Bruges, after there had not been a trace of them in Flanders for years, suggests that the importance of the city for the firm was increasing again by the beginning of the 1380s. Other facts back this up. For example, it can be concluded from the nation's register that in this period the Bruges branch of the company numbered as many staff as had the headquarters in Paris, sometimes even more.[35] When, in May 1383, factor Galico da Piastra had to be out of the office for more than three days and, as the rules of the community said, had to be replaced as consul, the interim consul was no one less than manager Dino,[36] who had not left his job in France to deal with business in the Naaldenstraat before.[37] It had been more than ten years since Bruges had enjoyed so much attention from the Rapondi.

It is not so surprising that the family were concentrating again on the commercial metropolis in the north, after having neglected their interests there for years. Not, as the beginning of this chapter might suggest, because of the Ceremonial Entries and other money-devouring festivities which would be staged in Bruges, the jewel in the crown of the new count, and from which merchants such as the Rapondi could gain a lot of profit, nor because of the return of the international business community after the terrifying events of 1379-1385, although both may have contributed to it. Before 1379, Philip the Bold had entertained the Bruggelings with expensive spectacles as well, attracting the foreign merchants en masse to the city, and at that time, Dino and his brothers where completely absent.[38] However, in the meantime, new and more fundamental events than annual revelry had taken place.

As long as Louis of Male wielded the sceptre over Flanders, the Flemings did not need Philip the Bold particularly, despite his services as a negotiator in the conflicts with their count.[39] For his part, the duke could do without the Flemish people, however eager he may have been to obtain their collaboration later. This all changed in 1384 on his succession to the throne, when a relationship of dependency came into existence between Philip and his new subjects. The Flemings were in want of an able and righteous ruler, who could offer them prosperity. The duke, on his side, needed to be able to use the military, economic, and financial capital of his people to realize his political ambitions, of which he had plenty.

In order to let this relationship develop smoothly, at least on the financial level, a third player was necessary in fourteenth-century reality. The financial capacity of the Flemings could not be mobilized fast enough to satisfy the constantly changing and often very short-term demands of rulers such as Philip the Bold. Consequently, the duke needed an intermediary, someone he could trust implicitly, given the enormous responsibility attached to this function. If the transfer point was to collapse or unable to function properly, the duke would lose one of his most important sources of income, which could have fatal consequences. To keep the gigantic capital flows between the duke and the Flemings moving, the intermediary in question better had access to considerable financial reserves as well.

---

[35] E. LAZZARESCHI (red.), *Il libro della communitá*, pp. 65, 83, 99, 122, 155.
[36] E. LAZZARESCHI (red.), *Il libro della communitá*, p. 116.
[37] See *supra*.
[38] See *supra*.
[39] See *supra*.

This profile almost seems to have been written especially for Dino and his colleagues. In the previous years, they had shown a willingness to efface their own ambitions for those of the duke that was changelled by few. Moreover, that willingness had made them so rich that they were perfectly suited financially for the job. That, due to their previous activities, they were very familiar with business practices in Flanders, and especially Bruges, which, as the richest city in the county, would play an important part in the relations between the new count and his subjects, was no handicap either.

Thus, it was the Rapondi who ended up in this key position in the Burgundian administration. In other words, the close partnership between the duke and his bankers transformed itself into a complex triangular relationship. However, the company's activities were not new. For Iolanda of Bar, for example, they had also acted as intermediaries in financial transactions.[40] What was new was the size of the operations they would perform. While 30 000 francs was a quite exceptional amount in the period up to and including 1385, after this date similar sums and larger ones would pass through Dino's hands regularly. The time of the gargantuan financial operations had begun, which is why the Rapondi had to be in Bruges.

We do not even have to wait until the death of Louis of Male for the Rapondi to return to Bruges' financial world. As the Ghent War had accelerated the arrival of Philip the Bold in Flemish politics, it also accelerated that of his loyal financiers. When the first financial issue arose in Flanders in which Philip was concerned, the Rapondi were present. After his victory in Westrozebeke on November 27, 1382, the French king Charles VI agreed to leave Bruges unpillaged if he was paid 120 000 francs.[41] The city yielded and the prince appointed an attorney to collect the money on the spot. He chose Giovanni Rapondi, the family's representative in Bruges and a protégé of Philip the Bold, who at that time completely determined the life of the king and was considered as the brains behind the French invasion in Flanders, primarily concerned about his own interests. Provided with the charter of the French king, Giovanni presented himself to the Bruges city council on December 19, 1382, where he collected the first instalment of 60 000 francs, to transfer it all to Paris.[42]

When the all but independently acting Charles VI later gave 30 000 francs of this sum by way of his counsellor and master of the Parisian *chambre des comptes* Nicolas de Plancy to Philip for his 'efforts' concerning the defence of Flanders, it was again the youngest of the Rapondi clan who would collect the sum. He passed on 6500 francs to Pierre Varopel, who was to make preparations for one of the duke's many expeditions against England, and handed over the rest, amounting to 699 francs, 12 shillings and 6 pennies, to the receiver general of Flanders,[43] whereupon he was rewarded with 500 francs for his work.[44] Giovanni did not have to concern himself with the 60 000 francs Bruges still owed, since the king remitted this amount, hoping to secure the goodwill of the city in the face of a new English threat.[45]

[40] See *supra*.
[41] R. VAUGHAN, *Philip the Bold*, p. 27.
[42] SAB, Cartularium Groenenbouc A, f° 109 v°.
[43] A. VAN NIEUWENHUYSEN, *Documents relatifs à la gestion des finances*, p. 108.
[44] G. BIGWOOD, *Le régime juridique et économique Tome I*, p. 188.
[45] R. VAUGHAN, *Philip the Bold*, p. 30.

It is important to note, however, that a part of the first 60 000 francs paid by the Bruggelings had been borrowed from the same people who came to collect the money. In the city accounts of 1383-84, Nicolais Scoorkin, the Bruges treasurer, is said to have received 100 francs from Dino in Paris on two occasions, "for the money of the king".[46] The sum was repaid some months later, together with the "loss of payment" that was made in this operation.[47] In this way, the Rapondi were not only responsible for the transfer of capital from the city to a higher level but also provided the city with the resources to make this transfer possible, by using the position they occupied on this higher level and the advantages and especially the foreknowledge this produced. This, however limited it may have been, was a prelude to what would happen later and what would be, mainly in the period after 1396, fundamental for the company's success.

Almost simultaneously, the Rapondi would reap the benefit of Philip's political insight a little furter south. The fine that Louis of Male had imposed on Ypres and the surrounding cities after Westrozebeke for their participation in the revolt against his authority, he assigned to his son-in-law, for his 'unselfish' help in the crushing of the uprising.[48] Now Dino Rapondi would do the honours in the name of the duke. For the costs he incurred in collecting the money and converting all the different currencies into gold francs, making a loss of 600 lb. gr.,[49] he was given 200 lb. gr.[50] Both 1382 operations make very clear who would be put forward to spearhead the duke's financial policies in Flanders. Moreover, in terms of size, they overshadow everything the Rapondi had done before and illustrate the new standards to which Dino and his relatives now made their accounts.

Yet, the large-scale transactions in Bruges and Ypres did not have direct consequences for the firm in Flanders. We only know that Giovanni served as a receiver for the duke in the period immediately after Philip's accession to the throne when the administration of finance was still unregulated. In this function he collected 5504 francs in January and February 1384, intended to pay the troops in the Ghent War.[51] The continuation of the struggle with Ghent and the danger of a new attack by the English however rendered the execution of these plans and the setup of a financial organisation impossible and left the Rapondi without work. In the meantime they were put forward to bring Philip's ambitions closer to another prey of the Burgundian prince: Brabant.

There, Philip the Bold had inherited the rights of Louis of Male, who after his successful invasion of the duchy in 1357[52] had obtained a concession from duchess Joan stipulating that his daughter, Philip's then future wife, would succeed her should the Brabantine ruler die without heirs. This possibility suddenly became a lot more probable when duke Wenceslas of Luxemburg died some months before the succession in Flanders and left Joan childless. For Philip, this was the signal to increase the pressure on the old and weak Joan in order to secure the principality. That he put his bankers into battle to this end

[46] SAB, Stadsrekening 02/02/1383-02/02/1384, f° 3 r°.
[47] SAB, Stadsrekening 02/02/1383-02/02/1384, f° 135 r°.
[48] L. MIROT, *La société des Raponde*, p. 345.
[49] J. RAUZIER, *Finances et gestion d'une principauté*, p. 628.
[50] J. RAUZIER, *Finances et gestion d'une principauté*, p. 686.
[51] A. VAN NIEUWENHUYSEN, *Documents relatifs à la gestion des finances*, p. 108.
[52] See *supra*.

can be understood, knowing that the duchess was short of money and that the offensive against Brabant also comprised an important monetary component.[53] The Rapondi would later earn their name as the architects of Burgundian monetary policies.[54]

Again, it seems to have been mainly Giovanni who was the most active, not surprisingly since, as the representative of the company in Bruges, he was the most available member of the temporarily rather under-employed family in Flanders. His first activities were directed towards strengthening the ducal grip on Antwerp, a strategically important border point with Brabant, of which it had been a part until 1357.[55] We see him travelling to this city with Philip's chamberlain and counsellor Olivier de Jussey and Jean de Blanchet at the end of 1383 and staying there for 34 days for "big issues", probably related to the succession. For Rapondi, this must have been one of the first steps in ducal service, since he only received 2 lb. a day, Blanchet four and the experienced Jussey six.[56]

Before visiting Tournai, Giovanni called at Antwerp again at the beginning of 1384, going on to Brabant and ending up in Brussels. Each time he attended the renewal of the bench of aldermen,[57] probably trying to ensure that the new magistrates were favourable to the Burgundian cause. In the meantime he had received a fine of 2400 lb. paid by a certain Henry of Borselen in the name of the Antwerp governor by way of a money-changer.[58] Finally, in the first months of 1385, we meet him in Hainaut, "concerning the death of the duke of Brabant".[59] Possibly he was there to talk with Albert of Bavaria, the local ruler who fully supported the Burgundian plans[60] after he had been able to marry his son and his daughter to Philip's children,[61] about what had to be done now that attractive prospects arose in Brabant with the death of Wenceslas of Luxemburg.

If for the young Giovanni the events of 1383-84 were the moment at which he could step into the foreground, for manager Dino they were an incentive to leave the Rapondis' activities in Paris and concentrate completely on the developments in the Low Countries. After his visit to the Lucchese nation in Bruges and his stay in Ypres, the head of the firm seems to have contributed to Philip the Bold's Brabant policy as well. In March 1383 he transferred the advance of 4000 francs that Antwerp had assigned to the duke on the revenues of the excise taxes; in December he did the same with the *aide* of 3000 francs the city had to give to receiver general Amiot Arnaut.[62] In March 1384, Olivier de Jussey, the knight Guy de la Trémoïlle, Odinet de Chaseron, an

---

[53] R. VAUGHAN, *Philip the Bold*, pp. 95-96.
[54] See *infra.*
[55] See *supra.* For the Flemish counts' Antwerp policy, see J. VAN GERVEN, "Antwerpen in de veertiende eeuw. Kleine stad zonder toekomst of opkomend handelscentrum?" in: *Belgisch Tijdschrift voor Filologie en Geschiedenis*, Brussel, 1998, 76, pp. 907-938.
[56] J. RAUZIER, *Finances et gestion d'une principauté*, p. 447.
[57] P. VAN DEN BROECK, *De diplomaten onder de regering van Filips de Stoute als graaf van Vlaanderen (1384-1404): hun bevoegdheid, opleiding en sociale achtergrond.*, Rijksuniversiteit Gent (onuitgegeven licentiaatsverhandeling), 1978-1979, annexes.
[58] A. VAN NIEUWENHUYSEN, *Documents relatifs à la gestion des finances*, p. 106.
[59] P. VAN DEN BROECK, *De diplomaten onder de regering van Filips de Stoute*, annexes.
[60] R. VAUGHAN, *Philip the Bold*, p. 87. Albert served as regent of Hainaut for his brother, count William V, who showed signs of insanity.
[61] See *infra.*
[62] A. VAN NIEUWENHUYSEN, *Documents relatifs à la gestion des finances*, p. 109.

old acquaintance Benedic du Gal[63] and Dino Rapondi formed an important embassy to Brabant,[64] some weeks before Philip the Bold himself would arrive in Brussels with his wife and an impressive retinue.[65]

Despite the assiduous cooperation from the Rapondi, the duke's efforts were not that succesful. Joan did give him the small duchy of Limbourg and after a couple of years appointed him as her heir, but the Estates of Brabant, the representatives of the three estates,[66] as yet refused to recognize the Burgundians, even after Philip had sacrificed his own ambitions to rule the duchy himself and had proposed his second son Anthony as a successor.[67] Nevertheless, the diplomatic offensive went on,[68] albeit without Dino, Giovanni and their relatives after 1385. With the Peace of Tournai, Brabantine affairs went back into cold storage, to make way for that first priority, namely Flanders.

3.2 Between the city and the Duke

Although the Rapondi have always been occupied with the financial policy of the duke throughout the whole of Flanders, and other cities and regions would require their attention as well, the biggest share of their time and efforts would be focused on Bruges. That they lived and worked there, having made themselves familiar with the affairs in the city and making them able to combine their own activities with 'civil service', was partially responsible for this. Even more important is the fact that Bruges' financial capacity was much larger than that of the rest of Flanders because of its economic activities. For the Burgundian treasury, it was of the utmost importance to address this potential in an efficient way. This importance and the role of the Rapondi already became clear in the spring of 1385.

3.2.1 The Big Debt Settlement of 1385

The new relations between the city, the duke and their banker were shown clearly for the first time on the occasion of the settlement of the big debts which Bruges had piled up during five years of war, consisting of fines, outstanding taxes and other obligations. In the spirit of reconciliation which took hold in most of Flanders after Westrozebeke[69] and which was necessary for both parties to be able to act normally again, it was agreed in January 1385 in Lille that the city could buy off these arrears of payments, fixed at 44 314 francs,[70] for 30 000 francs, to be redeemed in monthly instalments.[71] To make

---

[63] See *supra*.
[64] J. RAUZIER, *Finances et gestion d'une principauté*, p. 447.
[65] R. VAUGHAN, *Philip the Bold*, p. 96.
[66] For this institution, always anxious about maintaining Brabantine autonomy, see A. UYTTEBROUCK, *Le gouvernement du duché de Brabant au bas moyen âge (1355-1430)*, Bruxelles, Editions de l'Université de Bruxelles, 1975, pp. 429-469.
[67] R. VAUGHAN, *Philip the Bold*, pp. 99-100.
[68] Which in the end, in 1403, would yield a result, see *infra*.
[69] R. VAUGHAN, *Philip the Bold*, pp. 32-33.
[70] L. MIROT, *La société des Raponde*, p. 372.
[71] SAB, Stadsrekeningen 02/09/1385-02/09/1386, f° 24 r°. There seems to have been no connection with the special monthly war tax that most Flemish cities and districts granted to the duke on May 10, 1382 to pay for the struggle with Ghent, since the instalments as well as the amounts of these payments are quite different from those of the debt settlement. W. PREVENIER, "De beden in het graafschap Vlaanderen onder Filips de Stoute (1384-1404)" in: *Belgisch Tijdschrift voor Filologie en Geschiedenis*, Brussel, 1960, 38, pp. 349-350.

sure that each instalment reached the receiver general of Flanders in time, Bruges again hired the services of the Rapondi company, whom it had used for the payments to the French king some years before, and who were more able to manage this than the city, thanks to their technical knowledge and their familiarity with the ducal financial administration.

Dino transferred the first 1500 francs in February and equal amounts the following six months, bringing down the debt to 19 500 francs.[72] Although after August the redemptions disappeared from the communal accounts, the reason unknown, they probably continued, as we learn from the collection of charters in the Bruges City Archives. Included in this are four receipts in which Jacop of Screyhem, receiver general of Flanders and Artois, declares that he received 1000 francs in September, October, November and in December 1387 by way of Giovanni and Dino Rapondi from treasurer Johan Buerse.[73] From the financial year 1389-1390 onwards, the payments into the accounts start again, showing that the firm was now putting receiver Pierre de la Tannerie in possession of rather irregular sums, ranging from 212 lb. gr.[74] to 533 lb. gr.[75] For the last payment "in diminishment of xxx^{m} francs", amounting to 214 lb. 15 s. 10 d. gr., the city was given the receipt by Galico da Piastra, factor of the enterprise, in 1391.[76] There is no further trace of the agreements of 1385, which seem to have been respected completely.

Apart from the general debt settlement, Bruges still had to redeem some specific arrears that had resulted from the war years. It concerned the 'octroi' among others, the lump sum paid by the city each year to the count for the right to impose excise taxes. Even though there are no precise numbers, the debt caused by neglecting this tax seems to have mounted up considerably. The Bruges treasurers redeemed this off with only three, consequently quite big, payments, spread over some three years. In 1388-89, they hired Dino's services to deliver respectively 1317 lb. 14 s. 2 d. gr. and 996 lb. 17 s. 10 d. gr.[77] to Jacob of Screyhem; in 1391 Pierre de la Tannerie received another 50 lb. gr. by way of Galico da Piastra.[78] The gargantuan size of this effort only becomes fully clear when shown on a diagram of transfers of Bruges funds to the duke executed by the Rapondi.[79] On this, the enormous peak in ordinary payments at the end of the 1380s, especially in 1388, is immediately obvious, with amounts that would not appear again in the next thirty years of the firm's financial activities in the city. After these outliers, the payments of the octroi followed their normal pattern again, with four annual instalments, each time amounting to 66 lb. 13 s. 4 d. gr., which the Rapondi transferred to the receiver general.[80]

These were the regular movements of capital from Bruges to the ducal authority, together with the Transport, the tax the Flemings needed to pay to their count since 1312.[81] Unlike the octroi, no traces are to be found of debts relating to the Transport and the sources only contain indications of the normal

[72] SAB, Stadsrekeningen 02/09/1385-02/09/1386, f° 24 r°.
[73] SAB, Politieke Oorkonden, reeks 1, n° 696 B, C, D, E.
[74] SAB, Stadsrekeningen 02/09/1390-02/09/1391, f° 47 v°.
[75] SAB, Stadsrekeningen 1389-1390, f° 48 r°.
[76] SAB, Stadsrekeningen 02/09/1390-02/09/1391, f° 47 v°.
[77] SAB, Stadsrekeningen 02/09/1388-02/09/1389, f° 50 r°.
[78] SAB, Stadsrekeningen 02/09/1391-02/09/1392, f° 41 r°.
[79] See annexes.
[80] See, for example, SAB, Stadsrekeningen 02/09/1392-02/09/1393, f° 45 v°.
[81] See *supra*.

1217 lb. gr. the city had paid since Christmas Eve 1388.[82] The transfers of these amounts were also Rapondi's work. Often the revenues of the octroi as well as the Transport stayed in Dino's hands. This happened, as can be concluded from many charters in the City Archives, when the receiver had ordered Bruges by way of an assignment to pay these sums directly to the Rapondi, as a compensation for what the duke still owed them.[83] In this way, one player disappeared out of the triangular relationship between the city, the financier and the sovereign lord, something that would happen again later on.

More than once, the city rewarded the Rapondi clan for what it did. In 1388, for example, it gave Dino 100 francs for "the several involvements and good services he has often done".[84] Two years later he was even honoured in the presence of the mayor, the treasurers and other notables who wished to thank him.[85] The Rapondi, as were most ducal functionaries, were also excluded from the payment of the excise taxes on wine, the value of one barrel.[86] Bruges' appreciation for the family can be understood because of its importance in operations, such as the one described above. For the city, Rapondi was a power broker, who gave it access to power by making possible contacts at ducal level and maybe, given his familiarity with the authorities, could even find the city advantageous agreements, as suggested by the reason given for the 100 francs honorarium.

Sometimes, the services of the Lucchese went even further in helping Bruges find the resources needed to supply the duke's demands, as had already happened in 1385.[87] For a bill of exchange, to be paid back in four months, the city obtained 2000 francs from Dino in 1392, necessary for the payment of its Transport taxes[88] which the Rapondi transferred to the receiver.[89] Until 1396, however, the Rapondis' work was mainly limited to the execution of the capital movements from the city to the duke, which took place "by the hand of Dine Raponde".

3.2.2 The Monetary Reform of 1389-90

When Galico da Piastra transferred the last instalment of Bruges' big debt repayment in 1391 to the receiver general of Flanders, the Bruges treasurer pointed out in his accounts that the payment had been made "in new money".[90] This note concerned the big monetary reform Philip the Bold had carried out at the end of 1389 and the beginning of 1390 and which would be the next occasion for the Rapondi to take up their role as go-betweens for the city and the duke. For the Lucchese were very much involved with the monetary politics of the Burgundians, not the least with the operation of 1389, which was preceded by a true monetary war with Brabant. In his efforts, explained above, to strengthen his grip on the neighbouring duchy, Philip also made use of the minting of coinage. Just a couple of months after the death of his predecessor

[82] See, for example, SAB, Stadsrekeningen 02/09/1388-02/09/1389, f° 50 r°.
[83] SAB, Politieke Oorkonden, reeks 1, n° 701, 702, 766.
[84] SAB, Stadsrekeningen 1387-1388, f° 21 r°.
[85] SAB, Stadsrekeningen 02/09/1390-02/09/1391, f° 112r°.
[86] See, for example, SAB, Stadsrekeningen 02/09/1391-02/09/1392, f° 8 v°, 9 v°, 10 v°.
[87] See *supra*.
[88] L. GILLIODTS-VAN SEVEREN, *Inventaire des archives de la ville de Bruges. Tome troisième*, p. 248.
[89] SAB, Stadsrekeningen 02/09/1391-02/09/1392, f° 41 r°.
[90] SAB, Stadsrekeningen 02/09/1390-02/09/1391, f° 47 v°.

Louis of Male, when the Ghent War was still raging, he tried to persuade Joan of Brabant to issue common gold and silver coins in their two regions. The monetary agreement would clear the way for a bigger unity – for which read 'Burgundian dominance' – on the political, institutional and economic levels. Joan yielded and agreed a pact with the duke until June 1389.[91] The Rapondi, whom we already suspected of being used in Brabant for financial and monetary activities, were of great use to Philip in these developments. In May 1386 Dino provided the 200 and 180 marks which made it possible for the mint in Malines to strike the common coins.[92]

Once the agreement was concluded, the duke started the second phase of his attack. The treaty of 1386 did not prevent him from minting his own coin. This he did, making sure that the double groot he arranged to be struck in Ghent contained considerably less precious metal or bullion than their common counterparts.[93] Given that, according to Gresham's law, the bad money (with a smaller proportion of precious metals) drives the good money (with a higher proportion of precious metals) out of circulation,[94] the inferior Flemish coins crowded out the superior Brabant ones which, with their large proportion of precious metals, were drawn to Philip's mint. Consequently, Joan was left with an ever-decreasing amount of bullion, having to incur more and more expenses to keep her coinage at the same level. The duke thus used the weapon of monetary manipulation to realize his political ambitions, as so many of his contemporaries did and as his father-in-law had done, also in relation to Brabant.

Again, he could rely on the support of the Rapondi clan. This, for instance, was the case when Dino provided his compatriot Alderic Interminelli with 1000 francs in 1387, so that he could pledge himself for Jean Thomas, mint master of Ghent,[95] where the bad Flemish coins were to be produced. Against this money, with a lower intrinsic value, Joan eventually tried to strike a new groot with even less precious metals, but soon she had to acknowledge Philip's superiority, to the detriment of the Brabant monetary system. When the monetary agreements ended, in June 1389, it had become so unprofitable for the duchess to keep her mint running that she had no other choice than to accept Philip the Bold's proposition to unite the mints of both principalities under his authority.[96]

Only now, when Philip the Bold had the Brabant coinage completely under his control, was he free think again of a revaluation of the Flemish groot, quite necessary since the continuous declines were not good for economic life and made the people prefer foreign, more stable currencies, making the duke miss out on a lot of revenue. When we look at the Rapondis' activities, we learn that the preparations for this revaluation had been going on for some time. Already in March 1388, Dino and several other counsellors met the officers of the *Chambre des Comptes* to discuss how to obtain a strong mint. Crucial to this was the *ristorno*, the amount offered to money-changers and merchants to bring

[91] H. VAN WERVEKE, "De Vlaamsche munthervorming van 1389-1390" in: *Nederlandsche Historiebladen*, Antwerpen, 1938, 1, p. 338.
[92] L. MIROT, *La société des Raponde*, p. 348.
[93] H. VAN WERVEKE, *De Vlaamsche munthervorming*, p. 339.
[94] M. BOONE, "Muntgeschiedenis middeleeuwen" in: J. ART (red.), *Hoe schrijf ik de geschiedenis van mijn gemeente? Deel IIIa Hulpwetenschappen*, Gent, Centrum voor Geschiedenis Universiteit Gent, 1995, p. 151.
[95] M. DEHAISNES and J.M. FINOT, *Inventaire sommaire des archives départementales. Tome I*, p. 396.
[96] H. VAN WERVEKE, *De Vlaamsche munthervorming*, pp. 338-339.

in their precious metals, mostly in the form of foreign coins, which was necessary for the striking of the new, superior money.[97]

The decision that was eventually reached must have made little difference, seeing that the duke issued an ordinance in January 1389 suggesting that the *maîtres des comptes* raise the *ristorno*. Apparently it was not high enough to motivate the merchants to deliver their gold and silver. To continue discussions, Philip sent Dino, who seems to have developed into his authority on Burgundian monetary policy, to Lille. Together with Benedic du Gal and Symon van der Zickelen, Rapondi arrived on February 2 in the Chambre des Comptes, where the consequences of the rise in value for the relationships with the neighbouring regions were high on the day's agenda. After long debates, all parties came to an agreement, whereupon Dino and van der Zickelen travelled to Ghent to settle affairs on the spot. In the afternoon, the final message arrived stating that the *ristorno* question had been settled.[98] Now the amount was clearly high enough, since Philip the Bold could start the production of his new groot, containing 1,07 grams of silver instead of 0,81 grams, on December 10, 1389.[99] A few weeks later Dino brought the letters to Lille in which the duke informed the Chambre des Comptes of his decision.[100]

Once again Dino contributed to the material execution of the resolution as well. He presented 3000 francs to pledge himself for Renaut de Gaudry, mint master of the new mint in Malines, which was established as a new depot to receive precious metals from merchants for whom Ghent was too far away, a means of ending the bullion flow abroad.[101] Dino would be one of Gaudry's most important connections in subsequent years as well. A letter which arrived at the Chambre des Comptes one year later allows us to conclude that the manager of the Malines mint was not allowed to make any payment before he had granted the Lucchese merchant-banker the 7000 francs that had been assigned on his revenues.[102] A similar arrangement was probably made for Bernard Bonot, mint master of Flanders and possibly not coincidentally Dino's compatriot[103] for whom Rapondi gave a pledge of 4000 francs in 1393[104] and to whose appointment he had contributed.[105]

Besides the ordinances that announced the decision to strike a stronger groot and the providing of the resources necessary to produce it, other measures were needed to make the transition to the new money as smooth as possible.[106] The ducal authority still had to fight the use of foreign money, because this hindered the spread of their own coinage and represented large amounts of precious metal that could otherwise be lodged in the Burgundian treasury. In

---

[97] L. MIROT, *La société des Raponde*, p. 353.

[98] J. BARTIER, P. BONENFANT (ed.) and A. VAN NIEUWENHUYSEN, *Ordonnances de Philippe le Hardi, de Marguerite de Male et de Jean sans Peur 1381-1419. Tome I contenant les ordonnances de Philippe le Hardi et de Marguerite de Male du 16 octobre 1381 au 31 décembre 1393*, Bruxelles, Koninklijke Commissie voor de uitgave der Oude Wetten en Verordeningen van België, 1965, pp. 309-311.

[99] H. VAN WERVEKE, *De Vlaamsche munthervorming*, p. 339.

[100] L. MIROT, *La société des Raponde*, p. 349.

[101] J. BARTIER, P. BONENFANT (ed.) and A. VAN NIEUWENHUYSEN, *Ordonnances. Tome I*, pp. 397-399.

[102] M. DEHAISNES and J.M. FINOT, *Inventaire sommaire des archives départementales. Tome I*, p. 397.

[103] As Barthelemi Spifame had once opened ducal doors for Dino and other Lucchese, the leader of the Rapondi company probably did the same for merchants coming from the same city.

[104] M. DEHAISNES and J.M. FINOT, *Inventaire sommaire des archives départementales. Tome I*, p. 399.

[105] L. MIROT, *La société des Raponde*, p. 353.

[106] H. VAN WERVEKE, *De Vlaamsche munthervorming*, p. 341.

May 1396, Dino joined other functionaries in a commission of the Chambre des Comptes to forbid the circulation of foreign coins.[107]

Thanks to these and other measures, the reform was a comparative success, laying the foundations for a monetary stability in Flanders that was to last for seventeen years, although it took four years before it was in full force, and labourers and tribute and annuity payers protested, as with every revaluation. This created a favourable climate for economic activities in cities such as Bruges, where the Rapondi were implementing the duke's decisions and served as a point of approach for monetary matters.[108] In Brabant, the monetary system remained battered and very dependent on the Flemish system after 1390,[109] as was shown on January 11, 1393, when Dino had to explain Philip's intentions in this area to Joan.[110]

Finally, the Rapondi felt the impact of the reform personally as well, in their purse. While their remunerations were still paid in francs of 42 groot in 1384, the francs they received after 1384 were worth 34 new, strong groot.[111] Furthermore, they were affected by the consequences of the change in trade, in which they were still active alongside their work for the duke. In that way, they were positioned extremely well to experience the implications of the decisions they helped along. After 1390, Dino remained one of the foremost architects of Burgundian monetary policy, a policy that would undergo no fundamental changes until 1407. Then again, the Rapondi would be present.

3.2.3 The First *Aide* (1391-92)

The *recette ordinaire*, to which belonged the Transport payments already mentioned and the octroi, was responsible for only a part of the ducal revenues in Flanders. Almost as important as a source for the Burgundian treasury were the Flemish *aides*.[112] In contrast with the Transport and the octroi, the *aide* was not a regular contribution,[113] but it had to be requested by the duke when he was in need of money, something which happened quite often, given his ambitious political plans. Consequently, every time such a question arose, Philip presented a petition to the Four Members of Flanders, who could decide autonomously on the granting of the subvention for the whole county except the nobility and the clergy, who were both theoretically exempt from taxes.[114]

---

[107] J. BARTIER, P. BONENFANT (eds.) and A. VAN NIEUWENHUYSEN, *Ordonnances de Philippe le Hardi, de Marguerite de Male et de Jean sans Peur 1381-1419. Tome II contenant les ordonnances de Philippe le Hardi et de Marguerite de Male du 17 janvier 1394 au 25 février 1405*, Bruxelles, Koninklijke Commissie voor de uitgave der Oude Wetten en Verordeningen van België, 1974, p. 133.

[108] A. VAN NIEUWENHUYSEN, *Les finances du duc de Bourgogne. Economie et Politique*, p. 50.

[109] H. VAN WERVEKE, *De Vlaamsche munthervorming*, p. 341-345.

[110] L. MIROT, *La société des Raponde*, p. 349.

[111] A. VAN NIEUWENHUYSEN, *Les finances du duc de Bourgogne Philippe le Hardi (1384-1404). Le montant des ressources*, Bruxelles, Académie Royale de Belgique, 1990, p. 180. A. VAN NIEUWENHUYSEN, *Le transport et le change des espèces*, p. 64.

[112] M. MOLLAT, *Recherches sur les finances des ducs*, pp. 312-314.

[113] For the attempts of the Burgundian dukes to impose a substantial regular tax, see M. BOONE, "Les ducs, les villes et l'argent des contribuables: le rêve d'un impôt princier permanent en Flandre à l'époque bourguignonne" in : P. CONTAMINE, J. KERHERVÉ and A. RIGAUDIÈRE (reds.), *L'Impôt au Moyen Age. L'Impôt public et le prélèvement seigneurial fin XIIe-début XVIé siècle. II. Les espaces fiscaux. Colloque tenu à Bercy les 14, 15 et 16 juin 2000*, Paris, Comité pour l'Histoire Économique et Financière de la France, 2002, pp. 323-341.

[114] Although the dukes have asked the clergy repeatedly for a separate aide, as in 1394 and 1397. W. PREVENIER, "De verhouding van de Clerus tot de locale en regionale Overheid in het Graafschap Vlaanderen in de Late Middeleeuwen" in: *Bronnen voor de religieuze geschiedenis van België, Middeleeuwen en Moderne*

Since this body, for whom these discretionary powers were one of the most important pillars of its dominance over the smaller cities and castellanies, was completely free in this, it could also refuse the application by the duke, which happened more than once.

The fixing of the amount of the *aide* was done by the Members as well. Usually, the duke proposed a sum as high as possible, which was consecutively reduced by the Four to arrive at a lower contribution. Then the *aide* was divided among the Flemish cities and administrative districts, who would then have their say. This division was done by way of a quota, based on the repartition tables of the first Transport taxes from the beginning of the fourteenth century, which had been followed less and less rigorously however. Bruges was always very cooperative towards Philip the Bold and paid more than the table asked for.

When the repartition was done, the collection of the money could start in the cities, where the magistracy took the amount out of the city's reserves, and in the countryside, where special ducal collectors or 'pointers' collected the share imposed on each parish. For each of these districts the *aides* were a heavy burden on their finances, causing many of them to try to escape the total of the payments or to postpone them.[115]

During the first years of his rule, Philip the Bold convinced the Four Members three times to grant him an *aide*. In 1385, they agreed to a monthly war tax for the duration of the hostilities with Ghent, that should have yielded him some 279 300 francs.[116] 4000 of these were transferred from Bruges to Henry Lippin, receiver general of Flanders and Artois, by Dino Rapondi,[117] who thus was immediately involved in the first subvention, at the same time as being heavily preoccupied by the Bruges debt settlement. In 1386, the duke acquired 12 000 francs for the defence of the Flemish coast against the English and in 1388 he would obtain 100 000 gold francs to pay for his expedition against William of Gulik, the aggressive prince of Guelders who repeatedly invaded Brabant, very important to Philip the Bold. The last subvention in particular forced the cities to make a considerable effort. Bruges, however, hardly needed four months to pay the complete amount, notwithstanding the fact it had to raise a large loan from some of the most prominent citizens.[118] Remarkably, the city did not hire the services of the Rapondi, who already did most of its banking business and had been willing before to provide it with money when necessary. It is possible that Bruges did not want to depend on the Rapondi even more than it already did.

The firm's absence from the deal in 1388 was not at all an indication that Bruges had ceased its contacts with the Rapondi, as is witnessed by the *aide* of August 1391, the first in which the firm intervened on a large scale. The 60 000 nobles that the duke asked then, the purpose of which is no longer known, was brought down by the Members to 45 000 nobles.[119] Bruges' share in this amounted to 2858 lb. 6 s. 8 d. gr., or 22.7% of the total.[120] Twice Dino

Tijden. Verslag Colloquium over Religieuze Geschiedenis, Brussel 1967, Leuven, s.n., 1968, pp. 10-25. (Bibliothèque de la Revue d'Histoire ecclésiastique, 47).

[115] W. PREVENIER, *De beden in het graafschap Vlaanderen*, pp. 337-349.

[116] W. PREVENIER, *De beden in het graafschap Vlaanderen*, pp. 349-350.

[117] L. GILLIODTS-VAN SEVEREN, *Inventaire des archives de la ville de Bruges. Première section: inventaire des chartes. Première série: treizième au seizième siècle Tome quatrième*, Bruges, 1871, p. 11.

[118] W. PREVENIER, *De beden in het graafschap Vlaanderen*, pp. 351-352.

[119] W. PREVENIER, *De beden in het graafschap Vlaanderen*, p. 352.

[120] W. PREVENIER, *De beden in het graafschap Vlaanderen*, annex 1.

transferred 250 lb. gr. of this to the receiver general of Flanders and Artois in 1391-92.[121] One year later, the city again asked him to transfer consecutively 300 and 650 lb. gr., which was the last instalment for the *aide* of 1391,[122] the payment of which had dragged on for quite some time in Flanders. In the meantime, according to the Bruges collection of charters, another three payments had been made, of respectively 66 lb. 18 s. 4 d. gr., 68 lb. 15 s. gr. and 950 lb. 5 s. gr. In these the Rapondi do not seem to have had any part.[123] This means that of the 2858 lb. 6 s. 8 d. gr. Bruges contributed for the subvention, which Dino as Philip's financial advisor had probably helped to realize, and from which he could now gain the benefits in his relations with the city, certainly 1450 lb. gr., or almost 51%, had reached the ducal receivers through the Rapondi, a share that would only grow.

3.3 The End of the 1380s and the Beginning of the 1390s: Commercial Success and Personal Failure

In the midst of the Rapondi's financial activity in Flanders, there were some developments which were not directly connected with Bruges, but which were to have a big influence on the relations between the city and the firm. These were personal and family issues, as well as commercial.

3.3.1 Climax of Trade

Besides the transfers of Bruges funds and the many loans and *décharges* with which the Rapondi helped out the Burgundian authorities, the company apparently still had time to concentrate on commodity trade. They had a lot of time, if we look at this period's registers of the toll in Saint-Jean de Losne, imposed on the export of cloth from Burgundy to the Empire, as Dino is mentioned as being one of the main exporters.[124] In hindsight, the second half of the 1380s and the beginning of the 1390's could be considered as the climax of the firm's commercial activities. There is more than one reason for this. First, this situation was a logical consequence of the firm's evolution in the previous period, when the Rapondi had reinforced their commercial position with Philip the Bold as well as with the French king, year after year.[125] Moreover, around 1390 there had been yet no trace of the profound conflicts that were to tear apart the French royal family, the Rapondis' most important group of clients, forcing the Lucchese to choose for one customer and against another. There was also no hint yet of the gigantic financial operations that would present themselves from 1394 on in Sluis[126] and would not leave much space for activities other than those in the financial field. Finally, these years coincidentally offered many more chances to gain commercial success with a series of royal weddings and other one-off revelries that would never repeat themselves.

[121] SAB, Stadsrekeningen 02/09/1391-02/09/1392, f° 41 v°.
[122] SAB, Stadsrekeningen 02/09/1392-02/09/1393, f° 46 v°.
[123] A. SCHOUTEET, *Regesten op de oorkonden van het Stadsarchief van Brugge 1385-1420*, Brugge, Genootschap voor Geschiedenis, 1982, pp. 77-78.
[124] A. VAN NIEUWENHUYSEN, *Les finances du duc de Bourgogne. Economie et Politique*, p. 189.
[125] See *supra*.
[126] See *infra*.

3.3.1.1 The Draper's Shop of the French and the Burgundian Court

The sequence of festivities started spectacularly in 1385, with a double marriage in Cambrai. This masterstroke by the duke, of the utmost importance for the political development of the Low Countries, established an alliance between the two most powerful dynasties of the Netherlands, of Burgundy and of Bavaria. That this union took place and not to Philip's original plan to marry his eldest daughter to Leopold of Austria, seems to have been the work in particular of Joan of Brabant, who did not fancy the projected marriage of William of Bavaria, heir of Holland-Zealand and Hainaut, to an English princess, since this could lead to an increasing influence from England, the ally of her hereditary enemy Guelders, in the regions that surrounded her territory. Instead of this, she encouraged a contract between the Bavarian prince and Margaret of Burgundy, leading to a conference in Cambrai in January 1385. This seemed to fail when William's father Albert showed no enthusiasm for marrying his son to Philip's daughter without being able at the same time to bestow his daughter on the duke's eldest son, something the duke did not favour particularly. However, the opportunity to establish a union with one of his most important neighbours and, by this, acquire possible claims on these principalities prevailed over Philip the Bold's intention to connect his successor to the French royal house. Because of this, both parties reached an agreement concluding a double union, between William of Bavaria and Margaret of Burgundy on the one hand, and John of Nevers and Margaret of Bavaria on the other, to be settled in an ostentatious manner, on April 12, 1385, again in Cambrai.[127]

The magnificence in which the marriages in Cambrai were celebrated seemed exceptional even by Burgundian standards. In "the biggest feast and triumph seen in the city for five hundred years", according to contemporaries, some 20 000 well-wishers were astonished by the enormous number of honoured guests who arrived from all corners of Europe and, after the ceremony in the cathedral, were feasting on sumptuous banquets and enjoying lavish entertainments, followed by three days of tournaments and races. Philip had even been able to rope in the French king, which added even more lustre to the event. The unlimited luxury and the splendid clothing, jewellery and other accessories displayed by the guests but mostly by the hosts, dazzled the imagination of the public. Some of the female attendants shone in their cloth of gold. The duke, groom John of Nevers and their large retinue of knights all wore velvet. No less than 247 minstrels, court servants and falconers were dressed for the occasion in satin,[128] all this to the satisfaction of the Rapondi firm.

For the Lucchese company, the marriages at Cambrai were also far more than merely another manifestation of Burgundian power, for which they were providing the fabrics. Neither trouble nor expense were spared to accomplish what must have been one of their biggest deliveries ever. They made a special order from Italy of fourteen very fine gold cloths worth 1200 lb. gr.

[127] B. SCHNERB, *Jean Sans Peur. Le prince meurtrier*, Paris, Éditions Payot & Rivages, 2005, pp. 38-45. R. VAUGHAN, *Philip the Bold*, pp. 86-87.

[128] W. P. BLOCKMANS and W. PREVENIER, *De Bourgondiërs*, pp. 44-45. B. SCHNERB, *Jean Sans Peur*, pp. 46-49. R. VAUGHAN, *Philip the Bold*, pp. 87-88.

and a light red ruby of 1400 francs,[129] with Philip the Bold paying extra for the transport. The gift of gold cloth for the female retinue also originated from the Rapondi, as did the cloth of silk and velvet on silk that were used for the costumes of the duke and his daughter.[130] The French king, who would be united by Philip to another Bavarian offspring some months later, arrived with his brother in Cambrai dressed in sendal, satin and velvet: these fabrics had been bought from the Rapondi as well.[131] Furthermore, the cart in which the duchess travelled to her son and daughter's wedding was decorated with red cloth and provided with pillows and velvet fabrics, all from the Rapondi shop.[132] When the festivities ended at the end of April 1385, the company had earned several thousand francs.[133]

In 1386 and 1387, the crowned heads had to manage without parties, although this was partly compensated for by a planned expedition against England and by ducal operations in Brabant, which of course also required the right clothing. The first project was particularly lucrative for the Rapondi, since Philip the Bold was to honour the queen, the princes of Berry and Bourbon, his eldest son and his functionaries Jean de Vienne and Guy de la Trémoïlle with satin, blue cloth and velvet adorned with gold, all coming from Dino. Louis of Touraine, the future duke of Orléans, was even given an enamelled golden belt by his uncle, who used his financiers for the purchase of this little trinket too.[134]

In 1388, the festivities came back, starting with the marriage with the Austrian dynasty, which had been pushed aside by developments in 1385. Now that Margaret of Burgundy had left with William of Bavaria for The Hague, the Habsburghians had only the choice of Philip's younger daughter Catherine as a future spouse for their heir. In the meantime, the groom had changed too, since Leopold, the successor to the throne, had unfortunately died in 1386. His brother Albert took his place. Bride and groom pronounced their vows in September 1388 in Dijon,[135] where velvet, baldachin and gold and blue cloth furnished by the Rapondi served as gifts from the duke to the married couple and to several Burgundian nobles.[136] The firm was still enjoying orders placed by the king of France as well. In the same year, Charles VI bought lined satin and white and red sendal to make a corset for his wife Isabella of Bavaria, who had just given birth to their first child.[137]

1389 was a festive year again, with more family happiness for the French court and commercial happiness for the Rapondi. It started with the marriage of Louis, brother of Charles VI, with Valentina, daughter of Giangaleazzo Visconti, the duke of Milan[138] who had helped out Philip the Bold by way of a gigantic loan, which Dino knew all about,[139] and who could be strategically important in connection with the struggle with the Roman papacy.

---

[129] L. MIROT, *La société des Raponde*, p. 336.
[130] H. DAVID, "Jeunesse de Jean, second duc de Bourgogne. Le double mariage de Cambrai " in : *Miscellanea Prof. dr. D. Roggen*, Antwerpen, Uitgeverij De Sikkel N.V., 1957, pp. 70-71.
[131] L. MIROT, *La société des Raponde*, p. 326.
[132] H. DAVID, *Jeunesse de Jean*, p. 72.
[133] Probably rather more than the 5015 francs mentioned by Léon Mirot, because this amount does not include the royal orders. L. MIROT, *La société des Raponde*, p. 337.
[134] L. MIROT, *La société des Raponde*, p. 337.
[135] R. VAUGHAN, *Philip the Bold*, p. 84.
[136] L. MIROT, *La société des Raponde*, p. 338.
[137] L. MIROT, *La société des Raponde*, p. 327.
[138] R. VAUGHAN, *Philip the Bold*, p. 44.
[139] See *supra*.

Consequently Philip, a big supporter of the marriage, strongly favoured the union with the Milanese prince and welcomed him in France with blue sendal from the Rapondi company.[140] It would not take long for the Lucchese to deal with Visconti again. In November 1390 Charles VI, probably on the initiative of Philip the Bold, who now completely controlled the king's actions, sent a Rapondi to Lombardy to draw Giangaleazzo's attention to the fact that a part of his daughter's dowry still had not been paid, and to win him over to the idea of a French invasion of Italy, another brainchild of the Burgundian duke. Giovanni, as the Rapondi director in Avignon probably living the closest of the family to Milan, was put to work by the prince again.[141]

Shortly after the marriage of Louis of Touraine and Valentina Visconti, Paris turned topsy-turvy again, this time for the coronation and the Ceremonial Entry of Isabella of Bavaria. For Philip the Bold, who had pushed through the alliance between the king and the Bavarian princess, Isabella was then an important ally at the French court,[142] just as her family in the Low Countries was, so it was wise for him to make a good impression. Since show and display again seemed to him the most appropriate means, the Rapondi could expect new money to stream in. This time they supplied velvet decorated with gold that was given to the queen, tafetta to outfit the forty knights and twenty five courtiers who joined the count of Nevers in Paris, and satin and velvet to cover their saddles and armour. To this was added a gold ring with a diamond with which John of Nevers rewarded the daughter of Bureau de la Rivière for having joined him during the Entry.

After he had offloaded some silver drinking bowls to the duke to present to Pierre de la Haye for the baptism of his son,[143] Dino ended 1389 in the following of Charles VI when the king undertook a trip to the south of France. This shows the prestige and the confidence the Rapondi enjoyed at the French court, but can also be seen as a manoeuvre by Philip the Bold, giving his nephew a guard dog. When they arrived in Avignon, where they would try to convince pope Clement VII to abdicate, the king was struck with what could have been one of the first outbursts of the disease that would trouble him the rest of his life. To stop the attacks, he ordered Dino to arrange for a wax figure of himself to be put on the tomb of Saint Pierre of Luxemburg, for the benefit of his cure, serving as an ex voto. Rapondi was paid 160 francs for this.[144]

Later in the trip they were at Dijon, where the Burgundian duke gave the king a warm welcome, the most memorable spectacle of Philip the Bold's rule besides the double marriage. It was flavoured with classical ingredients: magnificent costumes, copious banquets, tournaments and wondrous scenes. Another familiar component was the hundreds of gifts with which Philip sought to impress Charles and the public.[145] Dino's presence in the king's procession had not prevented his firm from providing the presents. The Rapondi company supplied the cloth, satin and velvet with which Philip the Bold delighted Margaret of Male, his daughter Catherine, the duke of Austria, the Lord of

---

[140] L. MIROT, *La société des Raponde*, p. 338.
[141] L. MIROT, *La société des Raponde*, p. 329.
[142] R. VAUGHAN, *Philip the Bold*, pp. 41, 44.
[143] L. MIROT, *La société des Raponde*, pp. 338-339.
[144] L. LE ROUX DE LINCY and L.M. TISSERAND (eds.), *Le Paris de Charles V et de Charles VI*, p. 337.
[145] R. VAUGHAN, *Philip the Bold*, pp. 195-196.

Gruuthuse and all the ladies of Dijon.[146] It would be the last big delivery by the firm to the duke or the king.

In the months before 1390, when no big festivities were planned, the orders still kept streaming into the Rapondis' offices. In fact, these periods held their own with those in which marriages, royal visits and Ceremonial Entries took place. The duke and the king continued to buy all sorts of fabric and luxury objects for any occasion imaginable, parties or no parties. Gold or silk, red or azure cloth; velvet; baldachin, set off or not with gold; ribbons; green or black satin; gold brocade on damask; white, red, green or blue sendal; silver and gold to be converted into threads: all fairly flew out of the door, used for the creation of *houppelandes*, jackets, dresses and fur coats; the setting off of tapestries; the covering of saddles, books of hours and the sheaths of daggers; the decoration of the statue of Our Lady of Tournai, the duke's "velvet chamber", the room "powdered with turtle-doves" for the count of Vertus, the *Sainte Chapelle* in Dijon and the king's chapel on Pentecost and especially for the many presents given to useful connections and guests. The list of persons who enjoyed a gift bought from the Rapondi was almost endless, from the wine pourer to the queen of France,[147] and, with only slight exaggeration, makes one wonder if there were any acquaintances or functionaries of Philip the Bold or Charles VI who did not possess one of the firm's pieces of fabric.

Within the range of these high-end objects, one status symbol is missing on the pattern-card of goods the company had to offer. The firm not only sold the fabrics for the coverings of the horses' saddles, but also the animals themselves. This is not to say that the Rapondi were wholesalers on the Parisian horse market, but every time the duke needed an animal of high quality, they were one of the possible suppliers. They would provide him with eleven horses, most of which were very expensive, among which were four 'coursiers' (originating from the Italian region of Puglia), one ambler, a big 'troitier' and a mule.[148]

The sale of horses, silk, gold wire and other luxury articles to the king and the duke yielded more and more money to the Rapondi, year after year. While they had ended 1387 with 7503 francs on the counter, and 1388 with 7130, they made 8000 francs in 1389 and even amassed 11 213 francs in 1390.[149] After this the totals went down, for the reasons mentioned at the beginning of this chapter. From now on, the core business of the firm would no longer be situated in the commercial sphere, but in the financial one. Commercial activities did not disappear completely from their portfolio. However, they would never again reach the scale of commercial trading that they had had at the end of the 1380s. Moreover, in the future they would no longer managed by Dino Rapondi, but by his younger brother Jacopo. For the older manager, other occupations arose.

[146] L. MIROT, *La société des Raponde*, p. 339.
[147] L. MIROT, *La société des Raponde*, pp. 326-327, 336-339.
[148] N. CHERRIER, *Les chevaux de Philippe le Hardi*, p. 143.
[149] L. MIROT, *La société des Raponde*, pp. 337-339.

3.3.1.2 The Return of the Hanseatic League to Bruges

It seems striking that the last big commercial operations undertaken by the Rapondi were not restricted to the glorious courts in Paris where they had been familiar faces for years, but to Bruges, the 'new' surroundings which now would demand all of their attention. Most of the company's activities would no longer be handled through relations with the royal or ducal chamberlain, but with the city's magistracy. Remarkably, the presence of the duke was still needed. If he and the city came into contact, you can bet that the Rapondi were there too. However, where the duke does not appear in the city's accounts, we do not find the Rapondi either, no matter how attractive the possibilities Bruges offered to merchant bankers might have been. Consequently, instead of the interaction between a supplier and his customer, a triangular relationship between the city, the duke and the financiers was to dominate their work for thirty years.

The first and, as far is known, also the only time these relationships would have a commercial effect on a large scale as well, was in 1393, with the return of the Hanseatic League. Five years earlier, the League had used the weapon of the boycott once again and had withdrawn from Bruges, contesting its treatment by the comital authorities. Talks to bring back the Hanse staple, which was very important for the Flemish economy, only yielded results at the end of 1392 when the Easterlings were given the apologies demanded, financial compensations and more favourable privileges; they then agreed to resettle in the city.[150] One of those privileges concerned the import of the German "hoppinbier". In March 1392, Philip the Bold and the Germans had already decided that the Hanse would only have to pay eight groot of excise taxes, of which the duke would keep two groot for himself. Dino Rapondi, an expert when financial issues were at stake, was one of the counsellors who had given their advice on the matter during the negotiations.[151]

To celebrate the return of the Easterlings and the reconciliation, Philip the Bold also made his appearance in Bruges some months later. The city council showed its best side and showered the august visitors with gifts. A lot of them were bought from Dino, at that point only the city's banker, who in this way again reaped benefits from the actions of his own patron, for whom he had himself helped to bring about the occasion. To emphasize its esteem for the honoured guests, the city chose to give expensive jewellery from Paris, the important field of action of the Rapondi known for this. In that way, the duke received a gold cup with a sapphire, Philip of Bar, son of the famous Iolanda, took home twelve silver plates and Pierre and Guillaume de la Trémoille and Odard de Chaseron, colleagues of Dino, each acquired two silver drinking bowls. In exchange for all this, the Rapondi got 982 francs from the Bruges treasurer.[152] Although they would still provide the city with gold plates for the duchess' Ceremonial Entry one year later,[153] this marked the end of the family's commercial heyday.

---

[150] D.W. POECK, *Kontorverlegung als Mittel hansischer Diplomatie*, pp. 44-49.

[151] J. BARTIER, P. BONENFANT (eds.) and A. VAN NIEUWENHUYSEN, *Ordonnances. Tome II*, pp. 455-456.

[152] SAB, Stadsrekening 10/03/1394-02/09/1394, f° 61 v°-63 r°.

[153] SAB, Stadsrekening 02/09/1394-02/09/1395, f° 76 r°.

3.3.2 Banishment from Lucca

The huge success which the Rapondi enjoyed in the commercial sphere was disturbed abruptly at the beginning of the 1390s by ominous messages coming from their hometown Lucca, where the tensions that had accumulated in the former period erupted. The abolishment of the *conservatores libertatis* and the establishment of a new *balìa* with fewer competences and a less one-sided composition in 1386[154] had slowed down the growth of Guinigi power, the immediate cause of all the troubles, but the structural weakness of the opposing party, which was the modest representation of its leading families, had not changed at all. For the Rapondi, who took the lead in this opposition, Piero and Giovanni di Jacopo still had to manage alone. In this respect, it did not cost the Guinigi party much effort to regain control over Lucchese politics, first by its activities in the regular councils, where it had always been able to keep its majority, then in the new *balìa*, which it also bent more and more to its will.[155]

This resulted in a growing number of disputes, which took a sharper tone and prompted the party leaders to gather their own armed militia. Following a proposition by the Guinigi that was deliberately meant as an insult to Bartolomeo Forteguerra, a well-known member of the Rapondi faction, a peaceful solution was now totally out of the question. The confrontation was delayed for some months by an endless list of alterations of the law and measures with which both groups tried to curtail each other's political influence,[156] something in which Piero Rapondi, first in the *Consiglio dei Trentasei* and in 1391 as *gonfaloniere di giustizia*,[157] the highest office in the republic, played an important part.

A couple of days, on May 12, 1392, the long expected violence broke loose after another meeting had dispersed without results. One party gathered in the Rapondi house, to which all its partisans flocked. On the way to the central *Piazza San Michele*, they ran into the enemy's militia. A short but heavy skirmish followed, in which the Guinigi were clearly the stronger. The Rapondi fled and their adversaries conquered the *Palazzo dei Anziani*, where they murdered Forteguerra Forteguerra, an old friend and trade partner of the Rapondi and one of the leaders of the opposition faction, and threw him out of the window. They then took control of the rest of the city. A better fortune fell to Piero and Giovanni's lot than to Forteguerra, for they were spared by the Guinigi who hid them and several others in their houses from the masses who were running wild.[158] In this way, the rivalry which had dominated Lucca for years was settled.

As well as instituting a modest number of executions and fines, the Guinigi immediately consolidated their power by appointing their partisans to all important functions, and banned their most important opponents. One of these was Giovanni Rapondi, who had to leave for Avignon, where he must have been taken care of by the local branch of his family. Piero was allowed to stay, despite his remarkable role in the struggle with the Guinigi, but was excluded from every political office.[159] He still had to leave two years later, after his

[154] See *supra*.
[155] C. MEEK, *Lucca 1369-1400*, pp. 254-257.
[156] C. MEEK, *Lucca 1369-1400*, pp. 257-267.
[157] L. MIROT, *La société des Raponde*, p. 305.
[158] C. MEEK, *Lucca 1369-1400*, pp. 267-268.
[159] C. MEEK, *Lucca 1369-1400*, pp. 271-272.

involvement in a conspiracy, active since October 1392, became known. The plan was to overthrow the government of the Guinigi, who ruled the city unchallenged, and to make the return of the Rapondi and other exiles possible. For this purpose, Piero went to Paris to get his brothers' support. He also solicitated the collaboration of Giovanni, who apparently had connections with several military leaders. In the meantime, his colleague-conspirators would try to convince other citizens to participate in the coup. However, everything fell apart when one of the persons they approached made their plans public.[160]

As a reprisal, the Guinigi not only expelled Piero but they also confiscated all his belongings in the city. Piero's brother Dino suddenly did get interested in Lucca. In a brilliant example of administrative acumen, he drew up a fictitious confession of debt in which he declared to have handed over all his family's properties in Italy to Philip the Bold in exchange for the enormous sum of 25 000 florins.[161] The duke, 'owner' of the confiscated goods, ordered his bailiff and his sheriff to summon the consul and three of the most respected members of the Lucchese nation in Bruges on April 30, 1394 and made it clear to them that if the *signoría* of their mother city did not give back 'his' properties within three months, he would confiscate the goods and credit of all the Lucchese in Bruges. The representatives of the nation, where generally little notice was taken of activities on the Italian peninsula, were clearly impressed and hastily addressed their city council, begging it to end the confiscation of the Rapondi goods. On June 25, the grudging answer of the Lucchese *signoría* arrived, agreeing to all Philip's demands.[162] If a proof of Philip's appreciation of and his confidence in his bankers was still required, it was hereby furnished.

Less than five months after the discovery of Piero's conspiracy, a Rapondi was heard of again in the intriguing plans of intrigue against the Guinigi. This time it concerned Giovanni, who must have been visited by a messenger of the Lucchese countryside, telling him that if he could gather enough men, they could give him the control over the whole *contado*. The case seems to have yielded no results.[163] Piero kept hatching plots as well. Despite the explicit prohibition by the Lucchese authorities on his presence in Tuscany, he settled in Pisa, helping Giangaleazzo Visconti to obtain the rule of that city. The close bond between the duke of Milan and Philip the Bold, the patron of the Rapondi, probably made this connection. Nevertheless, the aim of Piero's activities was his return to Lucca, using violence if necessary. He did not succeed, and in one of his attempts, at the beginning of 1398, he was captured. Incarcerated, he had to collect 20 000 florins before the end of the month, if he wanted to remain alive. Thereupon, Dino again came to the aid of his brother and paid the amount, which his friends had already reduced to 10 000 florins. After his release on March 16, 1398, Piero appeared occasionally in Pontremoli and Pavia,[164] later dissappearing completely from sight.

Notwithstanding the numerous conspiracies and intrigues, Lucca was definitely lost to the Rapondi, and most certainly when Paolo Guinigi declared his dictatorship of the city in 1400.[165] It was also lost to most of their allies of

---

160 C. MEEK, *Lucca 1369-1400*, p. 294.

161 R. DE ROOVER, *La communauté des marchands Lucquois à Bruges de 1377 à 1404*, p. 79.

162 E. LAZZARESCHI (red.), *Il libro della communitá*, pp. 220-224.

163 C. MEEK, *Lucca 1369-1400*, p. 295.

164 L. MIROT, *La société des Raponde*, pp. 305-306.

165 C. MEEK, *Lucca 1369-1400*, pp. 333-343.

1392. These often belonged to an in-group of Lucchese who had collected together in Paris and Bruges,[166] and now had another feature in common. The Rapondi had only themselves to blame that it had come to this. For years only their work in the service of Philip the Bold had been important and they had hardly devoted any attention to their interests in Lucca. Only when the Guinigi had conquered the *Palazzo dei Anziani* did they swing into action, yet much too late and even then with surprisingly little effectiveness.

Nonetheless, the banishment had far-reaching consequences for Dino and his family. Apart from the pain this must have caused the Lucchese, celebrated for the love of their birth place, and the knowledge that by this they had been cut from their supplies, their activities in Bruges would have felt the effects of banishment as well.[167] This does not mean that the Rapondi were only able to make a succesful career in Flanders because they had nothing to do in their home city anymore, making it possible to concentrate totally on their affairs in the Netherlands. Such a view would be blind to the fact that the grounds of their success in the north had been laid before 1384 and that they had been doing prosperous business in Bruges for ten years before they had to leave Lucca. This does not alter the fact, however, that having no more interests in Italy could have strengthened their devotion to their work in Flanders and the success this produced. Perhaps it is no coincidence that the Rapondi company's main financial accomplishments took place precisely after 1392.

3.3.3 The Rupture with Giovanni Rapondi

In addition to the loss of their mother town, the Rapondi had to cope with the end of another relationship. In 1395, Dino's nephew Giovanni di Guglielmo left the company in Bruges and started his own firm with Guglielmo[168] and Marco, the sons of his sister Filippa and the respected merchant Giusfredo Cenami, and their partner Simone Schiatta. The records of the Lucchese nation can date this event approximately. In September 1394, Giovanni was still mentioned among the company's staff members.[169] In November of that year, as consul, he worked on good terms with counsellor Filippo,[170] Dino's youngest brother who had joined the firm a little earlier.[171] In September 1395, however, we no longer find his name with the partners of the Rapondi company, but somewhat further on, with his own mark, almost identical to that of his uncles, with the Cenami.

---

[166] See *supra*.

[167] For the considerable economic importance of the practice, common in Italian city politics, of the banishments, see J. HEERS, "L'exil politique, facteur de transferts économiques (Italie centrale. XIIIe-XVe siècle)" in : J. HEERS (ed.), *Exil et civilisation en Italie (XIIe-XVIe siècles)*, Paris, Presses Universitaires de Nancy, 1990, pp. 9-20.

[168] The father of Giovanna Cenami, who was to be immortalized by Jan van Eyck together with Giovanni Arnolfini in his portrait of the couple. For this, see E. HALL, *The Arnolfini bethrothal. Medieval marriage and the enigma of van Eyck's double portrait*, Berkeley/Los Angeles (California), University of California Press, 1994, p. 90. For a recent revision, disputing the identification of the woman as Cenami, see J. PAVIOT, "Le double portrait Arnolfini de Jan van Eyck" in: *Revue Belge d'Archéologie et d'Histoire de l'Art*, Bruxelles, 1997, 66, pp. 19-33.

[169] E. LAZZARESCHI (red.), *Il libro della communitá*, p. 227.

[170] E. LAZZARESCHI (red.), *Il libro della communitá*, pp. 229-230.

[171] E. LAZZARESCHI (red.), *Il libro della communitá*, p. 184.

According to Raymond De Roover, whose opinion has been followed by most authors, the reason for his departure concerned Giovanni's incompetence, driving Dino to distraction and finally leading to a confrontation. "Everything points to the fact that Giovanni had little talent for business", says this historian.[172] Let alone that such a cause does not really seem to correlate with such a drastic consequence, certainly not in an entourage where family solidarity was a high priority, it is a mystery where De Roover thinks he sees proof of incompetence. If someone had shown such a lack of talent for all those years why would he have been entrusted with the most important tasks of the company? Giovanni had executed the missions for the king of France and had fulfilled complex diplomatic work in the service of Philip the Bold,[173] who had never showed any discontent about his efforts.

Nevertheless, despite these marks of business acumen, Giovanni's uncles continued to treat him in a way which has to be called nannyish at the least. For example when, in 1379, he was finally given the organisation of the Bruges branch of the company, he was also given a baby-sitter in the person of Dino's brother Michele,[174] whereas Galico da Piastra, not a partner but only a factor, had run the office on his own before.[175] Some time later, just as affairs in Flanders became more important, Dino kicked him upstairs to Avignon, by that time a bit of a backwater. Hardly a year had passed before Giovanni had to leave there as well,[176] having to present himself again in Bruges.[177]

Maybe the ins and outs of the affair in 1395 had more to do with a rivalry between Giovanni, who perhaps after all these years had thought that his time had finally come to take the place in the company that he had earned, given his own accomplishments and his status as a son of the manager whom the firm had to thank for a large part of its rise, and Dino, who desperately tried to keep the control of the firm in his own hands and those of his brothers. This rivalry could have been present for some time before the actual rupture. In 1393, Galico da Piastra, the wise old operator who had been Giovanni's refuge during the 1380s, had sought other horizons and had embarked on his own and his relatives' new venture.[178] It is possible that he wanted to reap the benefits of his work himself, but discontentment with the way his apprentice had been treatened could have motivated his decision as well.[179]

Even though the Cenami belonged to an influential merchant family,[180] it was difficult for Giovanni to survive in competition with firms like those of his uncles. Looking at the number of times it is mentioned, his partnership must have had little success and cannot have survived very long.[181] We only know that in March 1397, with the visit of the duchess, the city of Bruges gave Pierre de la Trémoille six silver plates with gold feet and borders, bought from "Janne Raponde".[182] Although this may also have been his namesake, who had been

---

[172] R. DE ROOVER, *La communauté des marchands Lucquois à Bruges de 1377 à 1404*, pp. 76-77.
[173] See *supra*.
[174] E. LAZZARESCHI (red.), *Il libro della communitá*, p. 57.
[175] E. LAZZARESCHI (red.), *Il libro della communitá*, p. 11.
[176] See *supra*.
[177] E. LAZZARESCHI (red.), *Il libro della communitá*, p. 170.
[178] E. LAZZARESCHI (red.), *Il libro della communitá*, pp. 198-199.
[179] R. DE ROOVER, *La communauté des marchands Lucquois à Bruges de 1377 à 1404*, pp. 76-77.
[180] For this, see L. MIROT, *Les Cename*, pp. 101-160.
[181] According to the register of the Lucchese nation, it certainly existed in September 1397. E. LAZZARESCHI (red.), *Il libro della communitá*, p. 252.
[182] SAB, Stadsrekening 02/09/1397-02/09/1398, f° 92 r°.

banished from Lucca and who was still collaborating with Dino, Giovanni apparently tried to do business with the same kind of goods and for the same occasions that the company he had left in 1395 had always done. In doing so, he does not seem to have had a lot of success. In other respects too, he was not doing very well. He was given a thorough telling-off by the Lucchese nation because he had thought it necessary to claim the ground in the Augustinian church where Francesco Panisi had been buried.[183]

Giovanni's problems did not move his uncles to pity. The grudge, caused by the rupture between him and Dino, who immediately after the split had stipulated with a notary of the Lucchese nation in Bruges that he would only give back his nephew's goods over which he had had the custody, "at the time that suited him", only increased in successive years. The successful merchant would no longer have anything to do with his disloyal relative and did everything he could to keep him from his family and especially from his belongings. Some years before his death, Dino even wrote repeatedly in his will that he would leave 3200 lb. par. to Giovanni on the condition that the latter renounce all rights, annuities, houses and other goods to which he had right as the grandson of Guido Rapondi, Dino's father, as well as everything that was due to him from Bartolomeo, Dino's brother. In 1414, the rich legator increased the amount by 6000 ecus. If Giovanni agreed, the testamentary executors could give him the sum in cash, "so he has something to live on honourably in the years to come".

Once Dino had died, Giovanni, a beggarly "old and sick man", accepted the offer. However, for reasons that remain unclear, the attorneys were not willing to hand over the amount to him, whereupon both parties asked for arbitration from the Genoese Rafael Spinelli and the Lucchese Opizio Onesti. That they chose the side of the testamentary executors was a blow to Giovanni, "of whom no long life was expected". Shortly after, his miserable life ended.[184] His sister Filippa, his nephew and former trade partner Guglielmo and his great-nephews Dadulfo, Guglielmo and Goffredo, the latter two the sons of his other partner, Marco, took care of his case from then on.

In so doing, they were primarily confronted with Jacopo Rapondi, Dino's brother who looked after the execution of his will in Paris and had inherited his monumental mansion in the *Rue de la vieille Monnaie* there.[185] Some days before his death, in March 1432, Jacopo decided to bury the acrimonious feelings that divided his family and in an addition to his will he ordered the executors to pay the 6000 ecus and the 3200 lb. par. and use his goods as a pledge.[186] They refused again, whereupon the endless process started all over again.[187] Only in March 1442, more than twenty- five years after the death of Giovanni, was an agreement reached, with the Cenami obtaining the 6000 ecus and, instead of the 3200 lb. par., the house in the *Rue de la vieille Monnaie*, that served as a pledge.[188] Thus came to an end a bitter disagreement that had started half a century earlier as a conflict between an uncle and his nephew.

---

183 E. LAZZARESCHI (red.), *Il libro della communitá*, p. 247.
184 L. MIROT, *La société des Raponde*, pp. 380, 386-387.
185 See *supra*.
186 L. MIROT, *Les Cename*, p. 106.
187 L. MIROT, *Les Cename*, p. 153.
188 L. MIROT, *Les Cename*, p. 106.

3.4 The Building Site of Sluis

The most important enterprise the Rapondi ever undertook in the Bruges area was in Sluis. This opinion, which comes from Eugenio Lazzareschi, former archivist in Lucca,[189] can hardly be called exaggerated. What Dino and his brothers accomplished on the banks of the Zwin shadowed everything they had done before, in size as well as in complexity. The work was part of building programme with which Philip the Bold was to repair or rebuild Flemish fortifications, which had suffered during the Ghent War. This was to take place in several towns including Oudenaarde,[190] for which in 1387 the Rapondi handed over 500 francs from the receiver general to Jehan de Poucques, in charge of the repair work.[191] Yet by far the largest and most expensive of these building campaigns, and of all the architectural projects of Philip's government,[192] took place in Sluis. It comprised two phases.

3.4.1 The Works on the Castle

During the first phase of the works, Sluis's wooden fort had to be transformed into a full stone castle[193] that could give protection against the English but was also intented to keep the vanquished of Westrozebeke under the ruler's thumb, making the construction very unpopular with the locals.[194] The campaign began four months after the duke's accession with his acquisition of the land, which was in the possession of William of Namur but which Philip the Bold could exchange with Béthune.[195] The participation of the Rapondi remained quite modest during this period, in which Dino was merely one of many persons checking to see if the plans were being executed properly and keeping an eye on the castle's progress.

In this capacity he inspected the site in 1389, joined by architect Raymond du Temple, and in 1390, 1392 and 1393. What seems to have been most important was that the project advanced quickly. This meant that sometimes Dino had to cut Gordian knots. In 1391, for example, he hastened from Paris to Bruges with officer Jacob van Screyhem to discuss the state of the works on the castle and decide what had to be done.[196] This also required occasional advances of the necessary money, so that work on the site would not be delayed. Consequently, to cover Dino's costs in Sluis, in 1391 the mint master in Malines had to supply him with 7000 francs before he could make other payments. Two years later the merchant and van Screyhem opened their purses again, this time to compensate Henri Heuvins, the Sluis master mason, one of the services for which Dino was rewarded with 2000 francs in 1393.[197]

---

[189] E. LAZZARESCHI (red.), *Il libro della communitá*, p. XXVI.
[190] R. VAUGHAN, *Philip the Bold*, pp. 169-170.
[191] L. MIROT, *La société des Raponde*, p. 349.
[192] A. VAN NIEUWENHUYSEN, *Les finances du duc de Bourgogne. Economie et Politique*, p. 440.
[193] R. VAUGHAN, *Philip the Bold*, pp. 170-171.
[194] M. BOONE, "Brugge en de Bourgondische hertogen: shoppen op markten van geld en macht" in : A. VANDEWALLE, *Hanzekooplui en Medicibankiers. Brugge, wisselmarkt van Europese culturen*, Oostkamp, Stichting Kunstboek, 2002, p. 130.
[195] R. VAUGHAN, *Philip the Bold*, p. 170.
[196] A. VAN NIEUWENHUYSEN, *Les finances du duc de Bourgogne. Economie et Politique*, pp. 440-441.
[197] L. MIROT, *La société des Raponde*, p. 350.

When the duchess reported to her husband that the castle was a "very good piece of work",[198] she was also commending Dino Rapondi's accomplishments.

3.4.2 The 'Tour de Bourgogne'

After the alterations on the castle had been completed, the second phase, the building of a completely new construction on the other side of the Sluis harbour mound called the *Tour de Bourgogne*, began in 1394.[199] These activities ushered in a new chapter in the Rapondi company's history. For the first time, Dino personally took on the final responsibility for a large-scale ducal affair,[200] the execution as well as the financing of an important project. While his contribution to the castle had been limited to inspections, payments and a single decision, from now on he would have to concern himself with almost every aspect of the building of the tower.

He probably started this in April 1394, when he left Paris to go and look at the site in Sluis with the duke and the chancellor and make the last preparations. During the 137 days he stayed in Flanders afterwards,[201] this site would swamp him immediately with overwork, since the water repeatedly broke the dikes which were needed for the laying of the foundations on which the building had to stand.[202] Therefore, in September 1394, in concert with a certain Gilles de Schenghe, Dino ordered the construction of a new dike.[203] This must have given better protection against the waters of the Zwin, because, a few days later, John of Nevers came to lay the first stone of "the big tower that has to be made in the sea near the aforementioned castle".[204]

After this, the works seem to have advanced quite well. In 1395, this gave Rapondi the opportunity (and the money) to finance the repair of the dikes and the water courses further into the polders of the Franc of Bruges and the Four Ambachten, something which was normally done by the local communities.[205] In January 1396, Dino ordered 1000 francs worth of wood in Sluis, and two months later the masons declared him free of the remaining 69 lb. 8 s. gr. they were owed from a total of 200 lb. gr.[206] Finally, in December 1396, he gave his "big tower" a final inspection.[207] That Rapondi had completed the building project in scarcely two years has been taken by more than one author as proof of his capabilities and perseverance.[208] The Lucchese continued to keep an eye on affairs in Sluis. In 1405-06, he lent the funds for some works on the *Tour de Bourgogne*[209] and two years later, together with his colleague counsellor Erart de Taceville, he decided to put two guards in the tower.[210]

---

[198] R. VAUGHAN, *Philip the Bold*, p. 171.
[199] R. VAUGHAN, *Philip the Bold*, p. 171.
[200] A. VAN NIEUWENHUYSEN, *Les finances du duc de Bourgogne. Economie et Politique*, pp. 440-441.
[201] L. MIROT, *La société des Raponde*, p. 350.
[202] R. VAUGHAN, *Philip the Bold*, p. 171.
[203] L. MIROT, *La société des Raponde*, p. 351.
[204] R. VAUGHAN, *Philip the Bold*, p. 171.
[205] A. VAN NIEUWENHUYSEN, *Les finances du duc de Bourgogne. Economie et Politique*, pp. 116-117.
[206] L. MIROT, *La société des Raponde*, p. 352.
[207] P. VAN DEN BROECK, *De diplomaten onder de regering van Filips de Stoute*, annexes.
[208] See R. VAUGHAN, *Philip the Bold*, p. 171. L. MIROT, *La société des Raponde*, p. 352.
[209] ADN, B 1878, f° 39 v°.
[210] ACO, B 1554, f° 199 v°.

The numerous costs Dino had to cover between April 1394 and December 1396, as the decision-maker for the site, he probably advanced out of his own pocket, drawing on his huge financial reserves, getting them paid back afterwards. For this he had to address three sorts of money resources. The largest sums he obtained from the *Recette Générale de Toutes les Finances*. In March 1394 receiver Josset de Halle sent 15 000 francs, and his successor Pierre de Montbertaut another 10 000 francs in March 1395.[211] Dino also received direct gifts from the French king, who had been convinced by the duke of the utility of the fortifications in Sluis in the hostilities with the English, and who paid for the guarding of the tower with an annual grant from 1397 onwards. The 8000 francs that Dino was given in 1395 also came out of the *Trésor Royal*.[212]

The third resource was the 10 000 franc *aide* granted by the Bruges city council, as usual highly benevolent towards Philip the Bold, despite the strong resentment against the building among the people, the only city or region in Flanders so to do.[213] Rapondi could partly determine himself whether he would have the Bruges capital quickly at his disposal, since the city again addressed him to collect the money. The first 1000 francs of the *aide* was already paid a month after the start of the works, in May 1394,[214] the first of a series of visits the banker would make to gather the funds.

We can find the proof of these payments in the city accounts, in which they are recorded one after the other,[215] as well as in the collection of charters, in which all the receipts from Dino, or in two cases the ducal chancellery, are kept.[216] However, the instalments mentioned in the documents do not match at all. This may be because the Lucchese granted discharges for several payments at once and for payments that had not been made yet, which would be strange since it was in the interests of both parties to record exactly what they had already paid or received. A little more credibly, it may be that the neat monthly debits of exactly 500 francs recorded by the city treasurers in their *conti* took place a lot more irregularly and in a less orderly fashion in reality. In any case, both documents assure that the last collection took place in February 1396,[217] and, for the first time, that each penny Bruges paid for the *aide* was received by the Rapondi.

The fact that Dino Rapondi for the first time took upon himself the execution as well as the financing of ducal policies had some important consequences. First, this resulted in an increase in the amounts of money he had to handle. The Bruges contribution remained under that of 1391 and far under what the city had paid at the end of the 1380s to redeem its octroi debts,[218] but together with the capital from the royal treasury and the *Recette Générale de Toutes les Finances*, the Bruggelings were responsible for the largest totals the Rapondi had already made available for an Philip the Bold's undertakings.[219] Also, Dino's

[211] A. VAN NIEUWENHUYSEN, *Les finances du duc de Bourgogne. Economie et Politique*, pp. 438-439.
[212] B.-A. POCQUET DU HAUT-JUSSE, *Les dons du* roi, p. 137.
[213] W. PREVENIER, *De beden in het graafschap Vlaanderen*, p. 335.
[214] SAB, Stadsrekening 10/03/1394-02/09/1394, f° 35 r°.
[215] SAB, Stadsrekening 10/03/1394-02/09/1394, f° 35 r°-v°. SAB, Stadsrekening 02/09/1394-02/09/1395, f° 41 r°. SAB, Stadsrekening 02/09/1395-02/09/1396, f° 43 v°-44 r°.
[216] SAB, Politieke oorkonden, reeks 1, n° 772 A-D, 776, 802 A-F.
[217] SAB, Stadsrekening 02/09/1395-02/09/1396, f° 44 r°. SAB, Politieke oorkonden, reeks 1, n° 802 F.
[218] See *supra*.
[219] 1375 lb. gr. of the Bruges contribution and 4537 lb. 10 s. gr. from the king and the *Recette Générale*, together worth 5912 lb. 10 s. gr., against 1500 lb. gr. for the *aide* in 1391 and 2363 lb. gr. for the back octroi.

double function made his selection as the receiver of the Bruges *aide* self-evident, since the money would have had to have reached him in any case. Consequently, the position he occupied in the duke's building plans in Sluis served to reinforce his financial influence on the city.

Since Rapondi himself had to spend the money he collected, and in fact already had spent it, taking into consideration the advance of the costs, it is improbable that these funds still passed through the ducal treasury. So, what had already taken place quite modestly with the payment of the Transport and the octroi, now happened systematically and on a large scale: one player dropped out of the triangular relationship between Philip the Bold, Bruges and the Rapondi, which was now reduced to a relationship between the city and the banker. That Philip the Bold was no longer required in this affair gave Dino a hitherto unknown freedom in handling the city funds. However, this freedom also had its limitations. In 1395, the *Chambre des Comptes* reprimanded him because his accounts of the activities in Sluis were not detailed enough and did not make clear on what he had spent the amounts he had received. The *maîtres des comptes* turned over the case to the chancellor, who followed their judgement and would discuss the matter with the duke.[220]

Although the outcome is not known, between 1394 and 1396 these rumblings of criticism did not prevent the family from obtaining a control over the money flow from Bruges to Philip the Bold that they had never had before. In a sense, this makes Sluis the climax of twelve years of capital movements between the city, the duke and the financiers. Yet, to be able to speak of a complete triangular relationship between those three, something was missing. For twelve years, the Rapondi had stood between the city and the duke, occasionally even taking over the role of the duke as they had done in 1394, but they had never presented themselves as an independent player in this arrangement. For this to change, an unexpected event on the plains of Hungary was necessary.

---

220 L. MIROT, *La société des Raponde*, p. 352.

CHAPTER 4

"PAR LUI SE POVOIENT FAIRE TOUTES FINANCES" (1396-1415)

4.1 Nicopolis: the Duke's Disaster and the Banker's Triumph

Since the beginning of the fourteenth century, the Ottoman Turks had gradually expanded their power over large parts of the Near East. After they had acquired power over the larger part of Thracia, Bulgaria and Macedonia, the whole of the Balkans fell to them upon their victory in Kosovo Polje in 1389, followed by their conquest of the remaining areas south of the Danube. The advancing Muslim danger alarmed European princes and nobles[1] and made some of them think. Philip the Bold, never without an ambitious plan, saw in the Turkish advance the perfect occasion for a crusade, one of those recruiting ideas which had been historically able to mobilize people throughout the whole Middle Ages, but which was also an ideal means to boost the status of those who had inspired it, regardless of the outcome.

The Burgundian duke had been considering the idea for several years, when a pause in the Hundred Years War in 1394 permitted him to design the final plan, to be a joint expedition led by himself, the duke of Lancaster and the duke of Orléans. The destination point of King Sigismund's Hungary[2] was chosen at the expense of Prussia, that other field of battle in the war against the heathens. This goal was retained when the planned project with Orléans and Lancaster had to make room in the second half of 1395 for a primarily Burgundian enterprise, commanded by Philip's oldest son, John of Nevers.[3]

4.1.1 Financing the Crusade

John had to get through a considerable list of preparations before he could set off on his journey to the Danube area. Given that his father was in control, it is no surprise that the provision of equipment for the expedition was an important part of this, besides obtaining the papal bulls needed for confronting the heathens. Indeed for Philip the Bold, there was little difference between the crusade and the marriages and Ceremonial Entries which demonstrated the power and the wealth of the house of Burgundy. Hence it was a point of honour for him that his son would meet the infidel in full pontificals. This explains the cartloads of green satin tents, of painted banners and horse cloths and the green liveries worn by the hundreds of John's followers, everything elaborately worked with gold and silver.[4] Mirot's statement that part

---

[1] W. P. BLOCKMANS and W. PREVENIER, *De Bourgondiërs*, pp. 51-52.

[2] M. KINTZINGER, "Sigismond, roi de Hongrie, et la croisade" in: *Annales de Bourgogne*, Dijon, 1996, 68, 3, pp. 23-33.

[3] R. VAUGHAN, *Philip the Bold*, pp. 62-63. See also J. PAVIOT and M. CHAUNEY-BOUILLOT (eds.), "Nicopolis 1396-1996. Actes du colloque international organisé par l'Académie des Sciences, Arts et Belles-Lettres de Dijon et le Centre National de la Recherche Scientifique réuni à Dijon, au Conseil régional de Bourgogne, le 18 octobre 1996" in : *Annales de Bourgogne*, Dijon, 1996, 68, 3, pp. 1-99. For the broader context of this project, see J. PAVIOT, *Les ducs de Bourgogne, la croisade et l'Orient (fin XIVe siècle-XVe siècle)*, Paris, Presses de l'Université de Paris-Sorbonne, 2003, pp. 20-49.

[4] B. SCHNERB, *Jean Sans Peur*, pp. 68-70. R. VAUGHAN, *Philip the Bold*, pp. 64-65.

of these luxuries were supplied by the Rapondi[5] is credible given the firm's specialisation in such goods but it lacks proof and does not correlate with the company's less dominant activity at a commercial level in this period.

Of greater importance for the crusade than John's clothes was the financing of the enterprise. The ducal administration did a very exceptional thing in the pragmatic world of medieval finance at the end of 1394, by making an estimate of the revenues and expenses it expected during the coming year. From the 520 000 francs which Philip hoped to collect in 1395 but which he could not spend entirely on the trip to Hungary, the annual ordinary revenues from his territories ran to some 200 000 francs. A new loan from Visconti was expected to yield 50 000 francs, and another dip into the treasury of Charles VI was to produce the same.

The duke wanted to raise the remaining 220 000 francs by asking for an *aide* in his lands. As usual the main part of this extraordinary tax had to come from Flanders,[6] where the duchess and John of Nevers, on the instructions of Philip, who had other business, requested the Members for a subvention of 100 000 nobles in June 1394, before the destination of the crusade was even fixed. However, after a lengthy discussion, in which the smaller cities and castellanies participated as well, John had to be content with 65 000 nobles,[7] of which Pierre de la Tannerie, appointed especially to collect the *aide*,[8] would gather the first half in February 1395.

Bruges, whose share had been determined at 11 000 nobles,[9] handed over its first instalment in three payments, of which it paid two again long before the due date, coming in on top of its contributions for the *Tour de Bourgogne*. It may be that the city had bitten off more than it could chew in so doing, for it only made the first payment of the second instalment months after the fixed date, delayed itself until October 1395.[10] The last payment was an even bigger obstacle as Bruges could not make it without the help of financiers. The Rapondi, heavily occupied at the time in Sluis, which explains their absence from the negotiations and the first payments of the *aide*, stepped into the breach and made sure that their employer got the urgently needed money. This they did not by transferring funds to the ducal treasury as they usually did, but by paying the 550 lb. gr. to the receiver themselves.[11] Some four years after they had enabled Bruges to pay its Transport taxes for a bill of exchange,[12] they again supplied the resources it needed to meet the duke's expectations, something that would have further reaching consequences than the last time. In each case the city, obliged to pay back the advance four months later, was grateful to the Rapondi and rewarded Dino with 10 lb. gr.,[13] possibly a hidden interest. This was no luxury, since they would have to use the Lucchese more than once in the following months.

The last of Bruges's payments only reached the receiver general on the eve of John of Nevers' farewell to Charles VI, a week after the final briefing for

---

[5] L. MIROT, *La société des Raponde*, p. 356.
[6] R. VAUGHAN, *Philip the Bold*, pp. 63-64.
[7] W. PREVENIER, *De beden in het graafschap Vlaanderen*, pp. 353-354.
[8] R. VAUGHAN, *Philip the Bold*, p. 63.
[9] W. PREVENIER, *De beden in het graafschap Vlaanderen*, annex 1.
[10] W. PREVENIER, *De beden in het graafschap Vlaanderen*, p. 354.
[11] SAB, Stadsrekening 02/09/1395-02/09/1396, f° 44 v°.
[12] See *supra*.
[13] SAB, Stadsrekening 02/09/1395-02/09/1396, f° 86 r°.

the crusade had been done. After the ducal family and the citizens of Dijon had waved him goodbye as well, the 24-year-old successor to the ducal throne left for Hungary on April 30, 1396. In his footsteps followed an impressive host of servants, and the flower of the French and Burgundian nobility. His supporters included count of Eu and constable of France Philip of Artois, marshall Boucicaut, admiral Jehan de Vienne, Henry and Philip of Bar, Enguerrand de Coucy, Guy and Guillaume de la Trémoille and Odard de Chaseron. After a trip on which they were joined by Bavarian and English contingents, they reached Buda in August 1396, where King Sigismund welcomed them. From there, they went to the Ottoman stronghold Nicopolis. The French-Burgundian siege of the city, reinforced by the Hungarian troops, brought the Turkish sultan Bajezid in great haste to Hungary. A confrontation took place on September 25, 1396, just outside Nicopolis. Taking advantage of the ill-thought-out tactics of his adversaries, Bajezid crushed the European coalition. Thousands of Frenchmen and Burgundians, including most of the leading nobility and some important Rapondi customers, such as Guillaume de la Trémoille and Odard de Chaseron, were left dead on the battlefield. Only a small group of prominent knights, led by John of Nevers, could enjoy the mercy of the *Grand Turc*. For them, the glorious "voyage of Hungary", ended in Ottoman incarceration.[14]

4.1.2 The Release of John of Nevers

The tragic news of the disaster of Nicopolis only started trickling into France at the beginning of 1397. Immediately, several messengers left for the East, presenting themselves back in Paris on Christmas Eve, carrying with them letters from John of Nevers and the offer by Bajezid to start negotiations on a ransom for the prisoners. While new envoys travelled to Turkey to appease the sultan with gifts and ascertain the Burgundians' fate, the duke made the first steps leading to talks.[15] The Rapondi family's capacities once again would be of great value.

Because of the Rapondis' connections in the eastern Mediterranean, where they had obtained expensive fabrics and spices for years, and because of their friendships with numerous Genoese and Venetian merchants in the area, not the least of whom was Bartolomeo Pellegrino, an influential alum and mastic salesman on Chio,[16] Dino had at his disposal a much faster and much more accessible way of making contact with the Turks than was possible by official channels. The famous chronicler Froissart made the Lucchese say himself to Philip the Bold: "Venetian and Genoese merchants can be of great value in this".[17] Consequently, it was through these channels that the cooperation of the king of Cyprus, quite familiar with the Ottoman court, was obtained and he could mollifiy Bajezid with a gold miniature ship. According to Froissart the Genoese constantly informed Rapondi of these and other advances, whereupon the Lucchese reported them in his turn to Philip the Bold and Charles VI on one of the numerous meetings they had during these weeks.[18]

[14] B. SCHNERB, *Jean Sans Peur*, pp. 70-81. R. VAUGHAN, *Philip the Bold*, pp. 65-71.
[15] B. SCHNERB, *Jean Sans Peur*, pp. 83-91. R. VAUGHAN, *Philip the Bold*, pp. 71-72.
[16] L. MIROT, *La société des Raponde*, pp. 359-360.
[17] J. FROISSART, *Chroniques*, Bruxelles, Ed. Kervyn de Lettenhove, 1867-1877, vol. 15, pp. 336-337.
[18] J. FROISSART, *Chroniques t. 16*, pp. 31-32.

Dino's efforts were of consequence, because when a solemn embassy, consisting of Jehan of Vergy, governor of Franche-Comté, and the Flemish souvereign-bailiff Gilbert of Leeuwerghem, visited and charmed Bajezid in June 1397 in Mikhalidsh with offerings of exceptionnal presents, the sultan was willing to release his prisoners for 200 000 ducats. The Rapondi again proved their usefulness in the payment of this sum. The 28 000 ducats presented on the spot by John of Nevers were borrowed from the cousin of the Cyprian king and two Genoese businessmen from Pera. Other princes and merchants from Genoa's Aegean colonies pledged themselves for 110 000 ducats, which was enough for Bajezid to free the vanquished of Nicopolis. Once John of Nevers and his companions had promised their benevolent financiers that they would pay back the amounts advanced before they left Venice on the return trip, they could finally go home.[19] This happened without Enguerrand de Coucy, however, who, after having asked Dino Rapondi to look after his goods and debts in Paris and his jewels in Venice, had died in Bursa.[20]

While John travelled to Italy by way of Mitylene and Rhodes, his father took measures to complete the second phase of the release. For this, the duke had to get the necessary sums in Venice, where his son, who arrived there in October, had to remain until he had reimbursed the ransom money to his financiers. Therefore, on September 26, 1397, Philip ordered Oudart Douay to keep a special account with all funds used for these payments. The duke also established a particular commission to execute, control and confirm all transactions concerning the ransom, dominated by Dino and also including Douay.[21] Philip the Bold entrusted his capable banker with another key role and sent him on November 15, 1397, with his faithfull factor Francesco Accettanti, the Galico da Piastra of Paris, and a retinue of eighteen horses to Treviso, where John of Nevers and his court had settled after an outbreak of the plague in Venice.[22]

Having arrived scarcely ten days later, Dino first made sure that Douay had the 150 000 francs allocated to him from the Burgundian general treasury.[23] This he did by way of two prodigious bills of exchange, amounting respectively to 60 000 and 71 668 francs,[24] showing the seemingly limitless possibilities of the Lucchese at this level.[25] Rapondi also established part of the loan by which the remaining 50 000 was raised. With others, he pledged himself for two credits of 10 000 francs in total, granted by Genoese merchants.[26] In this way, Oudart Douay was able to reimburse several businessmen who had contributed in the ransom, which only used up one fourth of his 200 000 francs. He had to spend the largest part of his money on heavy interests on fresh loans, the costs incurred by John of Nevers' court in Treviso and Venice and the debts run up by the duke's son in Turkey and on his return.

---

[19] B. SCHNERB, *Jean Sans Peur*, pp. 91-94. R. VAUGHAN, *Philip the Bold*, p. 72.

[20] A. TUETEY (ed.), "Testaments enrégistrés au Parlement de Paris sous le règne de Charles VII" in: *Mélanges Historiques. Choix de documents*, Paris, 1880, 3, pp. 283-284.

[21] B.-A. POCQUET DU HAUT-JUSSE, "Le retour de Nicopolis et la rançon de Jean sans Peur. Compte inédit de maitre Oudart Douay pour le duc de Bourgogne 1397-1398" in: *Annales de Bourgogne*, Dijon, 1937, 9, pp. 297-298.

[22] L. MIROT, *La société des Raponde*, pp. 360-361.

[23] R. VAUGHAN, *Philip the Bold*, p. 73.

[24] B.-A. POCQUET DU HAUT-JUSSE, *Le retour de Nicopolis*, p. 298.

[25] B.-A. POCQUET DU HAUT-JUSSE, *Le retour de Nicopolis*, p. 298.

[26] L. MIROT, *La société des Raponde*, pp. 363.

During his stay on the Italian peninsula, another affair of great importance arrived on Dino's agenda. The Hungarian king Sigismund, who had hosted the crusaders and had been able to escape from Nicopolis himself, offered to pay half of the ransom. When the king did not seem to possess the resources necessary to keep his promise, Rapondi demonstrated his financial skills. The merchant issued the king 100 000 ducats, for the latter to pay to John of Nevers, and in exchange he would receive an annuity of 7000 ducats previously received by Sigismund from Venice each year.[27] On January 15, 1398 Dino's proxies Regnier Pot and Jacques de Courtiambles visited the Hungarian king to receive the annuity papers and hand over the fictitious capital. If we can believe the charters, they dropped by again a day later, this time as John the Fearless' proxies, and, again fictitiously, collected the promised 100 000 ducats,[28] which in reality must have gone directly from Rapondi to the Burgundian prince.

However, after Sigismund had reported the 'sale' of his annuity on June 15, 1398 to the *Serenissima Republicca*, the Venetians refused to pay it to Dino, claiming it had only been appointed to the Hungarian prince and could not be transferred. The king insisted one year later to the doge that Venice hand over the 7000 ducats to Rapondi with no results, although this did not prevent the Lucchese from mortgaging the annuity in 1400.[29] Even when Philip the Bold indemnified his faithful financier and took over the claim on the annual revenues, Venice did not soften.[30] The embassies John of Nevers would send as the future John the Fearless in 1405 and 1409 would not change anything, no more than his proposition to pay the forfeit sum of 100 000 ducats instead of the annuity. Since measures against the Venetian merchants did not seem a very good idea given the economic interests of his Flemish subjects, the prince left the affair where it was.[31] A definitive settlement would only be reached in 1424 under John's son Philip the Good after negotiations in which Dino's brother Filippo would take part.

Dino must have heard the news in Flanders that Venice had refused to pay him the annuity. After his job in northern Italy was done at the end of January 1398, he returned to Paris, where he arrived on February 15,[32] and then went on to Flanders, where important work awaited him. One week later, John of Nevers arrived in Dijon,[33] almost two years after his crusading departure. For him, the crusade was over. For the Burgundian tax payer it was not.

4.1.3 The Payment of the Ransom

In the spring of 1397, even before the first settlement of John of Nevers' release had been reached, Philip the Bold had started to look for the funds he would need. For this he addressed mainly his standard resources, which were the royal treasury, which he emptied of 124 000 francs,[34] and his subjects, from whom he requested another *aide*. In April 1397, the Members of

[27] B. SCHNERB, *Jean Sans Peur*, pp. 99-100. R. VAUGHAN, *Philip the Bold*, pp. 73-74.
[28] J. M. FINOT, *Inventaire sommaire Tome Septième*, p. 270.
[29] L. MIROT, *La société des Raponde*, pp. 361-362.
[30] B. SCHNERB, *Jean Sans Peur*, p. 100. R. VAUGHAN, *Philip the Bold*, p. 74.
[31] R. VAUGHAN, *John the Fearless*, p. 261.
[32] L. MIROT, *La société des Raponde*, pp. 361-362.
[33] B. SCHNERB, *Jean Sans Peur*, pp. 100-102. R. VAUGHAN, *Philip the Bold*, p. 76.
[34] R. VAUGHAN, *Philip the Bold*, p. 77.

Flanders, having just endured the heavy payments for the financing of the crusade, were presented with his request for a subvention of no less than 150 000 nobles. Nevertheless, in the discussions which followed, they succeeded in bringing this demand down to 100 000 nobles, agreed on July 13. One third of that amount needed to reach the ducal treasury on Christmas Day 1397, the second part on February 2, 1398 and the third on February 2, 1399.

Bruges again was an example of complaisance towards Philip the Bold, who had insisted it pay quickly given the urgent nature of the request, and the city made over its three instalments of 6077 2/3 nobles, altogether worth 18 233 nobles[35] or 5470 lb. gr. (18.2% of the total), far in advance.[36] Thus the April 1396 scenario repeated itself. When the city wanted to pay its contribution on October 22, two months too early, it was not capable of doing this. Therefore, it borrowed the entire 6077 2/3 nobles from Dino and gave him a bill of exchange which he discounted seven months later with a "loss" of 129 lb. 7 s. 5 d. gr. (7%).[37] The story repeated itself when Bruges wanted to make its second instalment long before the due date of February 2, 1398. This time it had to give the bill of exchange for 6077 2/3 nobles, paid back two months later with an interest of 72 lb. 8 s. 9 d. gr. (4%), to Filippo Rapondi,[38] for whom the *aide* of 1397 marked his first appearance on the stage of big financial operations, interestingly at the moment when his brother Dino was in Treviso. On April 6, 1398, when the city presented its third payment no less than ten months in advance, Dino had returned. For delivery of a bill of exchange, he granted the final 6077 2/3 nobles, supplied by himself, his compatriot and partner Francesco Totti and the Florentine Nerochio degli Alberti and immediately transferred the money to the receiver general.[39]

Not long after this, the Bruges city accounts speak of three other bills of exchange, amounting to 1020, 700 and 600 lb. gr. respectively. The statements by Gilliodts-van Severen and Bigwood that Rapondi received these letters for the payment of the city's octroi,[40] does not hold. First, the *conti* literally say that the documents relate to the subvention and not to the octroi. Secondly, the company mainly transferred the octroi money, as it did the Transport, in this period and did not advance them, whereas the three sums in the accounts correspond to more than fifteen years of normal octroi taxes.

Since the instalments of the exchanges follow seamlessly one after another and the amounts they represent decrease, it seems more probable that the city granted them each time to redeem a part of the debt caused by the previous. In this case, Bruges did not have at its disposal the full 1823 lb. gr. to pay back to the Rapondi on June 13, 1398, the due date of the bill it had given to obtain the money for the final instalment of the *aide*. Therefore, it immediately granted the company a new bill worth 1020 lb. gr., making up the deficit. To redeem this 1020 lb. gr., plus a loss of 79 lb. 9 d. gr. (7.8%) four months later, the city was short again, causing it to give the firm another paper payment to fill the 700 lb. gr. gap. The last bill took the place of the 600 lb. gr. it

---

[35] W. PREVENIER, *De beden in het graafschap Vlaanderen*, annex 1.

[36] W. PREVENIER, *De beden in het graafschap Vlaanderen*, pp. 354-355.

[37] SAB, Stadsrekening 02/09/1397-02/09/1398, f° 49 v°.

[38] SAB, Stadsrekening 02/09/1397-02/09/1398, f° 50 r°.

[39] SAB, Stadsrekening 02/09/1398-02/09/1399, f° 48 r°.

[40] L. GILLIODTS-VAN SEVEREN, *Inventaire des archives. Tome troisième*, p. 288. G. BIGWOOD, *Le régime juridique et économique Tome I*, p. 125.

was still unable to pay of this 700 lb. gr. and of the 14 lb. 19 s. 9 d. gr. interest imposed (2.14%) four months later.[41] Perhaps the 7 lb. 10 s. gr. Dino received from the city in 1400-1401[42] was the last of these consecutive debt redemptions.

In the frequency of these bills of exchange lies the big difference between Sluis and Nicopolis. What the Rapondi had done until 1396 was primarily facilitate the movement of capital between two main characters, the city and the duke, by transferring funds from one to the other. However, the amounts they made available on exchange between 1394 and 1396 did more than that. They were an indispensable element, without which the cash flow between Bruges and Philip the Bold simply could not have taken place. If the Rapondi had not provided the city with money, the latter would never have been able to meet the financial needs of the duke.[43] For the first time the family claimed a central role in the relation between Philip the Bold and Bruges, something which was not limited to a single event as in 1392.[44] Bruges's need for capital, caused by a combination of its complaisance towards the duke's requests and the eagerness with which Philip took advantage of that complaisance, did not disappear after 1398. Time after time, this would make the city approach Dino Rapondi, whose financial indispensability only increased. Or, in the words of Jean Froissart : "by him, all finances could be done".[45]

There were also smaller differences with Sluis. Nicopolis was one of these rare occasions on which the Rapondi could show their financial competence in other parts of Flanders besides Bruges. Filippo, who clearly made his breakthrough to the big time, transferred an instalment of the 1397-1398 *aide* for Ypres.[46] The 6000 nobles handed over by the Franc of Bruges for the same subvention in October 1397 were lent by him.[47] Remarkably, this payment, amounting to almost half of the 12 091 nobles the district had to give in total,[48] was also made months before the due date.[49] Thus the question emerges whether Bruges's willingness to pay more and earlier to Philip the Bold did not have something to do with the availability of financiers such as the Rapondi.

Although the history of the Rapondi from 1370 on reads like a succession of climaxes, the consequences for their relationship with the city and the duke, the involvement of places beyond Bruges, the size,[50] complexity and the duration of their operations make it hard not to consider Nicopolis as the family's *magnum opus*. This is testified to by the superlatives that Froissart showers on Dino. That the chronicler calls the Lucchese "wonderfully subtle"[51] and emphasizes that, without him, nothing could be done,[52] are just two examples of this. This is also witnessed by the remunerations Rapondi raked in concerning his work for the crusade. These rose to 2900 lb. gr.,[53] or more than

---

[41] SAB, Stadsrekening 02/09/1398-02/09/1399, f° 48 v°.
[42] SAB, Stadsrekening 02/09/1400-02/09/1401, f° 29 v°.
[43] That the duke was at the same time the employer of the Lucchese possibly explains the relatively low interest rates on the bills of exchange they accepted.
[44] See *supra*.
[45] J. FROISSART, *Chroniques t. 15*, p. 336.
[46] A. VAN NIEUWENHUYSEN, *Les finances du duc de Bourgogne. Economie et Politique*, p. 343.
[47] L. GILLIODTS-VAN SEVEREN, *Inventaire des archives. Tome troisième*, p. 292.
[48] W. PREVENIER, *De beden in het graafschap Vlaanderen*, annex 1.
[49] W. PREVENIER, *De beden in het graafschap Vlaanderen*, p. 355.
[50] See the graphs in the annexes.
[51] J. FROISSART, *Chroniques t. 16*, p. 60.
[52] J. FROISSART, *Chroniques t. 16*, p. 56.
[53] L. MIROT, *La société des Raponde*, pp. 360, 362-363.

double everything Bruges had paid for the *Tour de Bourgogne* in Sluis. This would even be testified to by the epitaph Dino ordered for his grave fifteen years later. If future generations had to remember only one of his accomplishments, it was that he "Joannem Ducum redemit a Turcis". Nicopolis, concerning which he had financed the crusade, negotiated the prisoners' releases and made possible the collection of the ransom, relying on his financial as well as his diplomatic capabilities, was the project with which the merchant made his name with the masses. He also made his name with John of Nevers, whom he had freed and who was to be the next duke. So, Philip the Bold's disaster was his banker's triumph.

4.2 The Old Duke and the New Duke

The last five years of Philip the Bold's rule went quite smoothly for the Rapondi company, compared to the bustle of Sluis and Nicopolis. One of the most important events that happened in this period was the gift from Bruges of 1000 nobles to the duke in 1404. Conform to the 1397-1398 scenario the city borrowed the sum from Dino for a bill of exchange worth 20 lb. gr. of interest (6.7%) four months later. The gift had two purposes,[54] corresponding with the Rapondis' two main activities in these years.

4.2.1 The Trade Negotiations with England

First, Philip the Bold was given 1000 nobles by the city for his role in the trade negotiations between England and Flanders. That trade did very well after a commercial agreement with the English had been reached in 1390 and especially after the famous twenty-eight year truce had been concluded in 1396. This provisionally ended the continuous and economically disastrous warfare between France and England and was sealed with the marriage between Richard II and Isabella, daughter of Charles VI.[55] To celebrate this happy event, a brilliant ceremony took place in Calais in October 1396, attended by both kings. Philip the Bold, as the most important man in the French government, the prince of a region for which trade with the English was of vital importance and the main architect of the agreements, was also present and, as usual, his presence was not unnoticeable. The impressive retinue with which he appeared included Dino Rapondi, who, together with 39 colleague courtiers, wore satin, bought by the duke for the occasion from Michele Mercati, another Lucchese.[56]

Despite its attendant pomp and circumstance, the truce ran into difficulties by the end of the fourteenth century because of the actions of elements in both countries who were hostile towards peace. Notwithstanding these efforts to end the truce, the inevitable reprisals and the continuous risk of military escalation, the parties kept talking. This was also the case for the English and the Four Members of Flanders in Calais, who primarily discussed compensations for damage inflicted to the economy by the warlike parties. Yet

---

[54] SAB, Stadsrekening 02/09/1403-02/09/1404, f° 52 v°.

[55] W. PREVENIER, "Les perturbations dans les relations commerciales anglo-flamandes entre 1379 et 1407. Causes de désaccord et raisons d'une réconciliation" in: *Economies et sociétés au moyen-âge. Mélanges offerts à Edouard Perroy*, Paris, Publications de la Sorbonne, 1973, pp. 480-481.

[56] P. de LICHTERVELDE, *Un Grand Commis des Ducs de Bourgogne. Jacques de Lichtervelde Seigneur de Coolscamp*, Bruxelles, Goemaere, 1943, pp. 28-29.

life was breathed into these talks from 1403 on, when Philip the Bold, after the repeated insistence by the Members on a promise of neutrality for his regions which would safeguard the all-important trade against the feared ravages of war, was given permission by Charles VI to negotiate a separate Anglo-Flemish treaty. From now on, the negotiations in Calais were held with the very active cooperation of the ducal envoys, which Bruges, who, as a commercial metropolis, could use an agreement to keep Flanders out of war,[57] tried to encourage with nobles. One of those envoys was Dino Rapondi, participating in the debates from August up to and until December 1398, the fate of which would have affected his own business as well.

At the beginning of May 1405, however, the talks threatened to fail again when one of those belligerent Burgundians, the count of Saint Pol, attempted to provoke the English by attacking their castle in Marck. John the Fearless, who had taken over the ducal sceptre from his father some months before, tried his best to dissociate himself from the action of his vassal, but England saw things differently and sent a reprisal expedition to the port of Sluis.[58] Therefore, the duke made all necessary preparations and summoned Dino to Ghent to settle the financing of the county's defence.[59] Consequently, the Rapondi lent the money to pay the salaries of the soldiers,[60] who, apart from some pillaging in the coastal area, succeeded in keeping the English at bay and prevented them from inflicting much damage. The hostilities did not damage the trade negotiations either. They simply continued in 1406, with the participation of the ducal deputies.[61] John the Fearless even took his deputation very seriously, extorting a loan of 2000 ecus à la couronne from Bruges in February 1406 to pay for it. Almost routinely now, when the duke drew on Bruges's finances, the city got the money from his bankers. In return a bill of exchange was given, which Filippo cashed four months later for the capital and 9 lb. 15 s. 1 d. gr. interest (2.9%).[62] For the rest of John the Fearless's rule, the trade talks between Flanders and England would be a regular feature, again bringing the Rapondi to Bruges, though in other circumstances.

4.2.2 The Succession in Brabant

The 'quieter' years between 1400 and 1405 permitted the Rapondi to concentrate again on a project they had ignored for years because of their work in Flanders, namely the succession in Brabant, also the second reason why Bruges had granted the 1000 nobles in 1404. By 1400 the many Burgundian efforts exerted there had not yielded much more than the secret handover of the area by duchess Joan to Philip the Bold and Margaret of Male, her gift to them of the small duchy of Limbourg and her recognition of Philip's second son Anthony as her successor. Although the proposed candidate offered the possibility of a separate dynasty with a resident prince, the Estates, the

[57] W. PREVENIER, *Les perturbations*, pp. 481-486.
[58] J. PAVIOT, *La politique navale des ducs de Bourgogne, 1384-1482*, Lille, Presses Universitaires de Lille, 1995, pp. 55-57.
[59] ACO, B 1547, f° 169 v°.
[60] ACO, B 1547, f° 212 r°.
[61] W. PREVENIER, *Les perturbations*, p. 481.
[62] SAB, Stadsrekening 02/09/1405-02/09/1406, f° 117 r°.

Brabantine people's representatives who were fond of their independence, refused to accept the Burgundian foreigners.[63]

Meanwhile, the duke tried to obtain a claim on another neighbouring principality, no matter how hypothetical. In 1402 he married Anthony to Joan, the eldest daughter of his vassal Waleran, count of Saint Pol, who aspired to the duchy of Luxemburg and had emphasized that aspiration more than once in a violent way.[64] Bearing in mind his ambitions in Brabant as well as Luxemburg, for Philip the marriage on April 25 in Arras was to be a proper demonstration of Burgundian power and wealth. As this cost money, Dino lent him various sums, of which the duke at his death still owed 380 nobles. In the meantime the financier had been given a reward of 3000 francs.[65]

However, Rapondi's loans were not enough to cover the expenses which Philip the Bold's big plans required and the burden of which he would pass on again to his subjects. Since the Four Members would no longer allow a general *aide* after the hard years at the end of the fourteenth century, the duke determined to win over several Flemish cities individually. Therefore Dino, whose inside knowledge of the victims' financial situation would be of great use, started a tour of the county in June 1401, with François de le Hofstede, Pierre de le Zype and Pierre de Montbertaut, to convince as many cities and castellanies as possible to grant Philip a loan, which they would be able to deduct from their share of the first future subvention. In Bruges, this resulted in a credit of 2000 nobles, for once not issued or transferred by the Rapondi. On the other hand Dino was able to move the smaller communities of Dunkirk, Kassel, Broekburg, Alost, Geraardsbergen and Ninove to contribute their share and made sure that these sums reached the receiver general. For covering the miles for this purpose, he was paid 100 and 340 francs.

Because of the work of Rapondi and other functionaries, Philip the Bold could spend 42 458 lb. par. extra to add lustre to his son's marriage.[66] Apparently, this was not enough though, since one year after the event, the duke asked for an *aide* of no less than 120 000 nobles to cover the costs he had for the feast. However, the Members refused his request and attempts by Dino, Jacques de Lichtervelde and Henri d'Espierres to win over the Franc of Bruges, did not change a thing.[67] Despite these expenses, the marriage did not really bring what Philip had expected, since the count of Saint Pol would never be able to realize his ambitions concerning Luxemburg. Anthony would obtain a much more effective claim on the region in 1407, when he married Elizabeth of Görlitz, the actual heiress of the principality.[68]

Anthony did not have to wait until 1407 to rule Brabant, although it did not really matter. In September 1403, Philip finally got the Estates to the point where they would recognise his son as the successor to duchess Joan, albeit at a heavy cost. The agreement had only been reached after Philip had promised to

---

[63] S. MUND, "Antoine de Bourgogne, prince français et duc de Brabant (1404-1415)" in: *Revue Belge de Philologie et d'Histoire*, Bruxelles, 1998, 76, pp. 321-322.
[64] R. VAUGHAN, *Philip the Bold*, pp. 89-90.
[65] L. MIROT, *La société des Raponde*, p. 365.
[66] A. VAN NIEUWENHUYSEN, *Les finances du duc de Bourgogne. Le montant des ressources*, p. 117.
[67] P. de LICHTERVELDE, *Un Grand Commis*, p. 108.
[68] S. MUND, *Antoine de Bourgogne*, pp. 343-345. For the festivities at the occasion of this event, see A. CHEVALIER, "Le Brabant à l'aube du XVe siècle: fêtes et solennités à la cour des ducs de la branche cadette de Bourgogne-Valois (1406-1430). Le mariage d'Antoine de Bourgogne et d'Elisabeth de Goerlitz" in: *Publications du Centre Européen d'Études Bourguignonnes (XIVe-XVIe s.)*, Dijon, 1994, 34, pp. 174-186.

reattach the important and lucrative trading centre of Antwerp to Brabant, which his father-in-law had only obtained in 1357, and add Limbourg, which he had only received himself from Joan in 1396. He did this even though he had already expended vast sums in convincing the Estates, something the money Bruges got from the Rapondi in 1404 had helped to cover. Moreover, little was left of Philip's original plan of annexing Brabant and Limbourg and ruling them. However, most important, as will be shown later, was the fact that the principality stayed in the Burgundian house. It would still take until the death of duchess Joan in 1406 before Anthony could really call himself duke of Brabant.[69] All this time, "the fact of the Lord of Brabant" would still cost the Burgundian treasury money. This money would still be advanced by Dino, but not to Philip the Bold.[70]

4.2.3 The Passing of Philip the Bold and the Beginning of the Rule of John the Fearless

On April 13, 1404, Dino was summoned by Philip the Bold to Ghent to discuss the finances of the activities he had planned for his next stay in Flanders.[71] The meeting did not take place, since the duke died some days later, on April 27, in Halle.[72] His death was a great loss for the Rapondi company. Thanks to his patronage the firm had grown big; he was responsible for almost every event it had lived through during the past thirty five years, from the orders of fabric it had sold for his wedding to the gigantic exchanges it had drawn for his crusade. The farewell was doubly painful, because some weeks before Jehan Canard had also died. As a chancellor he had helped to shape Burgundy, together with the duke and the banker, and had covered a lot of miles with Dino in Flanders, as is testified by the 2000 lb. t. the Lucchese still owed him at the moment of his death.[73] In hardly three months' time, the Rapondi company as well as the duchy had lost one of the most determining persons of the past decades.

Even the death of Philip the Bold required the service of his bankers. As a consequence of his numerous expensive projects and the luxury that had become an inherent part of his appearance, he left a considerable number of debts[74] and even the money for his funeral was lacking. However, the devotion of the Rapondi, who, with some exaggeration, had financed almost every step the duke had taken for twenty years, would help him out on his last trip as well. Dino advanced the 2024 ecus without which the funeral could not have taken place,[75] obtaining thereby a part of the ducal jewellery collection[76] in exchange for this service and the payment of various debts, illustrating the ducal family's grinding lack of money. His brother Jacopo arranged for the speedy delivery of several pieces of gold cloth from Lucca to decorate the twelve churches where Philip the Bold's body would rest during its transport from Halle to the

[69] S. MUND, *Antoine de Bourgogne*, p. 331.
[70] ACO, B 1547, f° 25 v°.
[71] L. MIROT, *La société des Raponde*, pp. 365-366.
[72] R. VAUGHAN, *Philip the Bold*, p. 101.
[73] A. TUETEY (ed.), *Testaments*, p. 402.
[74] W. PREVENIER, *De beden in het graafschap Vlaanderen*, pp. 331-333.
[75] L. MIROT, *La société des Raponde*, p. 366.
[76] ACO, B 1547, f° 207 v°.

Chartreuse de Champmol near Dijon,[77] as if they were silent witnesses to the vast share the Rapondi family had had in the rule of the deceased.

The succession of a new duke, after a one-year rule by duchess Margaret of Male, did not prejudice this Rapondi share. After their role in his release in Nicopolis,[78] they enjoyed even more confidence from John the Fearless than they had from his father and they probably could not do anything wrong in his eyes. Bruges, the Rapondis' most important business connection besides the duke, was less happy. Whereas the understanding between Philip the Bold and this city had always been very good, to the extent that it was willing to pay more than it actually had to, John the Fearless preferred to deal with Ghent, and Bruges learned to experience a less privileged, even harsh approach.[79] This would also occur at a financial level, not without consequences for the triangular relationship which had characterized the work of the Rapondi, and making clear once again which of the two other players had priority for the firm.

The Rapondi brothers immediately started working for their new employer. The Four Members did not leave the prince in much doubt as to whom he should reckon with, and used John the Fearless' Ceremonial Entry on Easter Day 1405 to present him with a list of grievances. In it they asked that the duke, his wife or his children regularly stay in the county, that John repair the privileges and the customs as they had existed under Louis of Male and that he pursue good commercial relations, primarily with England. The use of Flemish in administrative matters concerning the Flemish-speaking part of the county and the maintenance of the integrity of the Flemish territory were also included.[80] Dino Rapondi was one of the many counsellors who heard the requests in the Ten Walle court and who advised the duke to respond affirmatively to all questions.[81]

Some months later, Rapondi would meet the Members again. In September 1405 John the Fearless asked the Lucchese, still the government's specialist concerning finance as well as Flemish affairs, with Jehan Lengret and receiver-general Audrieu de Douay, to plead for one of his first *aide*s, the request for 12 000 nobles for the duchess' residence.[82] Around September 28 Dino got the message from Clais Utenhove and the bailiff of Ghent that the Four Members did not really fancy the idea of a subvention.[83] Not being discouraged by this, he visited Ypres at the end of October to present the duke's request for the contribution and to defend it. Thereupon, the envoys of the Members retreated to discuss the issue with their supporters. On November 3, they

---

[77] R. VAUGHAN, *John the Fearless*, p. 1.

[78] See *supra*.

[79] R. VAUGHAN, *John the Fearless*, pp. 25-26.

[80] B. SCHNERB, *Jean Sans Peur*, pp. 144-149. For the Members' demand to use Flemish, see M. BOONE, "Doen traitieren elken Vlaminc in Vlaemscher tale. Talige communicatie tussen machthebbers en hun onderhorigen in het Bourgondische Vlaanderen (1385-1505)" in: J. DE CALUWE, G. DE SCHUTTER, M. DEVOS, J. VAN KEYMEULEN (reds.), *Taeldeman, man van de taal, schatbewaarder van de taal, Gent Academia Press*, 2004, pp. 107-125.

[81] J.-M. CAUCHIES, *Ordonnances de Philippe le Hardi, de Marguerite de Male et de Jean sans Peur 1381-1419. Tome III. Ordonnances de Jean sans Peur 1405-1419*, Bruxelles, Koninklijke Commissie voor de uitgave der Oude Wetten en Verordeningen van België, 2001, pp. 5-9.

[82] A. ZOETE, *Organisatie en betekenis van de beden in het graafschap Vlaanderen onder de hertogen Jan zonder Vrees en Filips de Goede (1405-1467)*, Rijksuniversiteit Gent (onuitgegeven doctoraatsverhandeling), 1989-1990, vol. 2, p. 144.

[83] A. ZOETE, *Handelingen van de leden en van de staten van Vlaanderen (1405 – 1419) Excerpten uit de rekeningen der steden, kasselrijen en vorstelijke ambtenaren. Deel 1 (24 maart 1405 – 5 maart 1413*, Brussel, Koninklijke Commissie voor Geschiedenis, 1981, p. 53.

gathered again in Bruges, where they reported a negative verdict to Dino and his two companions.[84]

4.3 The Journey to Liège

When Philip the Bold concluded the famous double marriage with the Bavarian house in Cambrai in 1385,[85] one of his main intentions must have been to create bonds that he and his descendants could use later on. Those bonds would show their power in 1408 in Liège, the vast area between Brabant and Limbourg where a prince-bishop wielded the spiritual as well as the worldly sceptre. At the beginning of the fifteenth century, this function was in the hands of John of Bavaria, although he had to settle for the title of Elect since he had taken only sub-deacon's orders. In his continuous attempts to expand his power, John of Bavaria, the brother of William of Hainault and Holland-Zealand and the brother-in-law of John the Fearless, had irritated his subjects too much, who threw him out in 1406 and replaced him with the regent Henry of Perwez and the anti-bishop Thierry of Perwez. After they had conquered the whole prince-bishopric, John the deposed Elect called for the help of John the Fearless.[86]

The hesitant support offered initially by the Burgundian duke did not save John of Bavaria from retreating to Maastricht in July 1408, where he was besieged by his adversaries. Thereupon, John the Fearless concluded an alliance with William of Bavaria and delivered an ultimatum to the lords of Perwez, demanding that they lift the siege. Since they did not comply, preparations were made in August for a large expedition to show what would happen if the duke's family was aggrieved. The reinforcement of Burgundian influence in Liège and the intimidation of the rebellious Flemish cities were as much a consideration.[87] As usual, the financial part of the preparations was carried out by Dino Rapondi, who began looking for money from September 15 onwards.[88]

In the few days before the start of the expedition, the ducal receivers saw another tremendous demonstration of Dino's financial and networking capabilities. In very little time, the Lucchese made available 30 000 ecus by drawing bills of exchange on Venice and other places. For his efforts and the costs he had incurred, he received 1600 ecus,[89] with the loss on the bills of 241 gold francs being collected by Filippo.[90] Furthermore, Dino lent a part of the capital himself, for which he would be reimbursed 2000[91] and 1340 ecus.[92] Finally, Dino's financial presence in Bruges generated the necessary money. While other regions seem to have kept their purses closed[93] and the requested 6000 Flemish men of arms were probably not supplied either,[94] the merchant

---

[84] A. ZOETE, *Handelingen*, pp. 66-69.
[85] See *supra*.
[86] Y. CHARLIER, "La bataille d'Othée et sa place dans l'histoire de la principauté de Liège" in: *Bulletin de l'Institut archéologique liégois*, Liège, 1985, 97, pp. 144-172.
[87] Y. CHARLIER, *La bataille d'Othée*, pp. 173-184.
[88] R. VAUGHAN, *John the Fearless*, p. 55.
[89] ACO, B 1556, f° 170 r°.
[90] ACO, B 1556, f° 169 r°.
[91] ACO, B 1556, f° 10 v°.
[92] ACO, B 1560, f° 201 r°.
[93] For the contributions of those who did give money, see B. SCHNERB, "Un aspect de la politique financière de Jean sans Peur: la question des dépenses de guerre" in: *Publications du Centre Européen d'Études Bourguignonnes (XIVe-XVIe s.)*, Dijon, 1987, 27, p. 122, n. 52.
[94] A. ZOETE, *Organisatie en betekenis van de beden. Band 2*, p. 144.

was able to obtain a loan from some Bruges notables[95] amounting to 8950 ecus à la couronne, to be subtracted from the next contributions to the duke if they could "deliver it in ready money". Again, Dino helped the money-lenders by granting them a part of the amount, although this time it seems to have been more symbolic than actual, giving the modest sum of 500 ecus à la couronne for a bill of exchange on which the city would pay 3 lb. 150. gr. (3.3%).[96]

Thanks to the Rapondis' emergency services, the common troops of John the Fearless and William of Bavaria could enter the prince-bishopric on September 20, 1408. When Henry of Perwez heard the news, he left John of Bavaria in Maastricht and hastened towards the enemy. The two armies met on September 23 in Othée, where the militarily skilled John the Fearless and his ally crushed the Liégois. The rebellion completely collapsed and John of Bavaria was able to reoccupy the prince-episcopal throne once again. This is not to say that he was back in charge. John the Fearless and William of Bavaria used the success of their expedition, one of those typically Burgundian expressions of gratitude behind which lurked the promotion of their own interests, to take control of business in the prince-bishopric. They immediately showed who was boss by imposing a very heavy fine on the Liégois, which even John of Bavaria thought was exaggerated. The vanquished had to yield their rights, eliminate their guilds, pull down the city's reinforcements, and allow John and William's coins to come into circulation in Liège.

All the money Dino had supplied for the operation would repay itself so to speak, since the winners had rewarded themselves handsomely with 110 000 francs each, the fine from the beaten population. The collection of the funds started immediately afterwards,[97] led by Jehan du Buisson, especially appointed for the occasion, and executed by several 'commis'. One of those first attorneys who had to collect the money in the prince-bishopric, despite heavy resistance from the Liégois, was Filippo Rapondi.[98] It was in his own interests to do this properly, knowing that his brother Dino would be repaid various debts by assignments on the revenues of the fine.[99] In 1413, one year after John the Fearless and William of Bavaria had delivered their final common receipt,[100] the eldest of the Rapondi had still to receive 14 000 ecus of their dues.[101] The family was not only physically present at the collection. For John the Fearless, his 'commis' was as good an opportunity to emphasize the power and wealth of the Burgundian house as was a magnificent wedding, and therefore, in 1408, chamberlain Courralt de Jonghe made his appearance to the Liégois dressed in a red velvet robe, into which the fur of 300 martens, supplied by the Rapondi company, had been sewn.[102]

Besides being a significant Burgundian military accomplishment, the expedition against Liège was above all a new step in the subjection of the big cities, the principal competitors of the dukes in their struggle for power in the Netherlands. After Sluis, where a castle had been built at the entrance of Bruges's port complex, and Nicopolis, which had enabled Philip the Bold to

[95] Why the whole city did not contribute will become clear further on, see *infra*.
[96] SAB, Stadsrekening 02/09/1408-01/09/1409, f° 87 v°.
[97] Y. CHARLIER, *La bataille d'Othée*, pp. 185-220.
[98] ACO, B 1554, f° 37 r°.
[99] ADN, B 1894, f° 38 r°. ADN, B 1897, f° 209 v°.
[100] Y. CHARLIER, *La bataille d'Othée*, p. 217.
[101] L. MIROT, *La société des Raponde*, p. 370.
[102] ACO, B 1556, f° 100 r°.

cream off up to two-thirds of some city budgets despite, or just because of, the disastrous outcome of the crusade, the city dwellers had to cope with an even more direct blow on the battlefield of Othée. Three times communal aspirations had been curtailed, three times the Rapondi had been the financiers, and paradoxically this happened three times with city money, albeit in 1408 from a city some hundreds of miles further. In this paradox, the effects of the triangular relationship between Bruges, the duke and their bankers already prevailed. Due to the intervention of the Rapondi, the prince was able to use the city's potential to weaken that same city. Whereas this happened only implicitly under Philip the Bold, John the Fearless pursued this policy more openly. The Bruges inhabitants would soon experience the rather unpleasant consequences.

4.4 Armagnacs versus Bourguignons: the French Civil War

4.4.1 The Murder of Louis of Orléans

The call for help from John of Bavaria in the summer of 1408 came at an inopportune moment for John the Fearless. At that time, the Burgundian duke had other worries, the same as his father had had before him. Since both were in the first place French princes, those troubles had everything to do with their control over France. With some interruptions, the kingdom had been in the hands of Philip the Bold since 1380, assisted considerably by the mental instability of Charles VI and the passivity of other princes of the royal blood. By the end of the 1390s, however, the duke had had to deal more and more with Louis of Orléans, the king's brother. Dipping into royal resources as his uncle had always done, Orléans conducted a policy of obtaining allies and territories, more and more directed against Burgundian interests. He tried to gain control of the French government at the expense of Philip the Bold by, taking advantage of his trips to Flanders and Brabant, setting his partisans up in important places. In this, he succeeded so well that the Burgundian duke entered Paris with an army in December 1401 to change his nephew's mind. After feelings had calmed down, Louis simply continued his political offensive, countered by Philip's attempts to undo the consequences.

The duke of Burgundy dying in 1404 suited his nephew of Orléans quite well. The successor John the Fearless was only a cousin and not an uncle of the king, and could not equal the moral authority his father had had in the royal family, a situation that gave Louis the opportunity to seize power.[103] But the new Burgundian duke had an attribute denied Philip the Bold, the capability of handling an army. Firm in his intention of retaining his father's position in France, John the Fearless went to Paris in August 1405 with hundreds of men. There, he twarthed Louis of Orléans' attempt to removal the *dauphin*, the heir to the throne and the symbol of royal power, from the capital and brought him back to the Louvre, after which a paper war erupted with both dukes accusing each other of having kidnapped the king's son. A truce ended all of this, albeit for a short period. Rivalry reappeared during the following months, in which Louis succeeded in gaining the favour of most *princes des fleurs de lys*, made France agree a new English policy that was disastrous for Burgundy, and denied the

[103] B. SCHNERB, *Les Armagnacs et les Bourguignons. La maudite guerre*, Paris, Librairie Académique Perrin, 1988, pp. 44-57.

access to the royal treasury to his adversary.[104] The last manoeuvre was particularly successful at putting the knife to John the Fearless' throat, since the Burgundian state had always lived on gifts from the king. Only one option remained for the hard-pressed duke. An inhabitant of the *Rue Vieille-du-Temple* in Paris saw it happen.

When she looked through her window on the evening of November 23, 1407, she saw "a notable gentleman on horseback, joined by five or six riders and preceded by three or four men on foot, bearing two or three torches. They came from the direction of the queen's palace, in other words from the side of the *Porte Barbette*". Thereupon, the woman left her place at the window, but when she heard a noise outside, she hastened back to the street side. There, she saw "the gentleman, on his knees in the middle of the street, surrounded by seven or eight masked men, armed with swords and axes". They attacked the victim, who "collapsed on the street, while they kept beating on him". Then, they "left the gentleman, who did not move any more, and fled". The victim, who did not survive the attack, was Louis of Orléans. When the provost of Paris, burdened with the enquiry into the crime, revealed his findings to the royal princes, John the Fearless took the princes of Berry and Anjou aside and told his disbelieving audience that he had ordered the murder. The shock this caused enabled the duke to flee the capital in all haste and to retreat to his regions.[105]

Giovanni Sercambi, a Lucchese chronicler, stated that Dino Rapondi had a hand in the murder of Louis of Orléans.[106] He can hardly be regarded as neutral, since he was a notable member of the Guinigi party,[107] the hereditary enemies of the Rapondi in Lucca, and at the time he made his accusations he was involved in a serious conflict with the merchant concerning the inheritance of his father.[108] However, Dino also had some claims against him. At the moment of the attack, he must have been the Burgundian state's longest-serving counsellor, who had collaborated with and known the ins and outs of almost every important undertaking of Philip the Bold and John the Fearless over the past twenty years and enjoyed an unlimited amount of confidence from the duke. It would be strange if this confidence excluded him from the murder plans, the more so as one of its primary motives according to many historians was financial, the shutting down of the duke's royal resources.[109] Was Dino Rapondi not the outstanding financial expert in the ducal administration, who had always made sure the duke had access to sufficient revenues?

Suspicion thickens when we consider the testimony of Pierre Salmon, a writer in the service of John the Fearless who reported that a certain Giovanni Rapondi, probably Dino's second cousin, vindicated the murder in Lucca in January 1408, scarcely two months after the event, by pointing out the miserable state to which Louis of Orléans had brought France.[110] Even if Salmon's scribblings were only a fictitious construction which had to defend his

---

[104] B. SCHNERB, *Les Armagnacs et les Bourguignons*, pp. 58-69.
[105] B. SCHNERB, *Les Armagnacs et les Bourguignons*, pp. 70-74.
[106] G. SERCAMBI, *Le croniche di Giovanni Sercambi*, vol. 3, p. 127.
[107] C. MEEK, *Lucca 1369-1400*, p. 214.
[108] L. MIROT, *La colonie lucquoise à Paris*, pp. 81-82.
[109] See, for example, R. VAUGHAN, *John the Fearless*, p. 43.
[110] B. GUENEE, *Un meurtre, une société. L'assassinat du duc d'Orléans 23 novembre 1407*, Paris, Editions Gallimard, 1992, pp. 221-222.

employer's crime,[111] the question arises why exactly he brought the Rapondi family on the stage. It seems additionally damning when we know that the leader of the murderers in the *Rue Vieille-du-Temple*, a stone's throw of Dino's house, was Raoul d'Anquetonville, for years a regular business connection of the Rapondi in book illuminations, who had possibly become familiar with the duke, to whom he had sold some precious manuscripts, by way of the Lucchese.[112]

In the banker's favour is the argument that by condoning the murder he risked the commercial activities of his own Lucchese community in Paris, which was in fact to dwindle following the death of Orléans, causing considerable losses and division among the group's members.[113] Yet this in itself is negated by considering that the Rapondi had by the mid 1390s chosen a financial career exclusively in the service of the duke, at the expense of a commercial career with the several royal princes as clients,[114] and in this respect a downturn in the commercial climate would not have inconvenienced him that much, apart from possible lost opportunities through the misfortunes of others.

Whether the murder took place with or without the Rapondis' collaboration, their employer got away with it. John the Fearless's power and the support he still had in Paris kept the princes of the royal blood from taking action against him. What is more, he felt able to reappear in the capital in March 1408. After theologian Jean Petit had spoken out in justification of the murder, the duke succeeded in regaining control of the French government and eliminated various adversaries. With awkward timing, the call for help from John of Bavaria arrived at this moment, taking him from Paris and so giving the Orléans partisans the chance to launch a counterattack. The support they could gather did not suffice to stop the return of the victor of Liège, whereupon they retreated from the capital with the king. To get the prince, still the only representative of power for the Parisians, back in the Louvre, and to make further attempts to free himself from all guilt, John the Fearless began negotiations with the party in flight. These resulted in a big reconciliation ceremony in Chartres in March 1409. There, the Burgundian duke asked and was given a pardon by the two sons of the murdered Louis of Orléans. Peace returned to France, but a peace Bertrand Schnerb has not called "une paix fourrée" without good reason.[115]

4.4.2 The Rapondi as War Financiers

The glossy spectacle in Chartres probably wiped the hate that both parties felt for each other only in the minds of the credulous spectators. The adversaries themselves were more determined than ever to eliminate their enemy for good. This must have dawned on the most passionate advocate of Chartres in October 1409, as soon as John the Fearless, for whom the reconciliation had permitted him to maintain control over Paris, began the removal of all the

---

[111] Which is very probable since the Rapondi were not able to show themselves in Lucca at this time anymore.

[112] P.M. DE WINTER, *La Bibliothèque de Philippe le Hardi, duc de Bourgogne (1364-1404) Étude sur les manuscrits à peintures d'une collection princière à l'époque du « style gothique international »*, Paris, Centre National de la Recherche Scientifique,1985, pp. 98, 104.

[113] L. MIROT, *La colonie lucquoise à Paris*, pp. 83-84.

[114] See *supra*.

[115] B. SCHNERB, *Les Armagnacs et les Bourguignons*, pp. 74-97.

people who had been in his way during the months before the murder and reappropriated all power to himself. However, those who saw their interests threatened by the Burgundian offensive gathered around the new duke of Orléans in a party led by the elderly John of Berry, who had lost his government influence to his nephew,[116] named the Armagnacs after one of its most enthusiastic members.[117]

One of the few *grands seigneurs* whom John the Fearless could keep from joining this alliance was Louis II of Anjou. For this, he deployed his children, following his father in regarding them as the ideal material for the realization of his political calculations. The duke took advantage of the need for money Anjou's plans for a new invasion of the Italian peninsula caused, by offering him a dowry worth 40 000 ecus and a 90 000 ecu gift from the royal treasury,[118] over which he now had complete control, in return for a marriage between a daughter of Burgundy and a son of Anjou. Louis complied and in March 1410 his heir of the same name married Catherine, John the Fearless' eleven-year-old daughter.[119]

Transferring the 40 000 ecus, for which several Burgundian nobles pledged themselves, to the *Angevins*, was just the thing for Dino Rapondi, by now a specialist in ducal marriage finance. By way of three bills of exchange,[120] the Lucchese sent a first instalment of 4000 ecus in May 1411 from his office in Bruges to Montpellier, where Jehan Drogoli, chamberlain and attorney of Louis of Anjou's wife Yolanda, received the funds in cash.[121] Dino got the money back the same month with an assignment on the *Recette Générale de Toutes les Finances*,[122] followed by 200 ecus (his remuneration had been paid out in ecus of 40 groot while the coins he had spent himself were worth 42 groot), and 120 for the loss on the bills.[123] According to Léon Mirot, Rapondi collected another 115 ecus in November 1411 and 1866 ecus in March 1412 for further redemptions of the dowry.[124] But there were not to be many more, since in the summer of 1413, Louis II of Anjou exchanged his alliance with the Bourguignons for one with the Armagnacs and publicly dishonoured John the Fearless by sending Catherine back with an unconsumated marriage.[125]

Once the alliances had taken shape and Charles of Orléans had incarcerated the Burgundian knight Jean de Croy on an embassy to John of Berry,[126] for which Dino would advance the remuneration later on,[127] the hostilities would not be long in coming. How the duke would pay for the war efforts[128] seems to have been decided in the *Rue de la vieille Monnaie*. During the whole war, the Burgundian counsellors Pierre de Viesmille, Jacques de Courtiambles and the released Jean de Croy, treasurers and receivers Joceran

---

116 For the changes in his position, see F. AUTRAND, *Jean de Berry*, pp. 209-230.
117 B. SCHNERB, *Les Armagnacs et les Bourguignons*, pp. 101-105.
118 ADN, B 1894, f° 137 r°.
119 R. VAUGHAN, *John the Fearless*, p. 247.
120 ADN, B 1894, f° 147 v°.
121 ADN, B 1894, f° 137 r°.
122 ADN, B 1894, f° 13 v°.
123 ADN, B 1894, f° 147 v°.
124 L. MIROT, *La société des Raponde*, p. 371.
125 B. SCHNERB, *Jean Sans Peur*, p. 578.
R. VAUGHAN, *John the Fearless*, pp. 247-248.
126 B. SCHNERB, *Les Armagnacs et les Bourguignons*, p. 108.
127 ACO, B 1562, f° 104 r°.
128 For this, see B. SCHNERB, *Un aspect de la politique financière*, pp. 113-128.

Frepier, Jehan de Pressy, Jehan Despoullettes and Jehan Chousat stayed regularly in Dino and Jacopo's Paris mansion to discuss the financing of the military operations. There, they talked with counsellors of the king about the granting of royal *aides*,[129] with the chancellor, the *maîtres des comptes* and other ducal officers about the search for revenues[130] and with merchants about advances on those sums. Each day, the Rapondi paid for the "big dinners, suppers and other expenses" of their guests[131] with an occasional barrel of wine from John the Fearless.[132] Subsequently Jacopo presented the bill, verified by Pressy and Chousat, to the duke.[133]

One of the first war acts tackled by the counsellors in Dino's house took place in John the Fearless' southern possessions. In June 1411, the Armagnacs opened hostilities with an attack on the duchy of Burgundy, where John's old rival Louis of Chalon conquered various locations at the border. Because at that time the lion's share of the Bourguignon troops were in Flanders and Artois, Margaret of Bavaria, who ran the business in Dijon in the absence of her husband, had to call for help from the friendly duke of Lotharia.[134] For that, the latter needed to be paid and so John the Fearless gave his chamberlain Guillaume Gente 3000 francs, to be conveyed to Dino. The banker drew a bill of exchange for the same amount on another merchant and handed over the document to *échanson* Dauphin de Seris, who was to deliver it to Lotharia. However, the bill was protested there, so the Lotharian duke could not cash the sum and gave back the bill to Dino by way of Seris. Now, Guillaume Gente had to use the original amount in ready money to pay the salary of the Burgundian troops,[135] while Rapondi could repeat his operation, with 300 ecus coming from the *Recette Générale de Toutes les Finances*.[136] Those must have arrived, since at the end of August the Lotharian prince reversed all Louis of Chalon's conquests, campaigning with John the Fearless' youngest brother Philip of Nevers.[137]

In the North, the situation looked less bright for the Bourguignons. The Orléans party threatened Paris and had conquered Burgundian strongholds in Vermandois, from where they carried out raids in Artois. Yet, by the end of August 1411 John the Fearless had succeeded in raising an impressive army, far larger than that of his adversary, including an important contingent of Flemings.[138] The raising and the maintenance of such a military force evidently cost a fortune, and even on a distant battlefield in the north of France the duke could rely on his bankers. At his request, Dino Rapondi and his trade partner Bartolomeo Bettini transferred 3850 ecus using two bills of exchange to Jacopo Rapondi and Galvano Trenta in Paris, who delivered the sum to the duke, "somewhere in the fields".[139]

Jacopo and Galvano must have just started their return trip to the French capital when the Burgundian men began their march to Ham, which

[129] ACO, B 1560, f° 264 v°.
[130] ADN, B 1894, f° 305 r°.
[131] ACO, B 1560, f° 264 v°.
[132] ACO, B 1560, f° 177 r°.
[133] ADN, B 1894, f° 304 v°.
[134] B. SCHNERB, *Les Armagnacs et les Bourguignons*, p. 111.
[135] ADN, B 1894, f° 50 r°.
[136] ADN, B 4086, f° 93 v°.
[137] B. SCHNERB, *Les Armagnacs et les Bourguignons*, p. 111.
[138] B. SCHNERB, *Les Armagnacs et les Bourguignons*, p. 113.
[139] ADN, B 1894, f° 139 r°.

they captured from the Armagnacs. After Nesle and Roye had surrendered as well, John the Fearless crossed the Somme on September 20 and halted near Montdidier, waiting for the approaching Orléans army. On the eve of what could have been a decisive confrontation in the French Civil War, the Flemings decided to strike their tents and go home. Without the bulk of his infantry and part of his artillery, the duke had no choice but to sound the retreat.

When Charles of Orléans and his troops found the plain near Montdidier deserted, they could either pursue their enemy on his own territory or put up a massive siege of the capital. They took the latter option, turning the Parisian city walls into the stage for fierce fighting over the following days.[140] Although Jacopo Rapondi had to pay 1000 lb. t. to repair the damage inflicted on the ducal residence,[141] the siege had little result and John the Fearless, after regrouping his Montdidier troops, was even able to slip into the city in about the middle of October. From there, he broke the stranglehold of the Armagnacs on the capital, who retreated completely. After the relief of Paris, the Burgundian duke took the offensive again and gained victory after victory. This brought the Orleanists close to desperation, causing one of their leaders, John of Berry, ask for help from the English. The discovery of these contacts gave John the Fearless the opportunity to mobilize the royal army against the traitor and lay siege to Berry's capital of Bourges. This developed into a long-drawn-out battle for the besiegers as well as for the besieged, who finally opened negotiations. The result was a peace treaty between Armagnacs and Bourguignons, concluded on July 15, 1412.[142] For most people involved, this would be a pause in the *maudite guerre*; for the Rapondi it would be the end.

4.4.3 The Consequences of the War: Bruges in Need of Money

Even though the French Civil War was conducted hundreds of miles away from the Bruges city walls and the Bruges inhabitants only participated intermittently – and even then they thought it was necessary to escape – the circumstances of war would still lay a heavy burden on the city. For John the Fearless, the hostilities were a huge expense and since his relationship with Bruges was based on power rather than on cooperation, he saw no problem with the city paying for his war costs. Yet, not only the conflict between Armagnacs and Bourguignons caused problems with serious financial consequences between the city and the duke.

4.4.3.1 The Aftermath of the 'Calfvel'

For several years a ruling clique had been in power in Bruges which had been able to do business quite well with Philip the Bold. Some months after his death, however, they had displeased his son by refusing to grant him men he had requested for for the defence of the coast against the English, because of the unpopularity of such a decision with the population. Relations with the new duke did not improve when a conflict over the textile privileges arose between the city and the Franc of Bruges. The prince used this occasion to interfere in

---

[140] B. SCHNERB, *Les Armagnacs et les Bourguignons*, pp. 113-116.
[141] G. BIGWOOD, *Le régime juridique et économique Tome I*, p. 88.
[142] F. AUTRAND, *Jean de Berry*, pp. 233-238. B. SCHNERB, *Les Armagnacs et les Bourguignons*, pp. 116-121.

Bruges' politics, but saw his propositions rejected by the city magistracy, which was under pressure from the guilds not to touch the Bruges textile monopoly in any way. Nevertheless, an opposition faction whose leaders had been banished years before in a struggle for power with the ruling group and had been pardoned by the duke later, succeeded in convincing most of the guilds and submitted with them to John the Fearless. The duke saw a long-awaited opportunity to impose his will on the city, and did this with an unprecedented display of power.

The very next day he travelled to Bruges, where he relieved the ruling magistrates of their offices, confiscated their goods and banished them from the county. In their place he put his partisans, with a considerable number coming from the opposition group. Furthermore, the duke proclaimed the 'Calfvel', a charter with which he elevated the guilds back into full political and military bodies by giving them back their banners, albeit under such harsh conditions that the new entitlement was rather a weakening than a restoration of their position. They could never again claim the 'maendgheld', the remuneration every Bruges citizen received for his military duties but which had not been paid since the repression after Westrozebeke. The Calfvel also made it possible to banish them on the spot, with a trial before the aldermen only afterwards. Finally, John replaced the octroi for the excise taxes he received from the city every year with a tax of no less than a seventh of all Bruges revenues, the so called 'seventh penny'. On May 24, 1407, the new magistrates and the guilds put their seals to the two charters in which they accepted the duke's 'reforms'.[143] "Bruges was bullied into submission", as Richard Vaughan put it.[144]

The events of 1407 explain why the loans Bruges made for the duke's journey to Liège and for which the Rapondi supplied part of the money on a bill of exchange came only from "several citizens" and not from the city as a whole.[145] These faithful citizens were probably of the faction that had been given the city council by John the Fearless, and consequently tried to curry his favour. In providing the funds for this purpose, the Rapondi on the one hand made sure that the group favourable to their employer stood firm and stayed in power, a repeat of their actions since 1399 with their share in the annual renewal of the law.[146] On the other hand they exploited the zeal of these notables to please the prince financially, for their own benefit and that of the duke. It would not be the last time they did this. John the Fearless availed himself of Bruges' subjection and the submissiveness of the favoured ruling clique, to shift his heavy burdens, which would only increase because of the war in France, to the city. The result was a whirl of loans and *aides*, one after the other approved by a magistracy not in a position to refuse them. With every payment, the grip of the duke on the city grew stronger, the situation of Bruges got worse, and the influence of the Rapondi grew bigger. For it was the bankers who made sure that the city's treasurers had sufficient means to keep meeting the never-ending demands of the prince.

The first in a long series of contributions occurred when John the Fearless gave permission for the Four Members to impose 20 000 double ecus

---

143 J. DUMOLYN, *De Brugse opstand van 1436-1438*, Kortrijk-Heule, U.G.A., 1997, pp. 129-136.
144 R. VAUGHAN, *John the Fearless*, p. 26.
145 See *supra*.
146 See A. SCHOUTEET, *Regesten op de oorkonden 1385-1420*, p. 164 ff.

on the surrounding smaller cities to cover their costs in the trade negotiations with England. However, from the 14 400 lb. par. Bruges was able to collect in its district, not a penny was left. 2058 lb. 3 s. par. disappeared into the duke's pocket as the 'seventh penny'. 7542 lb. par. had to be given by the city to pay for its share in the *aide* granted by the Members to John in October 1408 to make good the loss on a subvention he had made because of the monetary reform in 1407. From this, the treasurers had to put aside 5100 lb. par. for Dino Rapondi, who had advanced this amount to the duke. The remaining 4799 lb. 17 s. par. went through the Lucchese to the receiver general, as part of a loan Bruges had issued to John on the revenues of the seventh penny and the payments to organize the 'Brugghemaerct', a city fair.[147]

Some months later, Rapondi was there again, this time to receive the loss of 6 lb. gr. (3.6%) he had made in ten months on a bill of exchange, supplied by the city for 1000 ecus à la couronne. Bruges needed this sum for a new credit to John the Fearless, the reason for which is unknown.[148] The treasurers did not have to wait long for the banker's next visit, since Dino provided them with 8000 ecus à la couronne on July 23, 1410 for the third loan in two-years' time.[149] In return he would get several bills of exchange, yielding an interest of 1000 ecus à la couronne (12.5%). It was intended that the city would pay back 1000 ecus à la couronne at the end of August 1410, followed by five three-monthly instalments of 1200 ecus à la couronne and a final instalment of 1000 ecus à la couronne in March 1412.[150] The Bruggelings seem to have only respected the first due date. Because of "missed payments", they owed 2200 ecus à la couronne in March 1411.[151] Yet, they guaranteed the Rapondi that they would use the revenues of the seventh penny (against which the loan to the duke had been secured) to redeem the debt.[152] This resulted in the payment of all late instalments in September 1411, after which the city was still 2200 ecus à la couronne in the red.[153] This shortage stayed in the accounts until 1412-1413, when Dino could record the final 445 ecus à la couronne in the income section of his *conti*[154] after numerous unpaid assignments on the seventh penny.[155]

In 1410-1411, the capital flow from the city to the duke temporarily became a capital flow from the city to the banker. Since the Rapondi had advanced more than 1333 lb. gr.[156] on the *aide* of 60 000 double ecus which John the Fearless, supported by Dino,[157] had been given by the Members for the costs of his war efforts in France, and which replaced the men-at-arms he had asked for first,[158] part of this subvention would end up with the Lucchese. Because the company again provided Bruges with the necessary money as well, a

[147] SAB, Stadsrekening 02/09/1408-01/09/1409, f° 103 v°.
[148] SAB, Stadsrekening 02/09/1409-01/09/1410, f° 105 v°.
[149] Three when we take into account the 8950 crowns supplied by the burghers for Liège, see *infra*.
[150] SAB, Stadsrekening 02/09/1409-01/09/1410, f° 114 r°.
[151] SAB, Stadsrekening 02/09/1410-01/09/1411, f° 125 v°-126 r°.
[152] SAB, Stadsrekening 02/09/1410-01/09/1411, f° 130 r°.
[153] SAB, Stadsrekening 02/09/1411-01/09/1412, f° 29 r°.
[154] SAB, Stadsrekening 02/09/1412-01/09/1413, f° 89 r°.
[155] SAB, Stadsrekening 02/09/1411-01/09/1412, f° 101 r°, 119 v°.
[156] A. ZOETE, "De beden in het graafschap Vlaanderen onder de hertogen Jan zonder Vrees en Filips de Goede (1405-1467)" in: *Verhandelingen van de Koninklijke Academie voor Wetenschappen, Letteren en Schone Kunsten van België*, Brussel, 1995, 56, nr. 149, p. 144.
[157] C. DE BORCHGRAEVE, *Diplomaten en diplomatie onder hertog Jan zonder Vrees. Impact op de Vlaamse politieke situatie*, Rijksuniversiteit Gent (onuitgegeven licentiaatsverhandeling), 1988-1989, p. 334.
[158] A. ZOETE, *Organisatie en betekenis van de beden. Band 2*, p. 145.

unique situation arose in which the Rapondi were financing themselves. From the 1885 lb. 10 s. par. the city had to pay in three instalments,[159] Dino granted the first 250 lb. gr. for a bill of six weeks with a loss of 6 lb. gr. (2.4%)[160] and the last 628 lb. 60 gr. for a bill of four months with a loss of 10 lb. gr. (1.6%),[161] together worth 878 lb. 100 gr. (46.5% of Bruges' share). As to the amount of Bruges capital which streamed to the ducal treasury by way of the Rapondi, after only five years John the Fearless had already acquired 3204 lb. gr.

The uninterrupted loans and *aides* had a disastrous effect on Bruges's finances. As the case of Dino's 8000 ecus à la couronne credit already showed, the city was months behind with its payments and sank deeper and deeper into debt. Even for daily costs it was short of money. Because of this, the Bruges treasurers were forced to use two procedures, of which the Rapondi clan gratefully availed themselves. First, the city could collect "ready money" quickly by giving bills of exchange. In this way, it got 2000 ecus à la couronne from the company in 1409,[162] 400 lb. gr. in 1412[163] and 2600 ecus à la couronne in 1413.[164] As well as this, Bruges resorted to a kind of indirect loan, by buying goods only to be paid for after a certain period, but selling them immediately at a loss, which usually amounted to less than the high interest with the direct loans. For merchants, this was a highly attractive opportunity to obtain commodities for a lower price than they would cost in normal circumstances. Dino, together with Genoese and Catalan businessmen, saved 30 lb. gr. on the purchase of 33 Ypres, 30 Wervik and 40 Courtrai cloths in 1409.[165] Other bargains were the bales of wax he bought from the money-hungry Bruges treasurers in 1408[166] and 1410.[167] However, the banker's fortune only benefited from the misery of the city, who had to richly pay back the bills of exchange as well as the goods.

The effects soon made themselves felt. The people's discontent with the squeezing of their city grew and finally led to an eruption when the Bruges army came back from Montdidier at the beginning of October 1411. The militia would not enter Bruges unless the magistracy complied with their demands. First, those seemed to concern mainly an extra stipend, which was conceded by the aldermen. Yet, during the night, demands got more radical, and in the morning, besides a demand for the conviction of the ducal-minded city council, a call for the confiscation of Dino Rapondi's goods was heard as well. Nonetheless, the deans of the guilds could ease the unrest of the masses and reduce the demands to some seven points.

Those concerned the abolition of bannishment on the spot, the removal of the grain 'cueillote', the payment of the 'maendghelt' and a bigger salary for the trip to Montdidier, as well as the replacement of the seventh penny by a contribution for the excise taxes, the solemn tearing up of the Calfvel and exemption from confiscations. The city council only agreed to the first four points, as the last three could only be decided by the duke. Therefore, a

[159] A. ZOETE, *Organisatie en betekenis van de beden. Band 2*, p. 205.
[160] SAB, Stadsrekening 02/09/1410-01/09/1411, f° 108 v°.
[161] SAB, Stadsrekening 02/09/1410-01/09/1411, f° 116 r°.
[162] SAB, Stadsrekening 02/09/1408-01/09/1409, f° 89 v°.
[163] SAB, Stadsrekening 02/09/1411-01/09/1412, f° 95 v°.
[164] SAB, Stadsrekening 02/09/1412-01/09/1413, f° 77 r°.
[165] SAB, Stadsrekening 02/09/1408-01/09/1409, f° 93 r°-v°.
[166] SAB, Stadsrekening 02/09/1408-01/09/1409, f° 88 v°.
[167] SAB, Stadsrekening 02/09/1409-01/09/1410, f° 110 v°.

delegation travelled to John the Fearless' son Philip of Charolais in Ghent, who sent the envoys on to his father on a battlefield near Beauvais. Urged by the other Members of Flanders and with the growing unrest of the Bruges militia in the background, the duke gave in. He took the Calfvel out of his archives in Lille and gave it to the deans of the guilds, who destroyed the document. Thereupon, the Bruges army finally entered the city gates.[168] Although he maintained his most important trump card, for John the Fearless this was a step backwards in his centralistic aspirations for the city.

That the guilds vented their rage on Rapondi too can be understood. He had made his living out of the misery of the city and did his best business when Bruges was in heavy financial difficulties. In the eyes of the common people, he was doing this as a creature of the duke, who had already won himself an unpopular name with projects such as Nicopolis and Sluis, where the magistrates had to guard the buildings to protect them from sabotage. Rapondi had enabled the duke to reduce the city to the lamentable situation it was in at that moment and, as the financier who came to collect the money each month and to whom the Bruges people still had to pay innumerable debts, he was one of the most visible representatives of that hated ducal policy. Rather than being regarded as a gateway for Bruges to the ducal authorities, the population now saw him as a gateway for the duke to drain the city's finances.

The warnings to John the Fearless and Dino Rapondi met with no success. The payments simply continued. What, under Philip the Bold, had been a smoothly operating interaction among three parties, had degenerated into the milking dry of one of the players by the two others. However, in their relentless attempts to squeeze as much money out of the city as possible, the duke and the banker had to be careful not to strangle it financially. They came very close to this in September 1412, when Bruges was exactly 9381 lb. 11 s. 3 d. gr. in the red, more than one and a half times the amount of the entire city budget. Because of this, the city was forced to farm out all its revenues for a period of four years to a group of citizens, who would pay 4800 lb. gr. for this each year. The decision was approved by the ducal counsellors, including Rapondi, though not without having obtained the concession that the revenue farmers would continue to grant the exemptions from the excise taxes on wine that Dino and the other counsellors, as well as the clergy, enjoyed. The counsellors also made sure that the city would still have at its disposal the revenues of the seventh penny.[169] Bruges needed them to redeem its 8000-ecus à la couronne loan to counsellor Rapondi.

Even a city without income was not safe from John the Fearless' requirements. In 1413, by way of a bill of exchange and the purchase of goods bought in advance, Dino and some other merchants provided Bruges with the resources to issue a new loan of 400 lb. gr. to the duke[170] (how it was to pay this back is a mystery). Nevertheless, the contributions to the duke seem to have diminished substantially after 1412, which allowed the city to struggle free of this financial morass, albeit very slowly. For twenty long years,[171] it would have

[168] J. DUMOLYN, *De Brugse opstand*, pp. 138-140.
[169] SAB, Stadsrekening 02/09/1412-01/09/1413, f° 2 r°.
[170] SAB, Stadsrekening 02/09/1412-01/09/1413, f° 91 v°.
[171] J. DUMOLYN, *De Brugse opstand*, p. 141.

to endure the consequences of the teamwork of a greedy duke, a submissive city council and a substantial banker.

4.4.3.2 The Monetary Reforms of 1407 and 1410

On top of the redemption of the city's debts, the Bruges treasurers had some extra troubles in the course of 1407, again involving Dino. The inhabitant of the *Rue de la vieille Monnaie* would cooperate with the establishment of the new money which John the Fearless was about to introduce after seventeen years of monetary stability. First, the duke wanted to increase the price of silver, intending to attract precious metals to the Flemish mints. Then, hoping to make a profit for his costly activities in France, he intended to pusue an increase of the groot's nominal value, maintaining the intrinsic value of the coins at the same level. In April 1407, he presented his plans to the Four Members, who discussed the matter intensively with John's counsellors during the following weeks.[172] Next to the chancellor, Dino Rapondi sat on the ducal side of the negotiation table.[173] An agreement was reached on July 15, 1407, after which production of the new groot could start.

However, the operation resulted in total chaos. The raising of silver prices did not bring as much precious metal to the mints as expected, delaying the coinage until September and bringing too few new coins onto the market, whereupon these were overvalued and disappeared from circulation: here again we must bear in mind Gresham's law.[174] Moreover, the delay and the absence of an official ordinance caused uncertainty in the business world. Debtors, including Bruges, wanted to pay in the old, cheaper coins; creditors wanted to receive in the new, more expensive coins, which slowed down transactions. Finally, the common people understood soon enough that the new groot contained far less silver than the official rates would have them believe and after only two weeks reverted to using the old money.[175] It was one of the few times when a project involving Dino turned out to be a fiasco.[176]

Another monetary failure loomed. John the Fearless had not been at all discouraged at all and launched a new reform in 1410 in order to raise money. The Four Members were not opposed to this plan if they were able to participate in the preparation of the monetary ordinance.[177] In these preparations Dino seems to have played an even more active role than in 1407. For almost two years, from February 1409 until January 1412, he stayed in Flanders "for the fact of the money",[178] six months of which, from February to August 1410, were completely devoted to the negotiations with the Members in Ghent.

---

172 W.P. BLOCKMANS, "La participation des sujets flamands à la politique monétaire des ducs de Bourgogne" in : *Revue belge de numismatique*, 1973, 119, pp. 105-106. Although he agrees on its disastrous outcome, R. DE ROOVER gives a completely different interpretation of the reform. R. DE ROOVER, "The Bruges money market around 1400" in: *Verhandelingen van de Koninklijke Academie voor Wetenschappen, Letteren en Schone Kunsten van België*, Brussel, 1968, 29, p. 67-68.

173 ACO, B 1554, f° 174 r°.

174 Gresham's law implies that the bad money (with a smaller proportion of precious metals) drives the good money (with a higher proportion of precious metals) out of circulation.

175 H. VAN DER WEE, "L'échec de la réforme monétaire de 1407 en Flandre, vu par les marchands italiens de Bruges" in : *Studi in onore de Amintore Fanfani III Medioevo*, Milano, A. Giuffrè, 1962, pp. 583-587.

176 The Nicopolis crusade had been a disaster for the duke, but a triumph for the banker.

177 W.P. BLOCKMANS, *La participation des sujets*, pp. 106-107.

178 ACO, B 1560, f° 232 r°. ADN, B 1894, f° 86 v°. ADN, B 1897, f° 51 r°. ACO, B 1576, f° 218 v°.

He met the deputies of the Four for a first time from February 20 to 23, when they talked about the payment of debts, annuities and farms in the period of the revaluation,[179] something which had caused trouble in 1407. Henri Goethals[180] joined Dino for the talks from March 5 to 19, which led to new agreements concerning the mint and the publication of a new ordinance.[181] Yet, at the beginning of May, Rapondi had to run business alone again, when he had to sound the Members out on an interdiction of the import of foreign coins and they presented him in return with some complaints about the new groot.[182] The negotiations advanced, and Dino asked his interlocutors some weeks later to make the ordinance known and let it take effect on December 25, 1410.[183] He had to repeat his request on about June 20, whereupon the prohibition on the export of precious metals was brought up as well. Consecutively, two more negotiations sufficed to agree on the foreign currencies that the parties would permit in Flanders.[184] Dino and the Members parted for the last time on August 10 after the envoys had been given some advice on the introduction of the new groot.[185]

Despite Rapondi's intensive negotiations and the fact that he even seems to have made his personal financial reserves available to make the operation a success, the operation, which started on Christmas Day 1410, failed again. The nominal increase was again too strong in relation to the coins' intrinsic value, which made the public suspicious of the money. An exhortation to respect the monetary ordinance strictly did not change this state of affairs.[186] All efforts to impose rates which did not respond to economic reality were in vain, also when Dino Rapondi threw his weight onto the scale.

The affair lasted until 1412, when several principalities of the Low Countries, France and England, executed a devaluation. Since their mediocre coins drove the superior Burgundian pieces out of circulation,[187] Dino had to travel again to report an interdiction on this foreign money to the Four Members.[188] However, the next meeting with the Members on monetary policy would take place without him.

4.5 The Final Years of Dino Rapondi's Life

As his work for the monetary reforms already suggested, Dino Rapondi spent the last years of his life mainly in Flanders. With his house in the Naaldenstraat, which he certainly occupied from 1409 on, as headquarters, he concentrated on three big projects, only interrupted by the trip of the

[179] A. ZOETE, *Handelingen*, pp. 427-428.
[180] M. BOONE and J. DUMOLYN, "Henri Goethals, doyen de Liège: Un homme d'église gantois au service des ducs de Bourgogne Jean sans Peur et Philippe le Bon", in: *Publications du Centre Européen d'Études Bourguignonnes (XIVe-XVIe s.),* Dijon, 1998, 38, pp. 89-106.
[181] A. ZOETE, *Handelingen*, pp. 431-432.
[182] A. ZOETE, *Handelingen*, pp. 445-446.
[183] A. ZOETE, *Handelingen*, pp. 454-455.
[184] A. ZOETE, *Handelingen*, pp. 464-471.
[185] A. ZOETE, *Handelingen*, pp. 608-610.
[186] W.P. BLOCKMANS, *La participation des sujets*, p. 108.
[187] W.P. BLOCKMANS, *La participation des sujets*, p. 110.
[188] ACO, B 1576, f° 219 v°. C. DE BORCHGRAEVE, *Diplomaten*, p. 336.

Burgundian envoys to the council of Pisa in 1409-1410.[189] Besides the financing of ducal operations in the Civil War, for which he cooperated closely with his brother Jacopo in Paris, and his occupation in the monetary field, he was principally active in the regency council of Philip of Charolais.

Despite his constant presence in France, where the struggle for power took precedence, John the Fearless agreed to Flemish demands, for whom the relationship between prince and subjects had always been much more important than in the other Burgundian regions, by leaving his son, the future Philip the Good, in Ghent. Philip actually ruled the county from 1411 on, replacing his father. The inexperienced Philip was assisted by the chancellor and a regular regency council, occupied by various of the duke's counsellors.[190] The settlement of financial and economic questions in Flanders relied on John the Fearless's old banker Rapondi being part of the council.[191] Such an economic question was the status of merchants from Portugal, not unimportant for Flemish trade. Dino was one of the counsellors who confirmed the Portuguese privileges on December 26, 1411[192] and dealt with these matters again in May 1414.[193]

Could Dino Rapondi have really been of any use to Philip of Charolais? The years had started to add up for the Lucchese. According to Vaughan, he had only been able to travel in a carriage since 1402[194] and if we can believe the 15th-century doctor Jacques Sacquépée, he was already suffering from a disease of the bladder. Consequently it is not surprising that a certain Gilles Cousin released him in 1407 from the execution of his will, "taking into consideration his high age and weakness".[195] That Dino's weak health got worse during the following years is proved by his will of February 24, 1413. In view of his activities in Flanders and the state of war in France, it is remarkable he did this in Paris, before the notaries of the Châtelet. Perhaps the pause in the conflict between Bourguignons and Armagnacs in 1413 had encouraged him to return to the French capital, which after his banishment from Lucca had always been his second home, far more than Bruges. Possibly for the same reason, he wanted to be buried in Paris, in the chapel of Sainte Anne in the Augustines church, dressed in a habit of the order. Nevertheless, he still foresaw some work in Flanders, since he added that the *Volto Santo* chapel in Bruges Augustinian church had to serve as a final resting place in case death surprised him there.

After the choice of his burial place, an impressive list of legacies follows, illustrating his wealth and in which the absence of the Burgundian duke is especially remarkable. The French king's immeasurable treasury was enriched by exactly 16 s. par. In a religious flickering, typical of merchants in the face of death,[196] a series of churches, abbeys and charitable institutions, mainly in Lucca

---

[189] R.H. BAUTIER and J. SORNAY, *Les sources de l'histoire économique et sociale du Moyen Âge. 2 : Les États de la maison de Bourgogne. Vol. I Archives centrales de l'État bourguignon (1384-1500). Archives des principautés territoriales*, Paris, CNRS Editions, 2001, p. 53.

[190] R. VAUGHAN, *John the Fearless*, pp. 153-155.

[191] P. de LICHTERVELDE, *Un Grand Commis*, p. 194.

[192] J.-M. CAUCHIES, *Ordonnances*, pp. 253-259.

[193] J. PAVIOT, *Portugal et Bourgogne au XVe siècle (1384-1482) : recueil de documents extraits des archives bourguignonnes*, Paris, Centre culturel Calouste Gulbenkian, 1995, p 176.

[194] R. VAUGHAN, *Philip the Bold*, p. 221.

[195] L. MIROT, *La société des Raponde*, p. 376.

[196] For this, see J. CHIFFOLEAU, *La comptabilité de l'Au-delà. Les hommes, la mort et la religion dans la région d'Avignon à la fin du Moyen Age (vers 1320- vers 1480)*, Rome, École Française de Rome, 1980, pp. 209-425. (Collection de l'École Française de Rome, 47).

and France, were to enjoy an inheritance from "that big usurer", as historian Adriaan de But from the Dunes Abbey once called him. To be absolutely sure he would get into heaven, Rapondi also left 240 lb. par. for thirty Gregorian masses, 1000 requiem masses, and a pilgrimage each to Saint Jacob of Compostella, Rome and Jerusalem in his *comptabilité de l'Au-delà.* After these came the less Christian stipulations concerning his nephew Giovanni[197] and the sums for his staff and the young marriageable girls from his family. All these instructions were executed punctually by his brothers Jacopo, who inherited all his possessions in Paris, Andrea and Filippo. The latter received all Dino's goods in Bruges, 3200 lb. par. for his sons Jacopo and Dino, named after his uncle, and 800 lb. par. to find husbands for his daughters Caterina and Luisa. Other testamentary executors were Dino's faithful factor Francesco Accettanti, his cousin Paulo Buzzolini and his second cousin Jacopo di Giovanni.[198]

Dino Rapondi's statue in the Sainte Chapelle in Dijon
(Paris, Bibliothèque de l'Arsenal, Ms. 3901, c. 22)

Less than two years later, Dino's will would be executed. He died on February 1, 1415 in Bruges,[199] in ducal harness as he had been for most of his business life.[200] Some days later he was buried, not as he had asked in the

[197] See *supra.*
[198] A. TUETEY (ed.), *Testaments*, pp. 553-562.
[199] J. GAILLARD (ed.), *Inscriptions funéraires*, p. 160.
[200] ADN, B 4088, f° 153 v°.

Augustinian church, but in the majestic Saint Donatian's cathedral, perhaps as a last honour from his employer. Rapondi had left the settlement of his funeral and everything that came after in his will to his relatives and they spared neither trouble nor expense.

A month after the death of his brother, Filippo appeared at the Saint Donatian's chapter to make the necessary arrangements.[201] The first of these concerned the erection of a blue tombstone against the middle of the back wall of the chapel of Saint John the Baptist, the patron saint of the Lucchese. The monument was adorned with the Rapondi family arms and an epitaph which emphasized the origin and the accomplishments of the deceased.[202] A tile with another Latin inscription decorated the opposite wall.[203] Both stones left sufficient space for the future tombs of Filippo and his descendants in the chapel, where no one could be buried without the family's approval. Somewhat further from the burial place, a stained-glass window high in the nave of the church was to keep the banker's memory alive.

Filippo also discussed aspects of Dino's commemoration other than the ones in stone and glass with the canons. The result was one of the most extensive foundations in Saint Donatian's *Acta Capituli*, befitting the wealth of the deceased merchant. For example, an eternal requiem mass was to be celebrated in the chapel of Saint John the Baptist by one of the five vicars each day after communion. On the date of Dino's death each year, the canons were to sing a remembrance mass. During this service, accompanied from the beginning to the Agnus Dei by bell-chiming, two large lights would burn on Rapondi's grave, ten small ones on the ceiling and two small ones on the altar of the chapel, as well as three ponds of candles. In particular on May 6, the name-day of Saint John, the chapter had work to do. On the eve of the feast the sexton was to open the chapel and decorate it with herbs, gold cloth and silk. On the day itself, a vicar and six altar boys, joined by an organ player and his prompter, would sing a polyphonic mass. Finally, this would be followed by a solemn celebration in the choir of the cathedral.[204] For these services, which are listed on Dino's death day as well as on May 6 in the church's obituary,[205] all involved would be compensated with 9 lb. gr. and the chapter receiving 200 lb. gr., with which it could buy an annuity.[206]

Dino's commemoration was not only cherished in Bruges. In Dijon, in the *Sainte Chapelle* of the dukes, whom the Lucchese had served his whole life, a statue was erected showing Rapondi, kneeling with bare head and folded hands. However, following the French Revolution, the new owner of the chapel of the dukes in Dijon made sure to demolish the monument to the "fanatic imbecile, called the Burgundian merchant",[207] while the new French prefect who governed the Départment de la Lys had the whole of Saint Donatian's church in Bruges razed to the ground.

---

[201] BAB, Acta Capituli 1414-1438, f° 12 r°.
[202] See annexes.
[203] V. VERMEERSCH (ed.), *Grafmonumenten, te Brugge voor 1578*, Brugge, Raaklijn, 1976, p. 117.
[204] BAB, Acta Capituli 1414-1438, f° 38 r°.
[205] L. GILLIODTS-VAN SEVEREN, "L' Obituaire de Saint-Donatien de Bruges" in : *Bulletin de la Commission Royale d'Histoire*, Bruxelles, 1889, 16, pp. 329, 335.
[206] BAB, Acta Capituli 1414-1438, f° 38 r°.
[207] L. MIROT, *La société des Raponde*, p. 304.

CHAPTER 5

THE FADING OF A TRIANGULAR RELATIONSHIP (1415-1430)

5.1 The Bruges Branch under Filippo Rapondi: a New Course or Business as Usual?

Dino's death must have represented a major transition for the Rapondi company. It was such a transition that historians usually speak of the periods before and after 1415 or, to be more accurate, they do not speak of a period after 1415 at all.[1] However, some of the most important developments for the firm's history did take place without the celebrated manager at its head. Those were mainly taken care of by Dino's brother Filippo, who took charge of the family's business in Bruges. Active in Flanders since the middle of the 1390s, having been involved in the company's largest undertakings, such as Nicopolis and Liège, and having led several of these operations himself, the business could hardly be called new to him. As had happened before, when Guglielmo and Dino took over the firm's direction,[2] some sweeping changes in its policy occurred after Filippo had settled into the manager's seat. Although they had to do with different aspects of the company's business, these changes seem to have had a common factor. All of them, to a certain extent, led to a reduction in risks and an increase in security. Now this was something new for a firm that had participated in some of the most financially hazardous operations in Burgundian history.

5.1.1 Changing the Firm Structure

As Dino had stipulated in his will,[3] his brother Jacopo, supported by his nephew Guidotto,[4] took over his possessions and activities in Paris[5] and Filippo was to conduct business in Bruges. Both maintained very close contacts and regularly informed each other of economic and political developments in a continuous stream of letters.[6] Yet, unlike in the previous period, they seem to have worked independently from each other, each having his own juridically autonomous firm. The coordinating direction that Dino had provided for thirty years by constantly travelling between the company's branches, albeit residing more permanently in Flanders for the last five years of his life,[7] was missing. According to John F. Padgett, the company had already been split into two

[1] Léon Mirot, for example, devotes more than seventy pages of his article on the firm to Dino and only four to the period after his death.
[2] See *supra*.
[3] See *supra*.
[4] L. GALOPPINI, *Mercanti toscani e Bruges nel Tardo Medioevo*, Universiteit Gent, unpublished PhD dissertation, 2002-2003, p. 173. In 1418, Jacopo and Guidotto swore fealty to John the Fearless and in 1419, they were part of an embassy sent by Philip the Good to the English king Henry V. P. BONENFANT, *Du meurtre de Montereau au traité de Troyes*, Bruxelles, Académie Royale de Belgique, 1958, pp. 39-40. (Mémoires, 52).
[5] He would do this until his death in 1432. See, for example, J. FAVIER (ed.), *Les contribuables parisiens à la fin de la Guerre de Cent Ans. Les rôles d'impôt de 1421, 1423 et 1438*, Genève, Librairie Droz, 1970, p. 18.
[6] E. LAZZARESCHI and L. MIROT (eds.), "Lettere di Mercanti Lucchesi da Bruges e da Parigi" in: *Bollettino Storico Lucchese*, Lucca, 1929, 1, pp. 165-199.
[7] See *supra*.

separate entities in 1396, since the consular register of the Lucchese merchant guild of that year mentions a firm led by Dino in Paris and one directed by his second cousin Jacopo di Giovanni in Bruges.[8] Nevertheless, there was no question of splitting up in this case, as Jacopo di Giovanni's business house had always been a completely independent firm with its headquarters in Lucca.[9] Its presence in Bruges was only a temporary measure, probably to help out the partnership of the Rapondi brothers, which remained intact. The latter was clearly not the case in 1415, corresponding with a more general trend in the world of commerce at the end of the fourteenth and the beginning of the fifteenth century. To protect themselves against growing risks and insecurity in international trade, many firms developed from centralised, unitary entities (with the super companies of the Bardi and the Peruzzi as most distinct examples)[10] into decentralised bodies consisting of juridically separated components (with the fifteenth-century Medici as the prototype).[11] Whereas the bankruptcy of one branch could throw the whole company into crisis in the first case, in the second case the firm's other branches would be relatively unaffected.[12] In this respect, Filippo and Jacopo conducted a more secure policy than Dino had ever done.

5.1.2 Changing Alliances

5.1.2.1 The Duke's Three Lucchese

In 1417 Filippo Rapondi, Bartolomeo Bettini and Marco Guidiccioni issued a loan to John the Fearless.[13] Each of the three money-lenders was a Lucchese banker and silk merchant, as well as a *maître d'hôtel* and a counsellor in the ducal household. Working closely together, they would be responsible for the final years of Lucchese predominance in ducal finance, although each also did business on his own account. However, their relations with the Rapondi family were not new, on the contrary. Guidiccioni, active in Bruges from 1393 onwards,[14] had been appointed as one of the executors of Dino's will in 1413, and Bettini, who had been present in Flanders from 1397 onwards,[15] even owed his ducal career to the famous Lucchese. He had worked as a clerk for the eldest Rapondi brother in 1413,[16] had transported marten furs and pieces of damask cloth to John the Fearless's chamberlain for him[17] and had sent money in cash to the duke on the battlefields of France together with him.[18] Yet, while it is clear that Dino was in charge when doing business with Guidiccioni and Bettini, Filippo's partnership with them was more based on equality. He even left the

[8] P.D. MCLEAN and J.F. PADGETT, "Organizational Invention and Elite Transformation: the Birth of Partnership Systems in Renaissance Florence" in: *American Journal of Sociology*, 2006, 111, s.p.
[9] See *supra*.
[10] For them, see E.S. HUNT, *The medieval super-companies*, passim.
[11] See R. DE ROOVER, *The rise and decline of the Medici bank, 1397-1494*, Cambridge (Masachusetts), Harvard University Press, 1963, 500 p.
[12] E.S. HUNT and J.M. MURRAY, *A history of business*, pp. 154-156.
[13] M. MOLLAT (ed.), *Comptes généraux de l'État bourguignon*, p. 240.
[14] LAZZARESCHI (ed.), *Libro della Communitá*, p. 192.
[15] LAZZARESCHI (ed.), *Libro della Communitá*, p. 251.
[16] ADN, B 1903, f° 184 r°.
[17] ACO, B 1576, f° 176 r°.
[18] ADN, B 1903, f° 139 r°.

initiative, and the bulk of the risks, to Guidiccioni, often considered as the true successor of Dino Rapondi.[19]

With Bartolomeo Bettini, Filippo lent more than 800 lb. gr. to the duke.[20] When the ducal administration was in need of money, both galloped to Lille to make themselves available to the duke's functionaries[21] or profitably sold spices on credit to the receiver general who then tried to resell them on the spot.[22] Bettini bought annuities in the name of Filippo's daughters[23] and they represented their nation together in its financial dealings with the city of Bruges,[24] informing each other of these and other operations by way of numerous letters.[25] Their bonds were not restricted to bills of exchange and lending contracts. When Bettini died in 1420, it was Filippo who once again visited the Saint Donatian's chapter to arrange his friend's foundation. He thought the canons much too greedy in demanding 10 lb. gr., however, and was only prepared to pay 6 lb. gr.[26] Finally, after an arbitrator had intervened, Rapondi agreed to give them 9 lb. gr.[27] In 1424, Filippo again took care of the late Bettini's interests and made sure Bruges paid its many debts to his former partner's heirs.[28]

Marco Guidiccioni was the third of the duke's three important Lucchese, maintaining close business connections with the other two. In 1420, for example, he and Rapondi sold red baldachin embroidered with Lucchese gold wire to Philip the Good which the duke presented to Saint Peter's church in Ghent upon his Ceremonial Entry.[29] Again, their relations exceeded the world of economic transactions and again, the Saint Donatian's chapter was to play a role in them. Guidiccioni was married to Giovanna, the daughter of Filippo's brother Andrea. When she died, in January 1417, he wanted to give his wife a worthy funeral and ordered the canons of Saint Donatian to ring the bells of the cathedral. Afterwards, she was buried in the chapel of Our Lady he had bought in the church of the Clarissen and had rechristened as the chapel of the Holy Cross.[30] The good relations between Marco Guidiccioni and his in-laws lasted after Giovanna Rapondi's death. When, in 1424, he was arrested in Paris, it was Jacopo Rapondi who paid the pledge to get him freed.[31]

5.1.2.2 When the Old and the New Generations of Ducal Bankers Met

Not all faces were so familiar as those of Marco Guidiccioni and Bartolomeo Bettini. Filippo would engage in business with the Medici, the

---

[19] C. DE SMET, *Les emprunts de Philippe le Bon, d'après les comptes de la recette générale de l'État bourguignon*, Université de Lille, unpublished master's thesis, 1956, p. 149. L. GALOPPINI, *Mercanti toscani*, p. 183.
[20] C. DE SMET, *Les emprunts*, p. 148.
[21] ADN, B 1903, f° 218 v°. For the corresponding remuneration, see ACO, B 1903, f° 153 r°.
[22] C. DE SMET, *Les emprunts*, p. 36.
[23] ADN, B 4086, f° 22 v°.
[24] SAB, Stadsrekening 02/09/1415-01/09/1416, f° 23 v°.
[25] E. LAZZARESCHI and L. MIROT, *Lettere di Mercanti Lucchesi*, p. 184.
[26] BAB, Acta Capituli 1414-1438, f° 94 v°.
[27] BAB, Acta Capituli 1414-1438, f° 102 v°.
[28] SAB, Stadsrekening 02/09/1424-02/09/1425, f° 37 v°.
[29] L. MIROT, *La société des Raponde*, p. 387.
[30] L. GALOPPINI, *Mercanti toscani*, p. 346.
[31] L. MIROT, "Les Isbarre, monnayeurs royaux, Augustin Isbarre" in: *Bibliothèque de l'Ecole des Chartes*, Paris, 1927, 88, p. 307.

Florentine firm that would dominate ducal banking and international trade in years to come but at that time did not yet have a permanent branch in Bruges. In the meantime, the company worked with changing correspondents, one of whom presumably was Filippo Rapondi.[32] In the course of 1415, he was sent some extra funds by the firm's representative in Lübeck, Lodovico Baglioni, as the 228 lb. he had at his disposal was not enough to execute the transactions his principals expected of him.[33] One year later, Rapondi would receive 2350 Rhenish florins from German merchants resident in Bruges in the name of the Florentines, a sum the Medici factors had lent to ambassadors from Lübeck and the Hanseatic League attending the council of Constance some time before.[34] Notwithstanding the fact that rendering services to other firms was not uncommon in Italian merchant communities, this is the first time in the Rapondis' history that we see one of its members working on the account of another.

5.1.3 Changing Investment Patterns

In around 1415, Filippo used the family's capital to make some remarkable investments. He bought a piece of land of 111 roods on the northern side of the Naaldenstraat in Bruges, opposite the house of his late compatriot Paulo Domaschi, for 8 lb. 7 s. gr. The plot was to be used by Rapondi and his heirs for all time and it made it necessary to enlarge his adjacent mansion and give it a new façade. This was the house he had inherited in 1415 from Dino, who had lived there during the last years of his life.[35] Filippo went on to spend the considerable amount of 2800 ecus on the so-called 'right of two groot'. This was a tax of two groot on every sealed piece of cloth produced in the Flemish town of Wervik, to be paid by the merchant-entrepreneurs to the count. Despite the protests of the inhabitants that this tax could not be alienated, Rapondi obtained the right from John the Fearless, and granted it to his daughters Caterina and Luisa, who would enjoy it for the rest of their lives.[36]

In both cases, the family opted for large but secure investments with little risk involved but with little profit-gaining capacity either. Dino had acquired property like this as well. From 1387 until 1403, he had enjoyed the usufruct of the domain of Knesselare[37] and from 1394 on he had possessed the rights to be paid on the loading of ballast in all ships in the harbour of Sluis,[38] which were transferred to Filippo for the sake of his son Jacopo later on.[39] Still, both privileges had been bestowed on the Rapondi by Philip the Bold and although they may have served as a pledge for unrepaid loans by the family,[40]

---

[32] It would only open its first office in Bruges in 1439. R. DE ROOVER, *The Rise and Decline*, pp. 317-325.

[33] ASF, MAP 83, n° 51, c. 312.

[34] *Codex Diplomaticus Lubecensis. Lübeckisches Urkundenbuch. 1ste Abteilung. Urkundenbuch der Stadt Lübeck. Fünfter Theil*, Lübeck, Ferdinand Grautoff, 1877, pp. 633-634.

[35] SAB, Stadsrekening 02/09/1415-01/09/1416, f° 11 r°. See also J. MARECHAL, *Bijdrage tot de geschiedenis van het bankwezen*, pp. 84-85.

[36] ADN, B 4088, f° 22 v°. See also I. VANDECANDELAERE, *De lakennijverheid te Wervik : een prosopografisch overzicht (1382-1470)*, Universiteit Gent, unpublished master's thesis, 2001-2002, pp. 65-70.

[37] T. SOENS, *De rentmeesters van de graaf van Vlaanderen. Beheer en beheerders van het grafelijk domein in de late middeleeuwen*, Brussel, Paleis der Academiën, 2002, p. 283. (Verhandelingen van de Koninklijke Vlaamse Academie van België voor Wetenschappen en Kunsten, Nieuwe reeks, nr. 9).

[38] T. SOENS, *De rentmeesters van de graaf van Vlaanderen*, p. 317.

[39] ADN, B 4088, f° 32 v°.

[40] T. SOENS, *De rentmeesters van de graaf van Vlaanderen*, p. 83.

they had not been deliberate purchases. Dino's houses in Paris, on the other hand, clearly were. His mansion in the *Rue de la Vieille Monnaie* was one of the most luxurious of the capital[41] and must have cost a fortune. The point, however, is that this showpiece was bought in a period in which the Rapondi invested far larger amounts of money in high-risk ventures, notably finance and international trade, and that such real estate had to serve these ever-increasing financial and commercial interests. This was not exactly the case in 1415.

The Rapondis' commercial activities did not change radically after Dino's death. They remained what they had always been since the middle of the 1390s: the sideline of a firm that focused primarily on finance and banking.[42] Filippo managed to sell a grey horse[43] and some luxuries such as a feathered hat, a belt[44] and some pieces of satin and velvet[45] to the duke, and six large oak beams to the city of Bruges.[46] Much more important were the changes the new manager would bring about in the relations that had made up the core of his family's business for decades.

Between 1416 and 1419, the Rapondi, who for more than thirty years had been involved in almost every financial contribution from the city to the duke, would not transfer a single penny from Bruges to John the Fearless, nor would they advance the money.[47] Only in 1415 did Filippo enable the Bruggelings to rent the prince's seventh penny by providing them with 400 lb. gr. in exchange.[48] After that, four of the city's *aides* went through without any participation from the Rapondi.[49] As their collaboration with Bettini and Guidiccioni illustrated, they did still lend to John the Fearless, for example 10 000 lb. on the revenues of the 1417 *aide*.[50] The link with their activities in Bruges, however, was no longer apparent in the city accounts. Exactly this interaction, with the city using the Rapondi when addressing the prince because of their position and inside knowledge at the court and, vice versa, the duke resorting to them when dealing with the city-dwellers because of their position with the city, had secured the company's success for all these years.

In 1419-1420, the financial relations between the Rapondi, the city and the duke resumed, brought back together for the first time in five years by the seventh penny. Bruges rented this tax from Philip the Good but had promised to pay back advances made by money-lenders to the duke on its revenues. As Filippo was one of the most frequent to do the latter, a large share of the urban revenues went into his pocket.[51] Rapondi's most important financial achievement concerning the city and the duke, which can stand comparison with those of his brother, took place in 1424. Bruges paid the last instalment of its

---

[41] See *supra*.
[42] See *supra*.
[43] ADN, B 1903, f° 152 r°.
[44] ADN, B 4086, f° 191 r°.
[45] ADN, B 4086, f° 134 v°.
[46] SAB, Stadsrekening 02/09/1417-01/09/1418, f° 65 v°.
[47] See annexes.
[48] SAB, Stadsrekening 02/09/1415-01/09/1416, f° 114 v°.
[49] A. ZOETE, *Organisatie en betekenis van de beden. Band 2*, pp. 145-146.
[50] A. ZOETE, *De beden in het graafschap Vlaanderen*, p. 145.
[51] SAB, Stadsrekening 02/09/1419-01/09/1420, f° 57 v°, 59 r°, 127 r°-v°. SAB, Stadsrekening 02/09/1420-01/09/1421, f° 39 r°, 56 r°, 112 v°, 115 v°. SAB, Stadsrekening 02/09/1421-01/09/1422, f° 39 r°. SAB, Stadsrekening 02/09/1422-01/09/1423, f° 51 v°, 92 r°. SAB, Stadsrekening 02/09/1423-01/09/1424, f° 21 v°, 100 v°-101 r°. SAB, Stadsrekening 02/09/1424-01/09/1425, f° 37 v°, 52 r°, 53 v°. SAB, Stadsrekening 02/09/1425-01/09/1426, f° 48 v°. SAB, Stadsrekening 02/09/1426-01/09/1427, f° 48 v°-49 r°. SAB, Stadsrekeningen 02/09/1427-01/09/1428, f° 42 v°.

share of 49 494 lb. 7 s. 6 d. par. in the 150 000 ecus à la couronne *aide* the Four Members had granted to Philip the Good in 1421 for his Ceremonial Entry, the purchase of Namur and Béthune and the war efforts in France.[52] The city transferred the whole of this sum, 12 000 lb. par. or 1000 lb. gr., to Filippo, who had advanced it earlier to the duke.[53] Still supplying funds to the court independently from their connection with Bruges as well,[54] the Rapondi seemed to be back in business. Immediately afterwards, however, their loans to Philip the Good stopped completely. Characteristic of the close coherence with their activities in the city, the family's financial contacts with Bruges came to a standstill two years later,[55] this time forever.

5.1.4 Changing the Firm's Policy: an Explanation

Filippo Rapondi gave the company a more modest structure, left business initiatives to others, Lucchese or Florentine, invested the family's money in houses and annuities and reduced its involvement in ducal and urban finance until nothing of this remained: in a period of scarcely ten years, he had expelled almost every risk from the policies of a firm that for three decades had earned its living with hazardous undertakings. The question arises whether he did this deliberately, out of free will or by force. Which elements can have urged Filippo's decisions? As the Rapondis' resumption of financial transactions in 1419-1420 more or less coincides with the accession to the throne of duke Philip the Good, personal resentment between Filippo and Philip's predecessor John the Fearless could have caused the interruption of operations in the previous four years. Yet, during the same period, the Rapondi continued to issue loans to the court independent of their contacts with Bruges and to act as the duke's *maître d'hôtel* and counsellor.[56] Besides, this explanation does not hold for the definitive end of the financial enterprise in 1424.

Thinking about Bruges, the other factor in the Rapondis' success story, the way it was treated by John the Fearless and Dino around 1410[57] is brought to mind. Had the financial stranglehold imposed upon the city by the duke and the banker seriously mortgaged its ability to pay during the following years? Yet, everything points to the fact that Bruges continued to honour its financial obligations to John the Fearless without interruption,[58] though without the participation of the Rapondi. Had bad experiences with Dino caused the city to dissociate itself from the family and hire other financiers? If so, it is strange that it went to exactly the same kind of bankers with similar ties to the duke, such as Marco Guidiccioni. Moreover, trouble with Bruges, as well as with John the Fearless, does not explain why a company changed its structure.

Can Filippo's decisions have been inspired by increased competition with other bankers? We should be aware of the resurgence of the Florentines on

---

[52] A. ZOETE, *Organisatie en betekenis van de beden. Band 2*, p. 146.
[53] SAB, Stadsrekening 02/09/1423-01/09/1424, f° 50 r°.
[54] C. DE SMET, *Les emprunts*, p. 148.
[55] Although the repayment of the city's debts to Filippo still dragged on for some years. See SAB, Stadsrekening 02/09/1428-01/09/1429, f° 83 r°. SAB, Stadsrekening 02/09/1429-01/09/1430, f° 84 r°. SAB, Stadsrekening 02/09/1430-01/09/1431, f° 89 v°. SAB, Stadsrekening 02/09/1431-01/09/1432, f° 83 v°. SAB, Stadsrekening 02/09/1432-01/09/1433, f° 25 v°.
[56] See, for example, ADN, B 4088, f° 134 v°.
[57] See *supra*.
[58] A. ZOETE, *Organisatie en betekenis van de beden. Band 2*, pp. 145-146.

the Bruges market in the course of the 1420s, also bearing in mind the Rapondis' collaboration with the Medici in 1416.[59] Nevertheless, the Florentine firms only really start participating in Burgundian finance in the 1430s at the earliest. The same goes for the Genoese,[60] the Lombards[61] and other groups. Significantly, Filippo's share in the financial affairs of Philip the Good was not taken over by unknown merchants from other regions but by his direct business partner and compatriot Marco Guidiccioni,[62] which makes the assertion of fierce competition rather implausible.

The fact that it was one of his closest friends and associates who inherited his role in finance and, more generally, the absence of any form of constraint suggest that Filippo's attempts to reduce risks and, in the end, his withdrawal from banking and trade were made of his own free will. Elements in his correspondence with friends and colleagues lead to the same conclusion. Although we do not know to what extent his words were sincere, in his letter to Guido da Pietrasanta, dated June 3, 1418, he wrote that he and his brother "wanted to discharge themselves from a lot of things and live more quietly".[63]

Filippo clearly suited his actions to these words and in doing so he was not an exception in the commercial world. The famous historian Henri Pirenne stated that after two, at most three generations, most merchant families give up their hazardous profession and engage in less risky and more honorary activities, buying an office or investing in real estate, a theory which, sometimes in a slightly modified form, has been endorsed by dozens of scholars.[64] Although Pirenne's periodization does not apply to the Rapondi and the switch rather takes place within a generation, Filippo did what all these others had done: after he and his brothers had travelled the whole of Europe and had participated in every possible venture for more than fifty years, he considered the risks no longer worth pursuing the enlargement of the family's capital and decided instead to secure it.

Yet, a sentimental argument may have played a role as well. From Filippo's letters it can be concluded that the call of his native town started to sound stronger and stronger, possibly at the expense of his work in Bruges. The merchant was eager to receive news from Lucca and constantly asked his friends to recommend him to the *Commune*,[65] which had banished his family in 1392. In this respect it is no surprise to see him present at the first political meeting in the city after the overthrow of the Guinigi rule, in 1431.[66] The only Rapondi brother who had been able to return to his native ground in almost forty years died some months later.

---

[59] See *supra*.
[60] C. DE SMET, *Les emprunts*, pp. 149-152.
[61] C. DE SMET, *Les emprunts*, pp. 121-124.
[62] C. DE SMET, *Les emprunts*, p. 148.
[63] E. LAZZARESCHI and L. MIROT (eds.), *Lettere di Mercanti Lucchesi*, p. 185.
[64] See F. BRAUDEL, *Civilisation matérielle, Économie et Capitalisme. XVe-XVIIIe siècle. Tome 2. Les jeux de l'échange*, Paris, Librairie Armand Colin, 1979, pp. 426-429.
[65] E. LAZZARESCHI and L. MIROT (eds.), *Lettere di Mercanti Lucchesi*, p. 194.
[66] M.E. BRATCHEL, *Lucca 1430 – 1494, the reconstruction of an Italian city-republic*, Oxford, Clarendon Press, 1995, p. 118.

PART 3

BANKERS WITHOUT A DUKE (1430-1470)

CHAPTER 6

RAPONDI: THE NEXT GENERATION

At the end of 1432, some weeks after Jacopo had died as well, Philip the Good held a memorial service for the four Rapondi brothers[1] who had served him, his father and his grandfather so well. The mass marked the end of an exceptional generation of ducal bankers, who had played an indispensable role in the formation of the Burgundian state during the previous forty-five years. Yet, as these busy occupations were abandoned towards the end of their carreers, what was left for their offspring to accomplish? Filippo and his wife Jacoba Antelminelli had three sons and two daughters, and all lived the kind of life children of burnt-out merchant families were supposed to live, according to Pirenne's theory. All but one of them seem to have been piloted into this by their father.

Jacopo, born in Flanders, was Filippo's oldest son and headed the *parentado* from 1431 on. One year after his father's death, he acquired Bruges citizenship,[2] which gave him access to a range of local political offices and local and regional trading systems. Moreover, while foreigner law had always sufficed to furnish his family's business with legal security, citizenship enabled him to resort to Flemish juridical courts, which may indicate that activities in Bruges had become more important to him than international trade. Correspondingly, we only see him conclude a transaction with an international dimension once, when he transferred funds from London to Venice with Niccolò Burlamacchi in 1438.[3] A more substantial source of income was probably what his father had provided him with, the rights he possessed on the loading of ballast in the port of Sluis.[4] Yet, as the partnership with Burlamacchi as well as his marriage to Caterina Tieri[5] demonstrate, the absence of regular commercial long-distance relations does not mean that Jacopo no longer maintained ties with Lucca. In 1439, he even served the town of his ancestors as *Gonfaloniere di Giustizia*,[6] the highest office in the republic. Since he handed over his ballast rights in Flanders in 1447,[7] Italy may also have become a more permanent place of residence during the last years of his life.

The second son, Alessandro, seems to have been introduced into the ecclesiastical administration by his father. In 1422 he was promised a prebend in Saint Donatian's chapter, not yet vacant, by the pope,[8] who shared the appointment of benefices with the local dean. These expectancies were usually granted by the intercession of powerful patrons with whom it was important for

---

[1] L. MIROT, *La société des Raponde*, pp. 388-389.

[2] SAB, Poorterboek 1418-1434, f° 134 r°. SAB, Stadsrekening 02/09/1431-01/09/1432, f° 12 r°. See also A. JAMEES, *Brugse Poorters, opgetekend uit de stadsrekeningen en ingeleid. Deel 2: 1418-1478*, Handzame, Familia et Patria, 1980, p. 111. R.A. PARMENTIER (ed.), *Indices op de Brugsche Poorterboeken*, Brugge, Desclée De Brouwer en Cie, 1938, dl. 1, pp. 162-163.

[3] ABIB, BLon, f° 167.3.

[4] See *supra*.

[5] E. LAZZARESCHI and L. MIROT (eds.), *Lettere di Mercanti Lucchesi*, p. 185.

[6] G. MANSI, *I Patrizi di Lucca. Le antiche famiglie lucchesi ed i loro stemmi*, Lucca, Titania, 1996, p. 412.

[7] G. BIGWOOD, *Le régime juridique et économique Tome I*, p. 666.

[8] BAB, Acta Capituli 1414-1438, f° 122 v°.

the Holy See to maintain good relations,[9] in this case Filippo's employer Philip the Good. As the procedure required it, Alessandro officially informed the chapter of the pope's decision, by procuration of the notary Johannes Scadelin.[10] The registration of this notification in the *Acta Capituli* reveals that Rapondi, like every candidate-canon who wanted to stand a good chance, bore the title of *magister*.[11] As this referred to people who had enjoyed a university education,[12] it implies that he had been deliberately prepared for a career outside the business world. Yet, he fared as did the majority of expectants, who never realized their claim because the chapter resisted the pope's intervention, because others had more effective claims or because new opportunities had arisen during the long waiting period.[13]

Returning to Tuscany even sooner than his brother, Alessandro was probably in the latter case. In 1436 he acted as the Lucchese vicar in the subject town of Pietrasanta,[14] one of the most important and lucrative vicariates in the *contado*. Three years later, he continued his university career at the Studio lucchese, an institution where no teaching took place but whose colleges of doctors examined people who came to Lucca in search of degrees. He was able to obtain a docorate by becoming a member of the college of doctors of canon and civil law, who found it difficult to find sufficient men to examine graduands.[15] Lucca, where he lived with his wife Angela Sergiusti,[16] his children and his female slave,[17] would also be Alessandro's final resting-place. He died on November 11, 1464, buried in the San Agostino church.[18]

Dino, clearly named after his uncle, is the most enigmatic of Filippo's children. We only have one mention of him, yet one with important implications. In 1463, he was one of the ten participants in the jousts organized by the society of the *Witte Beer* in Bruges. Usually, these tournaments were only attended by the Bruges urban nobility but sometimes honoured guests from outside the city, such as members of the ducal family, made their appearance as well.[19] Dino's presence among the latter may indicate that the merchant's son had reached a status which was considered high enough to take part in a typically noble activity. Given his brother's history in ducal service in 1422 and that of his family in general, it is likely that he too had made a career at the duke's court, which settled on a massive scale in Bruges in 1463.[20] However, no evidence of this has been found.[21]

---

[9] R. DE KEYSER, *Het St. Donaaskapittel te Brugge (1350-1450): bijdrage tot de studie van de hogere geestelijkheid tijdens de Late Middeleeuwen*, Katholieke Universiteit Leuven, unpublished PhD dissertation, 1972, vol. 1, pp. 48-87.
[10] On him, see J. MURRAY, *Notaries public in Flanders in the late Middle Ages*, Ann Arbor, Xerox University Microfilms International, 1985, pp. 381-382.
[11] BAB, Acta Capituli 1414-1438, f° 122 v°.
[12] R. DE KEYSER, *Het St. Donaaskapittel te Brugge*, pp. 203-207.
[13] R. DE KEYSER, *Het St. Donaaskapittel te Brugge*, pp. 61-87.
[14] M.E. BRATCHEL, *Lucca 1430 – 1494*, p. 243.
[15] J. DAVIES, "A 'Paper University'? The Studio lucchese, 1369-1487" in: *History of Universities*, Oxford, 1997-1999, 15, pp. 269-271, 282, 306.
[16] E. LAZZARESCHI and L. MIROT (eds.), *Lettere di Mercanti Lucchesi*, p. 185.
[17] M.E. BRATCHEL, *Lucca 1430 – 1494*, p. 281.
[18] L. MIROT, *La société des Raponde*, p. 300.
[19] A. VAN DEN ABEELE, *Het Ridderlijk Gezelschap van de Witte Beer. Steekspelen in Brugge tijdens de late Middeleeuwen*, Brugge, Uitgeverij Walleyn, 2000, pp. 59-70, 115-118.
[20] E. VAN DEN NESTE, *Tournois, joutes, pas d'armes*, p. 326.
[21] An analysis of the Prosopographia Burgundica database of the Deutsches Historisches Institut in Paris, containing the *écroes* of the several courts under Philip the Good and Charles the Bold did not yield any result.

Filippo Rapondi also had two daughters, Caterina and Luisa. In 1415 he had bought the rights of two groot on the cloth production in Wervik for both girls to enjoy for the rest of their lives. These revenues remained under the control of their father until they were marriageable.[22] On April 22, 1419, a proud Filippo celebrated the engagement of his daughters with two Lucchese-born businessmen active in Bruges, the marriages to take place within a year. Caterina went to Michele Burlamacchi, Luisa would have Lorenzo Trenta as her husband.[23] However, conjugal bliss was very short-lived in the latter case, as Luisa died on March 18, 1431. Her share in the Wervik rights returned to the duke, who gave it to her uncle Jacopo di Guido in recognition of services rendered. Caterina enjoyed her marriage and her income until her death on October 20, 1470.[24]

Two things become apparent looking at the lives of Filippo's children. First, the fact that their family's town of origin had become accessible again for the first time in a very long period, not only affected their father. Despite some indications of integration into the Bruges social fabric, at least two of them seem to have returned to Lucca. Second, their evolution from active merchants towards a more bourgeois life, initiated by Filippo, continued. While Jacopo and Alessandro collected offices, Caterina and Luisa lived on their private means and Dino even competed with the nobility, very little evidence of commercial or financial dealings remains. Yet, this period did not distinguish itself from the previous ones because of the absence of business activities. Trade and banking transactions would still keep the family busy, though not the part of the family that one would expect. The prevailing difference with the previous decades, however, is that these transactions would no longer take place with the involvement of the duke, who had been the determining factor in the financial and commercial success in the past. In this respect, the post-1430 years bear remarkable resemblances to what had happened before 1369.

---

[22] I. VANDECANDELAERE, *De lakennijverheid te Wervik*, pp. 67-68.
[23] E. LAZZARESCHI and L. MIROT (eds.), *Lettere di Mercanti Lucchesi*, p.
[24] I. VANDECANDELAERE, *De lakennijverheid te Wervik*, pp. 67-68.

CHAPTER 7

GOFFREDO RAPONDI: A MERCHANT IN SEARCH OF A PRIVILEGED RELATIONSHIP

In January 1445, Johan Reppin, the Grand Merchant of the German Order, left for Bruges. The purpose of his journey was to solve some problems caused by the fraudulent behaviour of one of the Order's representatives, Thomas Shenkendorf. Having arrived in Flanders, however, the Grand Merchant discovered that Shenkendorf's victims had a different idea of problem-solving than what he had in mind. "Yesterday morning, when I was to enter the church", he wrote home, "two Lombards approached me and had me arrested, as if I was a criminal, forcing me to look for a pledge". One of these two Lombards was the Lucchese Goffredo Rapondi. He and his partner Carlo Gigli[1] had sold silks for 260 lb. gr. to Thomas Shenkendorf, who had fled from the city without having paid them. By arresting his superior, the two merchants hoped to be compensated for their loss. After the affair had been brought before the Bruges magistracy, a juridical battle dragged on for nearly two years. Only in January 1447, did the aldermen decide that Johan Reppin could not be held responsible for the crimes committed by his representative.[2]

The Grand Merchant's story shows that fifteen years after the death of Filippo, the Rapondi were still conducting trade on the Bruges market. Not Jacopo, Alessandro or any of his other children followed in their father's commercial footsteps but Goffredo, son of Giovanni di Jacopo and Filippo's third cousin. Just as his grandfather had done with his father,[3] he must have been sent to his relatives in Bruges to learn the profession with his brother Gherardo, who probably ran errands for Dino in 1415.[4] Making use of the Rapondi brothers' clientele, such as the duke of Burgundy in 1417,[5] and their partners, such as Bernardo Bettini - brother of Bartolomeo - in 1423,[6] they would take their own first steps in business. Ten years later, the economic reputation of the illustrous Rapondi family was theirs to defend.

---

[1] On Gigli, see C.H. CLOUGH, "Three Gigli of Lucca in England during the Fifteenth and Early Sixteenth Centuries: Diversification in a Family of Mercery Merchants" in: *The Ricardian. Journal of the Richard III Society*, London, 2003, 13, pp. 121-147.

[2] J. SARNOWSKY, "Der Fall Thomas Schenkendorf. Rechtliche und diplomatische Probleme um die Königsberger Grosschäfferei des Deutschen Ordens" in: *Jahrbuch für die Geschichte Mittel- und Ostdeutschlands*, München, 1995, 43, pp. 187-206.

[3] See *supra*.

[4] M. MOLLAT (ed.), *Comptes généraux de l'État bourguignon*, p. 247.

[5] M. MOLLAT (ed.), *Comptes généraux de l'État bourguignon*, p. 65-66. Is it a coincidence that the one to receive the duke's purchase, Bartolomeo Bettini, was a close connection as well ?

[6] SAB, Cartularium Groenenbouc A, f° 137 r°. See also L. GILLIODTS-VAN SEVEREN, *Inventaire des archives. Tome deuxième*, Bruges, Louis de Plancke, 1871-1878, p. 323.

7.1 Bruges: the Node in Goffredo's Network

Bruges was to remain the node of the Rapondis' business network. Certainly from 1423 on, Goffredo owned a house in the city's Sint Jacob's district.[7] Apart from some time in 1450, when it seems to have been confiscated[8] and Rapondi was probably forced to rent property from his personnel,[9] the mansion served as headquarters for his commercial activities as well as those of fellow Lucchese. After having directed these activities with his brother Gherardo for some time,[10] Goffredo continued alone, supported by factors recruited from among his younger compatriots.

One of the Lucchese employed in this way was his distant relative Martin Cenami.[11] In the period before 1452, he made payments and received funds for Rapondi and watched over his boss's interests and belongings when he was absent. In exchange, Cenami received a salary and was given accomodation, either in his employer's house, where he could eat and stable his horse, or in a hostel paid by the company. After having done this job for at least eight and a half years, the factor seems to have been promoted to become a partner in the business. In order to strengthen their commercial ties, Goffredo allowed Cenami to marry his daughter Caterina and made all possible efforts to make the union work. He spent 700 lb. gr. to present her with a respectable dowry and, as bride and groom were relatives, obtained the papal dispensation. Yet, the marriage bond did not prevent the merchant and his son-in-law from falling out. Numerous differences had arisen between Rapondi and Cenami concerning commercial as well as matrimonial issues. These were only solved thanks to the judgement of the Bruges bench of aldermen, pronounced in October 1452.[12]

Francesco Micheli, originating from Lucca as well, was Goffredo's other factor. Already maintaining close commercial relations with him the year before,[13] he was certainly in Rapondi's service in 1439.[14] At some point, however, he must have joined the business of his brother Nicolo and the Borromei, which perhaps caused his former employer to hire Martin Cenami instead. Francesco's new job would not prevent him from having to deal with Rapondi, much of which would take place, again, in court.[15] In one case, dated 1436, Giovanni Arnolfini is also referred to as a factor.[16] If this assertion, only to be found in one source, is true, it must have concerned Giovanni di Nicolao and not his cousin Giovanni d' Arrigo Arnolfini.[17]

Giovanni d'Arrigo Arnolfini, the male subject in the famous Jan van Eyck double portrait, was already an established businessman by 1436 who

---

[7] C. FERRI, "I rapporti fra Lucca, Bruges e le Fiandre dal XV alla metà del XVI secolo, quali emergono dagli atti notarili esistenti nell' Archivio di Stato di Lucca" in : H. COLE, T. COLE, C. FERRI, G. LERA (eds.), *Lucca e le Fiandre. Brugge 2002. Capitale Europea della Cultura*, Lucca, Istituto Storico Lucchese, 2002, pp. 10-16.
[8] SAB, Civiele Sententiën, Register 1453-1460, f° 135 r°.
[9] SAB, Civiele Sententiën, Register 1447-1453, f° 304 v°.
[10] C. FERRI, *I rapporti fra Lucca, Bruges e le Fiandre*, pp. 14-16.
[11] He was the great-grandson of Guglielmo Rapondi, Goffredo's third cousin. L. MIROT, *Les Cename*, annex.
[12] SAB, Civiele Sententiën, Register 1447-1453, f° 304 v°. A new compromise, however, was necessary in 1456. SAB, Civiele Sententiën, Register 1453-1460, f° 142 r°, 153 r°.
[13] ABIB, BBr, f° 18.2, 60.2, 66.1, 86.3, 110.2.
[14] SAB, Memoriaal van de Kamer, Register 1439-1441, f° 27 v°.
[15] SAB, Civiele Sententën, Register 1453-1460, f° 134 v°, 135 r°.
[16] L. GALOPPINI, *Mercanti toscani*, p. 217.
[17] On the two Giovanni Arnolfinis, see L. GALOPPINI, *Mercanti toscani*, pp 206-213.

appeared in Goffredo's books, yet not as an employee.[18] Like the Burlamacchi,[19] the Di Poggio[20] and the Bernardini,[21] he was one of the many Lucchese trading partners of Rapondi, who remained a faithful member of the Lucchese nation.[22] The rest of the commercial network in Bruges mainly included other Italians, such as Bernardo Cambi[23] and Bernardo Portinari, the first manager of the Medici in Bruges,[24] and from some local citizens.[25] Goffredo also kept in touch with Jacopo Rapondi, who made cash tranfers[26] and handed over his ballast rights in Sluis to him.[27] Yet there seemed to be no long-term commercial relations between the two, and while the former was determined to succeed in trade, the latter was determined to withdraw from it.

As his family had always done, at least in those periods when commercial activities prevailed, Goffredo and his partners concentrated on the trade with silk, velvets and other expensive fabrics. Some of these still went to the ducal court. In 1436, for example, Arnolfini and Rapondi sold precious cloth to the duke.[28] The fact that Philip of Saveuse, Philip the Good's counsellor and chamberlain, handed over property to Goffredo in 1440,[29] also suggests the existence of relations with the duke. Still, regular and large-scale capital movements involving other centres of financial power, such as the city, no longer occurred. This is not to say that Goffredo never tried to restore them. Again in 1436, instead of lending money, he presented 10 lb. gr. to Bruges to help it pay for the siege of Calais by Philip the Good.[30] This had been undertaken by the duke to counter English aggression, who were displeased with the Burgundians for exchanging their old alliance with them for one with the French in signing the treaty of Arras in 1435. Just as the military campaign ended as a fiasco,[31] Goffredo's attempt to re-establish financial relations with the city and the duke were in vain.

Other reasons may have inspired Rapondi's generosity towards Bruges. In 1429, the English Crown had issued the Staple Ordinances. With the purpose of bringing as much precious metal as possible into the country, these prescribed that prices at the wool staple in Calais be increased, that all payments be made in cash and that one third of the wool price in bullion be delivered to the mint after each sale.[32] As these restrictive measures hindered the wool trade very much, an attack on Calais, which might have persuaded the stubborn

---

[18] ABIB, BBr, f° 110.2. SAB, Civiele Sententiën, Register 1447-1453, f° 304 v°. SAB, Civiele Sententiën, Register 1453-1460, f° 135 r°.
[19] SAB, Civiele Sententiën, Register 1447-1453, f° 304 v°.
[20] ABIB, BLon, f° 22.2.
[21] C. FERRI, *I rapporti fra Lucca, Bruges e le Fiandre*, pp. 10-12. SAB, Civiele Sententiën, Register 1447-1453, f° 304 v°.
[22] ABIB, BLon, f° 22.3.
[23] ABIB, BBr, f° 18.2, 66.1. For him, see R. DE ROOVER, *The rise and decline of the Medici bank*, pp. 199, 348, 351.
[24] ABIB, BBr, f° 18.2, 66.1. For him, see R. DE ROOVER, *The rise and decline of the Medici bank*, pp. 59-60. These contacts may have been a continuation of the early bonds with the Medici in 1416, see *supra*.
[25] Among them were Thideman Bonin, Denis Haghelsteen and Josse de Bul. SAB, Civiele Sententiën, Register 1447-1453, f° 304 v°.
[26] ABIB, BLon, f° 167.3.
[27] G. BIGWOOD, *Le régime juridique et économique Tome I*, p. 666.
[28] L. GALOPPINI, *Mercanti toscani*, p. 216.
[29] SAB, Memoriaal van de Kamer, Register 1439-1441, f° 91 v°.
[30] SAB, Stadsrekening 02/09/1435-02/09/1436, f° 15 r°.
[31] R. VAUGHAN, *Philip the Good*, pp. 75-82.
[32] J. MUNRO, *Wool, Cloth and Gold. The Struggle for Bullion in Anglo-Burgundian Trade. 1340-1478*, Bruxelles, Editions de l'Université de Bruxelles, 1973, pp. 84-92.

English into a little more complaisance or even force them to alter their staple policy completely, may have seemed a good idea to anyone engaged in these activities. As toll accounts reveal, Goffredo Rapondi had important interests in the wool traffic from England.[33]

7.2 London, Venice, Lucca and Antwerp: the International Dimension of Goffredo's Network

Although Bruges was Goffredo's business base, his activities were by no means restricted to the city walls. One of his most effective tools for looking after his interests in other, often distant, parts of Europe and for linking his local and international networks together, was the Bruges bank of the Milanese Borromei family. Like about four hundred other clients, Rapondi had an account with this institution, founded in 1435 and providing three types of services. First of all, it was possible to make payments by way of journal transfers, something Goffredo commonly resorted to when doing business with his partners in Bruges. Furthermore, drawing on Borromei branches and correspondents in other cities, the bank enabled its clients to make international money transfers, using bills of exchange, and undertook commodity trade on their behalf.[34] Together with other sources, the extant Borromei ledgers from Bruges and London allow us to make a fairly detailed reconstruction of the way in which a Lucchese merchant, residing in Bruges, constantly used these three procedures to organize long-distance trade in a quickly changing economic environment.[35]

Goffredo primarily offered an astonishing variety of silks, velvets, damasks and satin, sold in all possible colours and sizes.[36] Notwithstanding the fact that, in doing so, he was reverting to the great Lucchese tradition of trade in precious cloth, a considerable share of his stock did not originate from Lucca. By the middle of the fifteenth century, the Tuscan city was no longer the dominant centre for silk manufacture that it had been during the previous two centuries. Due to constant political turmoil during the 1400s, many entrepreneurs and artisans had left for Venice, Milan, Florence and Bologna, which had thankfully adopted the immigrants' capital and knowledge to develop their own silk industries.[37] This explains why Rapondi, besides the supplies from his native town, imported large quantities of silk from Milan, Florence[38] and especially Venice, where the presence of long-time friends and relatives of the family, such as the Burlamacchi, was very helpful.[39]

---

[33] M.-R. THIELEMANS, *Bourgogne et Angleterre. Relations politiques et économiques entre les Pays-Bas bourguignons et l'Angleterre. 1435-1467*, Bruxelles, Presses Universitaires de Bruxelles, 1966, p. 199.
[34] J. L. BOLTON and F.G. BRUSCOLI, "When did Antwerp replace Bruges as the commercial and financial centre of north-western Europe? The evidence of the Borromei ledger for 1438", Unpublished article, 2004, pp. 4-7.
[35] These ledgers are held in the Borromeo-Arese family archive on Isola Bella, Archivio Borromeo Isola Bella or ABIB, libri mastri 7 (London) and 8 (Bruges). At Queen Mary College, University of London, Professor J. Bolton and Dr. G. Bruscoli have been granted permission to create electronic database versions of them, planning to make these available on CD-ROM.
[36] See for example ABIB, BBr, f° 134.1.
[37] For Venice, see L. MOLÀ, *La communità dei lucchesi a Venezia. Immigrazione e industria della seta nel tardo Medioevo*, Venice, Istituto veneto di scienze, lettere ed arti, 1994, 354 p.
[38] ABIB, BBr, f° 134.1.
[39] SAB, Civiele Sententiën, Register 1453-1460, f° 135 r°.

The *Serenissima Repubblica* occupied a key position in Goffredo's trade system in more than one respect. In order to pay for his many silk purchases, he needed to have money at his disposal in Italy. For this purpose, he provided the Borromei branch in Bruges with a steady stream of bills of exchange, whereupon the bank made capital available through its partners and correspondents in Venice, the most important money market in the south. Most of the liquidity was furnished by a limited number of substantial bankers and money dealers, predominantly of Florentine origin, including Antonio Cionelli and company,[40] Cecco de' Tommasi and brothers,[41] the Pisan-born Mariano and Zebedeo de Colti,[42] Nicolo Ranghiadore,[43] the Milanese Arrighino Panigarola[44] and of course the local representatives of the Borromei family themselves.[45]

Once the goods had been bought and paid for, they were carried to Bruges by sea or overland, by way of Milan. Often, however, deliveries were delayed and commodities were damaged,[46] stolen or lost.[47] A way to avoid these problems was to charge the Borromei with the purchase and transport of the merchandise, as with the risks involved in it, as Goffredo did in 1438.[48] Occasionally, mostly when trading Lucchese silks, Rapondi sent his factor or even travelled to southern Europe himself in order to lay in supplies. In the latter case, his books were left with Martin Cenami, who was instructed to continue his business and watch over his house and furniture in Flanders.[49]

A number of the silks was sold in Bruges to Italian colleagues, local businessmen and the Burgundian court.[50] Another share of the stock was entrusted to the Borromei and sent to London, where Rapondi did not have a representative of his own. The bank took care of the transport to England, paid customs[51] and brokerage fees[52] and made sure the fabrics were sold to local merchants, most of whom were mercers[53] such as William Cantelowe,[54] and to a minority of English noblemen and courtiers, among whom were Lord Thomas Percy[55] and the Earl of Dorset.[56] Revenues and expenses made as well as a commission[57] were charged on the account Goffredo had with the Borromei in London, from where funds could be easily transferred to places where the bank needed to provide their client with cash. Things did not always operate that

---

[40] ABIB, BBr, f° 66.1. ABIB, BBr, f° 86.3. ABIB, BBr, f° 110.2.
[41] ABIB, BBr, f° 18.2. ABIB, BBr, f° 86.3. ABIB, BBr, f° 110.2. On them, see R.C. MUELLER, *The Venetian money market. Banks, panics, and the public debt, 1200-1500*, Baltimore, Johns Hopkins University Press, 1997, pp. 274, 335.
[42] ABIB, BBr, f° 18.2. ABIB, BBr, f° 86.3. ABIB, BBr, f° 110.2. On them, see R.C. MUELLER, *The Venetian money market*, p. 482.
[43] ABIB, BBr, f° 18.2. ABIB, BBr, f° 66.1. ABIB, BBr, f° 86.3. ABIB, BBr, f° 110.2.
[44] ABIB, BBr, f° 18.2. ABIB, BBr, f° 110.2. On him, see R.C. MUELLER, *The Venetian money market*, p. 275. He was the father of Giovanni Panigarola, Milanese ambassador at the court of Charles the Bold. R.J. WALSH, *Charles the Bold and Italy (1467-1477). Politics and Personnel*, Liverpool, Liverpool University Press, 2005, p. 206.
[45] ABIB, BBr, f° 18.2. ABIB, BBr, f° 66.1. ABIB, BBr, f° 86.3.
[46] C. FERRI, *I rapporti fra Lucca, Bruges e le Fiandre*, pp. 10-14. The references in this text are inaccurate.
[47] SAB, Civiele Sententiën, Register 1447-1453, f° 304 v°.
[48] ABIB, BBr, f° 134.1.
[49] SAB, Civiele Sententiën, Register 1447-1453, f° 304 v°.
[50] See *supra*.
[51] ABIB, BLon, f° 22.1.
[52] ABIB, BLon, f° 22.2. ABIB, BLon, f° 167.3.
[53] J. L. BOLTON and F.G. BRUSCOLI, *When did Antwerp replace Bruges*, p. 7.
[54] ABIB, BLon, f° 153.8.
[55] SAB, Civiele Sententiën, Register 1453-1460, f° 135 r°.
[56] SAB, Civiele Sententiën, Register 1447-1453, f° 62 v°.
[57] ABIB, BLon, f° 22.2. ABIB, BLon, f° 167.3.

smoothly though. In 1452, Goffredo summoned both staff members of the Borromei London branch, Felice da Fagnano and Nicolo Micheli, who was represented by his brother and former Rapondi factor Francesco, to appear in court.[58] Most disputes concerned the revenues of the commission trade they had conducted on his behalf which, according to the plaintiff, had never been paid.

General economic developments did not only influence Goffredo's choice of supply centres but also that of his outlets. Around the middle of the fifteenth century Bruges was still by far the most important commercial gateway-city in northern Europe. Yet, at the same time, Antwerp, although still not a shadow of the economic metropolis it would become in the sixteenth century, was able to offer possibilities considered interesting enough by international traders to do business there. In particular the four annual fairs organized in the Scheldt port and in the neighbouring town of Bergen-op-Zoom attracted a growing number of foreign merchants and,[59] from a certain point in time, also seemed important enough for Goffredo Rapondi to make the trip to Brabant, accompanied first by Francesco Micheli,[60] later by Martin Cenami.[61] When the Lucchese could not leave his business in Bruges, he appointed an attorney to represent him, as he did in 1439.[62]

Goffredo, his factors as well as any other person working on his behalf, deposited the money they received in Antwerp and Bergen-op-Zoom in the cash account opened by the Borromei for its clients to use for the period of the fairs.[63] Although we do not know what lay behind these receipts, it is likely that the Rapondi visited the Scheldt towns to sell some of their luxury cloth. Since payments were made from the cash account as well, albeit to a lesser extent, they would not have returned to Bruges empty-handed either.[64] It seems safe to assume they bought wool, bearing in mind that Goffredo was one of the principal payers of the toll imposed by the Burgundian duke on the export of this raw material out of Brabant.[65] It served as an ideal return freight to Italy, closing the circle of Rapondis' trade network.

---

[58] For da Fagnano, see SAB, Civiele Sententiën, Register 1447-1453, f° 62 v°. For Micheli, see SAB, Civiele Sententiën, Register 1453-1460, f° 135 r°.

[59] W. BRULEZ, "Bruges and Antwerp in the 15th and 16th Centuries: an Antithesis?" in: *Acta Historiae Neerlandicae. Studies on the History of the* Netherlands, The Hague, 1973, 6, pp. 1-26. H. VAN DER WEE, *The Growth of the Antwerp Market and the European Economy (fourteenth-sixteenth centuries)*, The Hague, Martinus Nijhoff, 1963, vol. 2, pp. 18-23. For the Bergen fairs, see C.J.F. SLOOTMANS, *Paas- en Koudemarkten te Bergen op Zoom 1365-1565*, Tilburg, Stichting Zuidelijk Historisch Contact, 1985, 3 vol. (Bijdragen tot de geschiedenis van het Zuiden van Nederland, 65).

[60] SAB, Civiele Sententiën, Register 1453-1460, f° 135 r°.

[61] SAB, Civiele Sententiën, Register 1447-1453, f° 304 v°.

[62] SAB, Memoriaal van de Kamer, Register 1439-1441, f° 27 v°.

[63] ABIB, BBr, f° 60.2. ABIB, BBr, f° 66.1. ABIB, BBr, f° 86.3. ABIB, BLon, f° 171.1. In order to supply this account, the Borromei drew on their cash account in Bruges or used Antwerp moneychangers, such as Tidman Claisson. For their services at the fairs, see J. L. BOLTON and F.G. BRUSCOLI, *When did Antwerp replace Bruges*, pp. 9-12.

[64] ABIB, BBr, f° 18.2. ABIB, BBr, f° 110.2.

[65] M.-R. THIELEMANS, *Bourgogne et Angleterre*, p. 199.

CHAPTER 8

FRANCESCO RAPONDI AND THE END OF THE FAMILY'S BUSINESS ACTIVITIES

Goffredo Rapondi is mentioned for the last time in 1456. Eight years later, his son Francesco acquired citizenship in Bruges. He did this "on the condition that he would execute no other profession than that of broker",[1] the local intermediary assisting or representing foreign merchants. The latter were obliged to use them with every commercial transaction on a penalty of fines, something Goffredo had experienced, ironically enough, some thirty years before.[2] Francesco had already been active as a broker in London in 1463,[3] possibly related to his father's business. It is unclear, however, if he actually executed this job in Bruges as well. No sources witnessing his activities remain and, unfortunately, the members' register of the brokers' guild is missing for this specific period. We only know that he was no longer a broker in 1501, when the lists resume.[4]

Entrance to the brokers' guild was only allowed under very particular conditions. Members had to be born in the city, which had been the case for Rapondi, and, most importantly, they were expected to renounce every form of trade to be neutral mediators in commercial transactions.[5] Also when Francesco in the end did not conduct brokerage in Bruges, his citizenship of the city suggests that he preferred Flemish judicial institutions above the much more commercially oriented foreigner law. This, together with the actual absence of business activities after 1456, leads to the conclusion that he followed in the footsteps of his relatives some thirty years before, leaving the risks of active trade to others. This time, no other branch of the family was waiting to continue the Rapondi business as Goffredo had done in 1430. For the first time in more than a century, the city had to manage without the Rapondis' commercial activities. As the reason why the family had come to Bruges had disappeared, the family itself disappeared as well. Francesco's fourth cousin Caterina, who died in 1470,[6] was the last Rapondi to be recorded in Flanders.

In the decades following the Rapondis' disappearance, Bruges lost its primary role in European business. Political events, the continuous state of war in Flanders and the economically disastrous conflict between the city and archduke Maximilian in particular, accelerated the rise of Antwerp as a more efficient meeting place for international trade.[7] Apart from the Castilians,

[1] SAB, Poorterboek 1454-1478, f° 70 v°. SAB, Stadsrekening 02/09/1464-01/09/1465, f° 9 v°. See also A. JAMEES, *Brugse Poorters. Deel 2: 1418-1478*, p. 322. R.A. PARMENTIER (ed.), *Indices op de Brugsche Poorterboeken*, Brugge, Desclée De Brouwer en Cie, 1938, dl. 2, pp. 658-659.

[2] SAB, Stadsrekening 02/09/1432-01/09/1432, f° 14 r°.

[3] R. DE ROOVER, *The Rise and Decline*, p. 112.

[4] M. CATRY and A. VAN DEN ABEELE, *Makelaars en handelaars. Van Nering der makelaars naar Kamer van Koophandel in het XVIIde eeuwse Brugge*, Brugge, Kamer voor Handel en Nijverheid Brugge en het Noorden van West-Vlaanderen, 1992, pp. 99-103.

[5] M. CATRY and A. VAN DEN ABEELE, *Makelaars en handelaars*, pp. 22-25.

[6] See *supra*.

[7] R. VAN UYTVEN, "Stages of economic decline, late medieval Bruges" in: J.-M. DUVOSQUEL and E. THOEN, *Peasants and townsmen in medieval Europe. Studia in honorem Adriaan Verhulst*, Gent, Snoeck-Ducaju & Zoon, 1995, pp. 259-269. (Belgisch Centrum voor Landelijke Geschiedenis, 114).

foreign merchants moved from Bruges to the Scheldt port,[8] joined by new groups of traders. While some of the most active among them were compatriots and close relatives of the Rapondi, such as the Cenami, the Burlamacchi and the Arnolfini,[9] the family itself did not appear in Antwerp. The same appears to be true for other commercial centres that emerged from the end of the fifteenth century onwards, such as Geneva and Lyons.[10] Only in Paris a Giovanni Rapondi, probably Francesco's cousin, is known to have conducted business in 1492.[11] After that, the development of international trade and banking, which the Rapondi had helped to shape for one and a half centuries, proceeded without them.

---

[8] J. MARECHAL, "Le depart de Bruges des marchands étrangers (XVe et XVIe siècles)" in : J. MARECHAL, *Europese aanwezigheid te Brugge. De vreemde kolonies (XIVde-XIXde eeuw)*, Brugge, Genootschap voor Geschiedenis, 1985, pp. 180-210. (Vlaamse Historische Studies, 3).

[9] J. DENUCÉ, *Italiaansche koopmansgeslachten te Antwerpen in de XVIe-XVIIIe eeuwen*, Mechelen, N.V. Het Kompas, 1934, pp. 43-56. J.A. GORIS, *Étude sur les colonies marchandes méridionales (portugais, espagnols, italiens) à Anvers de 1488 à 1567*, Louvain, Librairie Universitaire, 1925, p. 80.

[10] See F. BAYARD, "Après les Buonvisi, les Lucquois à Lyon aux XVIIe et XVIIIe siècles" in: T. FANFANI and R. MAZZEI, *Lucca e l'Europa degli affari. Secoli XV-XVII*, Lucca, Maria Pacini Fazzi editore, 1990, pp. 133-146. L. MOTTU-WEBER, "Les activités des marchands-banquiers et des «entrepreneurs» lucquois à Genève aux XVI et XVII siècles" in: T. FANFANI and R. MAZZEI, *Lucca e l'Europa degli affari. Secoli XV-XVII*, Lucca, Maria Pacini Fazzi editore, 1990, pp. 133- 146.

[11] J. FAVIER, "Une ville entre deux vocations : la place d'affaires de Paris au XVe siècle" in : *Annales*, Paris, 1973, 28, p. 1250.

CONCLUSION: THE RAPONDI AND THE LATE MEDIEVAL FINANCIERS

Flanders and the Rapondi shared a common history for more than a century, from 1360 until 1470. For almost half of this period, from 1385 until 1430, the family dominated ducal and urban finance in the Low Countries, dealing with the duke of Burgundy as well as with the city of Bruges. If we revisit the first pages of this book, the question arises as to how they managed to remain at the top of the money-lending business for so long without being financially ruined as so many of their colleagues were. To answer this question it is useful to briefly compare the Rapondis' work with that of other financiers in the fourteenth and fifteenth-century Low Countries.

In some respects, the Rapondis' activities were a continuation of those of the officers employed by the Flemish counts throughout the fourteenth century. Because of their technical knowledge, a growing number of professional bankers and money-dealers, mostly of Italian origin, had been invested with the general receivership in Flanders from the end of the thirteenth century onwards.[1] In common with the Rapondi, many were involved in urban finance while working for and lending to the prince, having begun their career doing business in Bruges or Ghent. Donato Peruzzi, a member of the Florentine super-company of the same name, acted as receiver-general in 1328 when he was to acquire the penalty of 20 000 lb. par. levied on the city of Bruges after its defeat in Kassel and which had been advanced by Peruzzi to Louis of Nevers.[2] Before taking up a political career during the dictatorship of Jacob of Artevelde, the Lombard Simon de Mirabello issued loans simultaneously to the count of Flanders and the city of Ghent, holding the office of receiver-general himself briefly in 1329.[3] Conte Gualterotti and Vane Guy, both receiver-general under Louis of Nevers and both associated with the Florentine Guidi company, provided money to Ghent.[4] For most of these officers, however, financing both the city and the count was occasional and only occurred when their office required it. The Rapondi, on the other hand, performed this business on a daily basis for more than three decades and were given important offices because of these services, not the other way around.

During the period in which the Rapondi carried out these activities, banking was dominated by Lucchese citizens. Although several of them supplied funds to either the Burgundian duke[5] or the Flemish cities,[6] few are known to have maintained long-term and large-scale financial relationships with both. Two Lucchese who did were Bartolomeo Bettini and Marco Guidiccioni. It is difficult, nevertheless, to consider Bettini, who collaborated closely with Dino and Filippo during his entire life, as acting independently from the Rapondi. Guidiccioni did make a career of his own, taking the lead among his Lucchese colleagues after Dino's death and continuing the bonds with Bruges and Philip

[1] E. E. KITTELL, *From Ad Hoc to Routine. A Case Study in Medieval Bureaucracy*, Philadelphia, University of Pennsylvania Press, 1991, pp. 60-195.
[2] For a detailed analysis of the operation, see R. DE ROOVER, *Money, banking and credit*, pp. 84-85.
[3] G. BIGWOOD, *Le régime juridique. Tome I*, p. 115. E. E. KITTELL, *From Ad Hoc to Routine*, p. 157.
[4] E. E. KITTELL, *From Ad Hoc to Routine*, p. 157.
[5] See, for example, the credit granted to Philip the Bold by Silvestro Trenta in 1403. A. VAN NIEUWENHUYSEN, *Les finances. Economie et politique*, p. 346.
[6] See, for example, the loan by Forteguerra Forteguerra to Ghent in 1379. J.M. MURRAY, *Bruges, Cradle of Capitalism*, p. 235.

the Good for more than ten years after Filippo had given up business about the mid-1420s. Yet, his bonds with the city were never as intense as the Rapondis' had been. Giovanni Arnolfini, perhaps the most famous Lucchese merchant in this period because of the Van Eyck painting, did not have lasting financial relationships with the city or the duke at all. Instead of granting loans to Bruges or the Burgundian authorities, which he did only twice, he achieved an overwhelming domination in the trade in luxury cloth, that other Lucchese specialty.

After sixty years of Lucchese dominance and considerable but disparate efforts by Genoese merchants,[7] the Florentines regained their leading position in banking from the middle of the 1430s onwards. Companies like that of Bernardo Cambi and Antonio da Rabatta provided sources of money frequently used by the Burgundian dukes.[8] Yet none of these would be as important to ducal finance as the Medici would be over the next forty years. Founded in the beginning of the fifteenth century, this firm established an office in Bruges in 1437, which was subsequently governed by Bernardo Portinari, Gierozzo de Pigli and Agnolo Tani. Its most famous manager, however, was Tommaso Portinari, a member of one of the oldest Florentine families who, having come to Flanders as an office boy, became head of the branch in 1464. Christened as 'Charles the Bold's Dino Rapondi' by Richard Vaughan,[9] his business does have some remarkable similarities with that of the Lucchese financier half a century earlier. Also acting as a ducal counsellor, Portinari served the duke as a devoted jack-of-all-trades, supplying the court with luxuries, farming the ducal wool toll in Gravelines and selling Burgundian galleys to the Medici. He was able to arrange a treaty with Charles the Bold, who, in return for a share in the revenues, banned from his dominions the sale of all alum other than that produced in the papal mines in Tolfa, which was distributed exclusively by the Medici. Most important, Portinari, in whose favour the duke personally intervened when his belongings were seized by privateers, intensified the loans to the prince that his firm had been granting since 1455, keeping the machinery of ducal finance working at all possible levels. Because some of these activities proved disadvantageous to his Medici employers, Portinari has long been held responsible for the banktruptcy of the bank's Bruges branch in 1480, a view that has been reappraised more recently.[10]

Besides the less successful outcome of the Florentine's activities, there is another important difference between Portinari's and Rapondis' business. Apart from his investment in a block of annuities issued by the city of Bruges as a means of financing a loan to Charles the Bold in 1471, Portinari nor any of the previous Medici managers were ever involved in urban finance. In this respect, the Medici are just another example of James Murray's assertion that "urban finance was never more than an occasional, even accidental, sideline for Italian companies in Bruges".[11] The same goes, however, for indigenous money-dealers

[7] Arnolfini advanced funds to Philip the Good in 1436 and 1461. C. DE SMET, *Les emprunts*, pp. 149-150. A. ZOETE, *De beden*, pp. 145-146.
[8] C. DE SMET, *Les emprunts*, p. 154.
[9] R. VAUGHAN, *De Bourgondiërs*, Haarlem, Fibula-Van Dishoeck, 1976, p. 97.
[10] For the old, negative appreciation of Portinari, see R. DE ROOVER, *The rise and decline of the Medici bank*, pp. 338-356. For a more balanced appraisal, see M. BOONE, *Apologie d'un banquier médiéval*, pp. 31-54. R.J. WALSH, *Charles the Bold and Italy 1467-1477. Politics and personnel*, Liverpool, Liverpool University Press, 2005, pp. 120-136.
[11] J.M. MURRAY, *Bruges, Cradle of Capitalism*, p. 235.

who furnished the court. Despite their Bruges origin and their frequent involvement in the city's affairs, people like Louis de Backer, the money-changer Colard le Fevre or Pieter Bladelin, the Burgundian financial governor famous for his foundation of Middelburg, supplied money to the duke[12] but, as far as is known, not to the city. Although it is difficult to draw definitive conclusions without a detailed account of Bruges' financial history, systematically lending to the prince and systematically lending to the city did not go together for most financiers in the late medieval Low Countries.

For the Rapondi company, urban finance was not a sideline: on the contrary. For almost half a century, they were not only bankers to the dukes of Burgundy, but also to the city of Bruges. This book shows that the key to the continuing success of the Rapondi lay within the specific context in which these bonds were pursued. In the Burgundian period, the Low Countries were the stage for a steady increase of power of the central government at the expense of its most important counterpart, the cities. This extension of power, including the display of it so typical to the Burgundian dukes, required enormous amounts of money. To a certain extent, this money was provided by the Rapondi, who were able to charge heavy interest. Yet, the reinforcement of his position enabled the prince to increasingly shift his financial burdens to the cities, who had to pay either directly for the duke's activities or indirectly for the loans which financed these. Being the main suppliers of these funds, Dino and his relatives were able to make handsome profits again. In this way, the Rapondi were able to do lucrative business in the short term but, at the same time, helped to create new opportunities to do so in the long term. Their loans contributed to a further reinforcement of the position of the duke, who was thus able to continue his costly policy and demand new contributions from the city.

This was not only a lucrative, but also a relatively safe way to do business. The Rapondis' position with the city was a reason for the duke not to displease them while their position at the court urged Bruges to pay them back in time. As Andrée Van Nieuwenhuysen has emphasized,[13] their position with the city also gave the Rapondi a very clear overview of one of the duke's most important sources of income. Consequently, they knew exactly how much they could spend on Philip the Bold or John the Fearless without incurring the risk of not being repaid. It is true, however, that the loans granted to Bruges did not always cover those issued to the duke, which were usually larger.[14] Yet, often up to 65% of the amounts they lent to the court was advanced to or transferred from the city by them as well. In this respect, the relations between Bruges and the dukes were as much a means of risk management for the Rapondi as were a decentralized firm structure or marine insurance for others in this hazardous period.

To a large extent, the Rapondi's success was a result of an incomplete state formation. During their hundred years stay in Flanders, they sold cartloads of silks, granted gigantic loans to the French king and transferred hundreds of thousands of florins for the Avignon papacy. However, they were never as successful as when they maintained financial relationships with both the duke of

[12] Albeit not to the same extent as the Italians. C. DE SMET, *Les emprunts*, pp. 146, 159.

[13] A. VAN NIEUWENHUYSEN, *Les finances. Economie et politique*, p. 348.

[14] The Rapondi even provided funds to the duke for occasions which did not involve financial contributions by the city at all. Still, the financiers were usually paid back for these advances by way of assignments on the city, who owed money to the prince for other reasons.

Burgundy and the city of Bruges. The increase of power of the central government at the expense of one of the duke's most important cities provided Dino and his companions with a lucrative and comparatively safe way of doing business, enabling them to remain at the top of the financial world for an exceptionally long period.

Bibliography
Annexes
Index

BIBLIOGRAPHY

1. Inventories

AERTS, Erik, *Geschiedenis en archief van de Rekenkamers. Overzicht van de archieven en verzamelingen van het Algemeen Rijksarchief*, Brussel, Algemeen Rijksarchief, 1996, 534 p. (Overzichten en gidsen, 27).

BAUTIER, Robert-Henri and **SORNAY**, Janine, *Les sources de l'histoire économique et sociale du Moyen Âge. 2 : Les États de la maison de Bourgogne. Vol. I Archives centrales de l'État bourguignon (1384-1500). Archives des principautés territoriales*, Paris, CNRS Editions, 2001, 782 p.

BRUCHET, Max, *Archives départementales du Nord. Répertoire numérique. Série B. Chambre des Comptes de Lille*, Lille, 1921, 2 vol.

JANSSENS DE BISTHOVEN, Boudewijn and **DE BACKER**, Christian, *Inventaris van het Bisschoppelijk Archief van Brugge*, Leuven, KADOC, 1984, 190 p.

VANDEWALLE, André, *Beknopte inventaris van het Stadsarchief van Brugge. Oud archief*, Brugge, Gemeentebestuur, 1979, 266 p.

2. Unpublished sources

2.1 Archives Départementales du Côte d'Or (ACO), Dijon, preserved on microfilm in the Manuscript Reading Room of the University Library in Ghent

-Recette Générale de Toutes les Finances :

B 1547

B 1554 (22/11/1407-22/11/1408)

B 1556 (22/11/1408-22/11/1409)

B 1558 (01/02/1408-01/02/1409)

B 1560 (01/02/1409-01/02/1410)

B 1562 (01/02/1410-17/04/1411)

B 1570 (01/02/1410-17/04/1411)

B 1572 (1412-1413)

B 1573 (16/11/1412- 21/02/1413)

B 1576 (21/02/1413-31/12/1414)

2.2 Archives Départementales du Nord (ADN), Lille

-Recette Fénérale de Flandre et d'Artois :

B 4086 (24/06/1411-24/06/1412)

B 4087 (1401-1414)

B 4088 (24/06/1415-24/06/1416)

B 7793 (1405-1411)

-Recette Générale de Toutes les Finances :

B 1878 (05/11/1405-19/11/1406)

B 1894 (18/04/1411-30/04/1412)

B 1897 (30/05/1412-16/10/1412)

B 1903 (19/03/1414-18/04/1415)

2.3 Archivio di Stato di Firenze (ASF)

Mediceo avanti il Principato (MAP) 83, n° 51, c. 312

2.4 Bisschoppelijk Archief, Bruges (BAB)

Acta Capituli, register 1414-1438 (A 50)

2.5 Stadsarchief, Bruges (SAB)

Cartularium Groenenbouc A

Cartularium Groenenbouc C

Civiele Sententiën Vierschaar, registers 1447-1453 and 1453-1461

Memoriaal van de Kamer, register 1439-1441

Politieke Oorkonden, reeks 1

'Regesten oorkonden bewaard op het Brugse Stadsarchief 1420-1500' (manuscript from the inheritance of A. Schouteet) (K 4 XXIII)

-Bruges city accounts, preserved in original :

02/02/1360-02/02/1361

02/02/1361-02/02/1362

02/02/1362-02/02/1363

02/02/1363-02/02/1364

02/02/1366-02/02/1367

02/02/1367-02/02/1368

02/02/1368-02/02/1369

02/02/1369-02/02/1370

02/02/1370-02/02/1371

02/02/1371-02/02/1372

02/02/1372-02/02/1373

02/02/1375-02/02/1376

02/02/1379-02/02/1380

02/02/1380-02/02/1381

02/02/1382-04/05/1382

27/11/1382-02/02/1383

02/02/1383-02/02/1384

02/02/1385-02/09/1385

02/09/1385-02/09/1386

02/09/1386-02/09/1387

1387-1388

02/09/1388-02/09/1389

02/09/1389-02/09/1390

02/09/1390-02/09/1391

02/09/1391-02/09/1392

02/09/1392-02/09/1393

02/09/1393-10/03/1394

10/03/1394-02/09/1394

02/09/1394-02/09/1395

02/09/1395-02/09/1396

02/09/1396-02/09/1397

02/09/1397-02/09/1398

02/09/1398-02/09/1399

02/09/1400-02/09/1401

02/09/1401-02/09/1402

02/09/1402-02/09/1403

02/09/1403-02/09/1404

02/09/1404-02/09/1405

02/09/1405-02/09/1406

02/09/1406-02/09/1407

02/09/1408-01/09/1409

02/09/1410-01/09/1411

02/09/1411-01/09/1412

02/09/1413-01/09/1414

02/09/1414-01/09/1415

02/09/1415-01/09/1416

02/09/1416-01/09/1417

02/09/1418-01/09/1419

02/09/1419-01/09/1420

02/09/1420-01/09/1421

02/09/1421-01/09/1422

02/09/1423-01/09/1424

02/09/1426-01/09/1427

02/09/1429-01/09/1430

02/09/1430-01/09/1431

02/09/1431-01/09/1432

02/09/1432-01/09/1433

02/09/1433-01/09/1434

02/09/1435-01/09/1436

02/09/1436-02/09/1438

02/09/1439-02/09/1440
02/09/1440-02/09/1441
02/09/1441-02/09/1442
02/09/1442-02/09/1443
02/09/1443-02/09/1444
02/09/1444-02/09/1445
02/09/1445-02/09/1446
02/09/1446-02/09/1447
02/09/1447-02/09/1448
02/09/1449-02/09/1450
02/09/1451-02/09/1452
02/09/1452-01/09/1453
02/09/1454-01/09/1455
02/09/1455-01/09/1456
02/09/1456-01/09/1457
02/09/1457-01/09/1458
02/09/1461-01/09/1462
02/09/1463-01/09/1464
02/09/1464-01/09/1465
02/09/1465-01/09/1466
02/09/1466-01/09/1467
02/09/1467-01/09/1468
02/09/1468-01/09/1469
02/09/1469-01/09/1470

-City accounts, copies from the Algemeen Rijksarchief, Brussels (ARAB):

02/09/1407-02/09/1408
02/09/1409-01/09/1410
02/09/1412-01/09/1413
02/09/1415-01/09/1416
02/09/1416-01/09/1417
02/09/1422-02/09/1423
02/09/1424-02/09/1425
02/09/1425-02/09/1426
02/09/1427-02/09/1428
02/09/1428-02/09/1429

3. *Published sources*

3.1 Non-narrative sources

BARTIER, John, **BONENFANT**, Paul (ed.) and **VAN NIEUWENHUYSEN**, Andrée, *Ordonnances de Philippe le Hardi, de Marguerite de Male et de Jean sans Peur 1381-1419. Tome I contenant les ordonnances de Philippe le Hardi et de Marguerite de Male du 16 octobre 1381 au 31 décembre 1393*, Bruxelles, Koninklijke Commissie voor de uitgave der Oude Wetten en Verordeningen van België, 1965, 649 p.

BARTIER, John, **BONENFANT**, Paul (eds.) and **VAN NIEUWENHUYSEN**, Andrée, *Ordonnances de Philippe le Hardi, de Marguerite de Male et de Jean sans Peur 1381-1419. Tome II contenant les ordonnances de Philippe le Hardi et de Marguerite de Male du 17 janvier 1394 au 25 février 1405*, Bruxelles, Koninklijke Commissie voor de uitgave der Oude Wetten en Verordeningen van België, 1974, 1019 p.

BEAUNE, Henri, "État des officiers de Philippe le Hardi duc de Bourgogne d'après les comptes de ses Receveurs et Trésoriers, de 1384 à 1386" in : *Revue nobiliaire historique et biographique*, Paris, 1865, 1, pp. 49-56.

BOZZOLO, Carla and **LOYAU**, Hélène, *La cour amoureuse dite de Charles VI*, Paris, Le Léopard d'Or, 1982-1992, 2 vol.

CAUCHIES, Jean-Marie, *Ordonnances de Philippe le Hardi, de Marguerite de Male et de Jean sans Peur 1381-1419. Tome III. Ordonnances de Jean sans Peur 1405-1419*, Bruxelles, Koninklijke Commissie voor de uitgave der Oude Wetten en Verordeningen van België, 2001, 569 p.

COCKSHAW, Pierre, "Mentions d'auteurs, de copistes, d'enmumineurs et de libraires dans les comptes généraux de l'Etat bourguignon (1384 – 1419) " in : *Scriptorium*, Gand, 1969, 23, pp. 122-144.

Codex Diplomaticus Lubecensis. Lübeckisches Urkundenbuch. 1ste Abteilung. Urkundenbuch der Stadt Lübeck Fünfter Theil, Lübeck, Ferdinand Grautoff, 1877, 836 p.

DEHAISNES, M., *Documents et extraits divers concernant l'histoire de l'art dans la Flandre, l'Artois et le Hainaut avant le xve siècle*, Lille, L. Quarré, 1886, 2 vol.

DEHAISNES, M. and **FINOT**, Jules M., *Inventaire sommaire des archives départementales antérieures à 1790. Nord. Archives Civiles-Série B. Tome I*, Lille, L. Danel, 1899-1906, 2 vol.

DELISLE, Léopold, *Mandements et actes divers de Charles V (1364-1380)*, Paris, Imprimerie Nationale, 1874, 1046 p.

DE MAS LATRIE, M., "Commerce et expéditions militaires de la France et de Venise au Moyen Age" in: *Mélanges Historiques. Choix de documents*, Paris, 1880, 3, pp. 1-240.

EVANS, Allan (ed.), *Francesco Balducci Pegolotti. La pratica della mercatura*, Cambridge (Massachusetts), the Medieval Academy of America, 1936, 443 p.

FAVIER, Jean, *Les contribuables parisiens à la fin de la guerre de cent ans. Les rôles d'impôt de 1421, 1423 et 1438*, Genève, Librairie Droz, 1970, 365 p.

FINOT, Jules M., *Inventaire sommaire des archives départementales antérieures à 1790. Nord. Archives Civiles-Série B. Tome Septième*, Lille, L. Danel, 1892, 391 p.

GAILLARD, J. (ed.), *Inscriptions funéraires et monumentales de la Flandre Occidentale. Arrondissement de Bruges*, Bruges, Edw. Gailliard et Cie, 1861, pp. 160-161.

GILLIODTS-VAN SEVEREN, Louis, *Cartulaire de l'ancienne estaple à Bruges. Recueil de documents concernant le commerce intérieur et maritime, les relations internationales et l'histoire de cette ville*, Bruges, Louis de Plancke, 1906, 3 vol.

GILLIODTS-VAN SEVEREN, Louis, *Inventaire des archives de la ville de Bruges. Première section: inventaire des chartes. Première série: treizième au seizième siècle*, Bruges, Louis de Plancke, 1871-1878, 6 vol.

GILLIODTS-VAN SEVEREN, Louis, "L' Obituaire de Saint-Donatien de Bruges" in : *Bulletin de la Commission Royale d'Histoire*, Bruxelles, 1889, 16, pp. 283-371.

JAMEES, Alfred, *Brugse Poorters, opgetekend uit de stadsrekeningen en ingeleid*, Handzame, Familia et Patria, 1974-1980, 882 p.

LAZZARESCHI, Eugenio (red.), *Il libro della communitá dei mercanti Lucchesi in Bruges*, Milano, Rodolfo Malfasi, 1947, 313 p.

LAZZARESCHI, Eugenio and **MIROT**, Léon, "Lettere di Mercanti Lucchesi da Bruges e da Parigi" in: *Bollettino Storico Lucchese*, Lucca, 1929, 1, pp. 165-199.

LE ROUX DE LINCY, L. and **TISSERAND**, L.M. (eds.), *Le Paris de Charles V et de Charles VI vu par des écrivains contemporains*, Caen, Paradigme, 1992, pp. 15-36.

LIMBURG-STIRUM, Thierry de (ed.), *Cartulaire de Louis de Male comte de Flandre. Decreten van den grave Lodewyck van Vlaenderen 1348 à 1358 Tome I*, Bruges, Louis De Plancke, 1898, 663 p.

MARCHAL-VERDOODT, Monique, *Table des noms de personnes et de lieux mentionnés dans les plus anciennes comptes de la recette générale de Philippe le Hardi, duc de Bourgogne (1383-1389)*, Bruxelles, Commission Royale d'Histoire, 1971, 400 p.

MOLLAT, Michel (ed.), *Comptes généraux de l'Etat bourguignon entre 1416 et 1420*, Paris, Imprimerie Nationale, 1965-1969, 3 vol.

PARAVICINI, Werner und **WERNICKE**, Horst (eds.), *Hansekaufleute in Brügge. Teil 3: Prosopographischer Katalog zu den Brügger Steuerlisten (1360-1390)*, Frankfurt am Main, Peter Lang, 1999, 573 p. (Kieler Werkstücke, Reihe D, 11).

PARMENTIER, R.A. (ed.), *Indices op de Brugsche Poorterboeken*, Brugge, Desclée De Brouwer en Cie, 1938, 2 vol.

PROST, Bernard and **PROST**, Henri, *Inventaires mobiliers et extraits de comptes des ducs de Bourgogne de la Maison Valois, 1363-1477 Tome I*, Paris, Leroux, 1902, 480 p.

SCHOUTEET, Albert, *Regesten op de oorkonden van het Stadsarchief van Brugge 1340-1384*, Brugge, Genootschap voor Geschiedenis, 1979, 352 p.

SCHOUTEET, Albert, *Regesten op de oorkonden van het Stadsarchief van Brugge 1385-1420*, Brugge, Genootschap voor Geschiedenis, 1982, 319 p.

TUETEY, Alexandre (ed.), "Testaments enrégistrés au Parlement de Paris sous le règne de Charles VII" in: *Mélanges Historiques. Choix de documents*, Paris, 1880, 3, pp. 240-704.

VAN NIEUWENHUYSEN, Andrée, "Documents relatifs à la gestion des finances de Philippe le Hardi, duc de Bourgogne et comte de Flandre (1384-1404)" in: *Bulletin de la commission royale d'histoire*, Bruxelles, 1980, 146, pp. 69-312.

VERMEERSCH, Valentin (ed.), *Grafmonumenten, te Brugge voor 1578*, Brugge, Raaklijn, 1976, pp. 117-119.

WEALE, James, "Obituaire de l'abbaye de l'Eeckhout" in: *La Flandre Revue des monuments d'histoire et d'antiquités*, Bruges, 1869-1870, 3, pp. 299-382.

ZOETE, Antoine, *Handelingen van de leden en van de staten van Vlaanderen (1405 – 1419) Excerpten uit de rekeningen der steden, kasselrijen en vorstelijke ambtenaren. Deel 1 (24 maart 1405 – 5 maart 1413*, Brussel, Koninklijke Commissie voor Geschiedenis, 1981, 2 vol.

3.2 Narrative sources

BRUN, Robert, "Annales avignonnaises de 1382 à 1410, extraits des archives de Datini" in: *Mémoires de l'institut historique de Provence*, 1935, pp. 17-142.

DE REIFFENBERGH (ed.), *Mémoires de J. Du Clercq, sur le règne de Philippe le Bon, duc de Bourgogne*, Bruxelles, J.-M. Lacrosse, 1835, first volume, 502 p.

DESPARS, Nicolaes, *Cronijcke van den lande ende graefscepe van Vlaenderen, gemaect door Jor Nicolaes Despars, van de jaeren 405 tot 1492,* Brugge, Ed. De Jonghe (J.), 1839, 4 vol.

FROISSART, Jean, *Chroniques*, Bruxelles, Ed. Kervyn de Lettenhove, 1867-1877, 25 vol.

SERCAMBI, Giovanni, *Le croniche di Giovanni Sercambi Lucchese pubblicate sui manoscritti originale*, Lucca, Ed. S. Bongi, 1892, 3 vol.

4. Literature

AERTS, Erik, "Geld en krediet. Brugge als financieel centrum" in : VERMEERSCH, Valentin (ed.), *Brugge en Europa*, Antwerpen, Mercatorfonds, 1992, pp 57-71.

ARNADE, Peter, *Realms of Ritual. Burgundian ceremony and civic life in late medieval Ghent*, Ithaca, Cornell University Press, 1996, 298 p.

AUGUSTYN, Beatrijs, "Ontvanger-generaal van Vlaanderen" in: AUGUSTYN, Beatrijs and PREVENIER, Walter (eds.), *De gewestelijke en lokale overheidsinstellingen in Vlaanderen tot 1795*, Brussel, Algemeen Rijksarchief, 1997, pp. 188-195.

AUTRAND, Françoise, *Charles V le Sage*, Paris, Librairie Arthème Fayard, 1994, 909 p.

AUTRAND, Françoise, *Jean de Berry : l'art et le pouvoir*, Paris, Librairie Arthème Fayard, 2000, 552 p.

AVONDS, Piet, "Brabant tijdens de regering van Hertog Jan III (1312-1356). Land en Instellingen" in: *Verhandelingen van de Koninklijke Academie voor Wetenschappen, Letteren en Schone Kunsten van België*, Brussel, 1991, 53, nr. 136, 312 p.

BARDOEL, Agatha Anna, "The urban uprising in Bruges, 1280-81. Some new findings about the rebels and the partisans" in: *Revue Belge de Philologie et d'Histoire*, Bruxelles, 1994, 72, pp. 761-791.

BAUTIER, Robert-Henri, "Aspects politiques du Grand Schisme" in: *Genèse et débuts du Grand Schisme d'Occident*, Paris, Éditions du Centre de la Recherche Scientifique, 1980, pp. 457-465.

BAUTIER, Robert-Henri, "Les foires de Champagne" in: *La foire*, Bruxelles, Librairie Encyclopédique, 1953, pp. 97-147.

BAYARD, Françoise, "Après les Buonvisi, les Lucquois à Lyon aux XVIIe et XVIIIe siècles" in: FANFANI, T. and MAZZEI, R., *Lucca e l'Europa degli affari. Secoli XV-XVII*, Lucca, Maria Pacini Fazzi editore, 1990, pp. 133- 146.

BERGMANS, Ann, "Van Lucca naar Brugge. Een Volto Santo in de Speelmanskapel" in: *Monumenten en Landschappen*, Brussel, 1993, 12, nr. 6, pp. 17-24.

BIGWOOD, Georges, *Le régime juridique et économique du commerce de l'argent dans la Belgique du moyen âge*, Bruxelles, Maurice Lamertin, 1921-1922, 2 vol.

BLOCKMANS, Frans, "Le controle par le prince des comptes urbains en Flandre et en Brabant au Moyen Age" in : *Finances et comptabilité urbaines du XIIIe au XVIe siècle, Colloque international, Blankenberge (1962)*, Bruxelles, Pro Civitate, 1964, pp. 287-343.

BLOCKMANS, Willem Pieter, "Brugge als Europees handelscentrum" in: VERMEERSCH, Valentin (ed.), *Brugge en Europa*, Antwerpen, Mercatorfonds, 1992, pp 41-55.

BLOCKMANS, Willem Pieter, "Konfliktregelung der Hanse in Flandern (1393-1451)" in : MENKE, Hubertus (ed.), *Die Niederlande und der europaische Nordosten : ein Jahrtausend weitraumiger Beziehungen (700-1700)*, Neumunster, Waccholtz, 1992, pp. 209-219.

BLOCKMANS, Willem Pieter, "La participation des sujets flamands à la politique monétaire des ducs de Bourgogne" in : *Revue belge de numismatique*, Bruxelles, 1973, 119, pp. 103-134.

BLOCKMANS, Willem Pieter, "De volksvertegenwoordiging in Vlaanderen in de overgang van Middeleeuwen naar Nieuwe Tijden (1384-1506)" in: *Verhandelingen van de Koninklijke Academie voor Wetenschappen, Letteren en Schone Kunsten van België*, Brussel, 1978, 40, nr. 90, 671 p.

BLOMQUIST, Thomas, "The Early History of European Banking: Merchants, Bankers and Lombards of XIIIth-Century Lucca in the County of Champagne" in: *Journal of European Economic History*, Roma, 1985, 14, pp. 522-536.

BOIS, Guy, *La grande dépression médiévale: XIV-XVe siècles. Le précédent d'une crise systémique*, Paris, Presses Universitaires de France, 2000, 211 p.

BOLTON, James L. and **BRUSCOLI**, Francesco Guido, "When did Antwerp replace Bruges as the commercial and financial centre of north-western Europe? The evidence of the Borromei ledger for 1438", Unpublished article, 2004.

BONENFANT, Paul, *Du meurtre de Montereau au traité de Troyes*, Bruxelles, Académie Royale de Belgique, 1958, 282 p. (Mémoires, 52).

BOONE, Marc, "Apologie d'un banquier médiéval : Tomasso Portinari et l'Etat bourguignon" in : *Le Moyen Age*, Bruxelles, 1999, pp. 31-54.

BOONE, Marc, "Brugge en de Bourgondische hertogen: shoppen op markten van geld en macht" in : VANDEWALLE, André, *Hanzekooplui en Medicibankiers Brugge, wisselmarkt van Europese culturen*, Oostkamp, Stichting Kunstboek, 2002, pp. 123-134.

BOONE, Marc, "Doen traitieren elken Vlaminc in Vlaemscher tale. Talige communicatie tussen machthebbers en hun onderhorigen in het Bourgondische Vlaanderen (1385-1505)" in: DE CALUWE, Johan, DE SCHUTTER, Georges, DEVOS, Magda, and VAN KEYMEULEN, Jacques (reds.), *Taeldeman, man van de taal, schatbewaarder van de taal,* Gent, Academia Press, 2004, pp. 107-125.

BOONE, Marc, "Dons et pots-de-vin, aspects de la sociabilité urbaine au bas Moyen Age. Le cas gantois pendant la période bourguignonne" in : *Revue du Nord*, Lille, 1988, 70, pp. 471-487.

BOONE, Marc, "Les ducs, les villes et l'argent des contribuables: le rêve d'un impôt princier permanent en Flandre à l'époque bourguignonne" in : CONTAMINE, Philippe, KERHERVÉ, Jean and RIGAUDIÈRE, Albert (reds.), *L'Impôt au Moyen Age. L'Impôt public et le prélèvement seigneurial fin XIIe-début XVIé siècle. II. Les espaces fiscaux. Colloque tenu à Bercy les 14, 15 et 16 juin 2000*, Paris, Comité pour l'Histoire Économique et Financière de la France, 2002, pp. 323-341.

BOONE, Marc, *Geld en macht : de Gentse stadsfinanciën en de Bourgondische staatsvorming (1384-1453)*, Gent, Maatschappij voor geschiedenis en oudheidkunde, 1990, 260 p.

BOONE, Marc, "Gent en de Bourgondische hertogen ca. 1384 - ca. 1453 : een sociaal-politieke studie van een staatsvormingsproces" in: *Verhandelingen van de Koninklijke Academie voor Wetenschappen, Letteren en Schone Kunsten van België*, 1990, 52, nr. 133, 281 p.

BOONE, Marc, "Muntgeschiedenis middeleeuwen" in: ART, Jan (red.), *Hoe schrijf ik de geschiedenis van mijn gemeente? Deel IIIa Hulpwetenschappen*, Gent, Centrum voor Geschiedenis Universiteit Gent, 1995, pp. 149-165.

BOONE, Marc, "Soeverein-baljuw van Vlaanderen" in: AUGUSTYN, Beatrijs and PREVENIER, Walter (eds.), *De gewestelijke en lokale overheidsinstellingen in Vlaanderen tot 1795*, Brussel, Algemeen Rijksarchief, 1997, pp. 115-122.

BOONE, Marc, "Een verstedelijkte samenleving onder spanning. Het graafschap Vlaanderen omstreeks 1302" in: VAN CAENEGHEM, Raoul C., *Feiten en mythen van de Guldensporenslag*, Antwerpen, Mercatorfonds, 2002, pp. 26-77.

BOONE, Marc, **DANNEEL**, Marianne and **GEIRNAERT**, Noël, "Pieter IV Adornes (1460 - ca.1496): een Brugs patricier in Gent" in: *Handelingen der Maatschappij voor Geschiedenis en Oudheidkunde te Gent*, Gent, 1985, 39, pp. 123-147.

BOONE, Marc and **DUMOLYN**, Jan, "Henri Goethals, doyen de Liège: Un homme d'église gantois au service des ducs de Bourgogne Jean sans Peur et Philippe le Bon", in: *Publications du Centre Européen d'Études Bourguignonnes (XIVe-XVIe s.),* Dijon, 1998, 38, pp. 89-106.

BOONE, Marc and **PRAK**, Maarten,, "Rulers, patricians and burghers: the Great and the Little Traditions of urban revolt in the Low Countries" in: DAVIDS, Karel and LUCASSEN, Jan, (eds.), *A miracle mirrored. The Dutch Republic in European Perspective*, Cambridge, Cambridge University Press, 1999, pp. 99-134.

BOONE, Marc and **PREVENIER**, Walter, "De 'stadstaat'-droom" in: DECAVELE, Johan, *Gent: apologie van een rebelse stad: geschiedenis, kunst, cultuur*, Antwerpen, Mercatorfonds, 1989, pp. 81-105.

BRATCHEL, M.E., *Lucca 1430 – 1494, the reconstruction of an Italian city-republic*, Oxford, Clarendon Press, 1995, 346 p.

BRAUDEL, Fernand, *Civilisation matérielle, Économie et Capitalisme. XVe-XVIIIe siècle. Tome 2. Les jeux de l'échange*, Paris, Librairie Armand Colin, 1979, 600 p.

BRULEZ, Wilfrid, "Bruges and Antwerp in the 15th and 16th Centuries: an Antithesis?" in: *Acta Historiae Neerlandicae. Studies on the History of the* Netherlands, The Hague, 1973, 6, pp. 1-26.

BUBENICEK, Michelle, *Quand les femmes gouvernent. Droit et politique au XIVe siècle : Yolande de Flandre*, Paris, Ecole des Chartes, 2002, 443 p.

BUETTNER, Brigitte, "Jacques Raponde « marchand de manuscripts enluminés » " in : *Médiévales. Langue, Textes, histoire*, St.-Denis, 1988, 14, pp. 23-32.

BUNTINX, Jan, "De Audiëntie van de graven van Vlaanderen. Studie over het centraal grafelijk gerecht (c. 1330-c. 1409)" in: *Verhandelingen van de Koninklijke Academie voor Wetenschappen, Letteren en Schone Kunsten van België*, Brussel, 1949, 11, nr. 10, 458 p.

BUNTINX, Willy, "Audiëntie van de graven van Vlaanderen" in : AUGUSTYN, Beatrijs and PREVENIER, Walter (eds.), *De gewestelijke en lokale overheidsinstellingen in Vlaanderen tot 1795*, Brussel, Algemeen Rijksarchief, 1997, pp. 123-130.

CASADO ALONSO, Hilario, "Brugge, centrum van uitwisseling met Spanje" in: VANDEWALLE, André, *Hanzekooplui en Medicibankiers Brugge, wisselmarkt van Europese culturen*, Oostkamp, Stichting Kunstboek, 2002, pp. 51-57.

CASADO ALONSO, Hilario, "La nation et le quartier des Castillans de Bruges (XVe et XVIe siècles)" in: *Handelingen van het Genootschap voor Geschiedenis*, Brugge, 1996, 133, pp. 61-77.

CATRY, Michaël and **VAN DEN ABEELE**, Andries, *Makelaars en handelaars. Van Nering der makelaars naar Kamer van Koophandel in het XVIIde eeuwse Brugge*, Brugge, Kamer voor Handel en Nijverheid Brugge en het Noorden van West-Vlaanderen, 1992, 208 p.

CHARLIER, Yves, "La bataille d'Othée et sa place dans l'histoire de la principauté de Liège" in: *Bulletin de l'Institut archéologique liégois*, Liège, 1985, 97, pp. 138-278.

CHATTAWAY, Carol M., "Looking a medieval gift horse in the mouth. The role of the giving of gift objects in the definition and maintenance of the power networks of Philip the Bold" in: *Bijdragen en mededelingen betreffende de geschiedenis der Nederlanden*, Den Haag, 1999, 114, 1, pp. 1-15.

CHERRIER, Noëlle, "Les chevaux de Philippe le Hardi (1371-1404)" in: *Annales de Bourgogne*, Dijon, 1995, 67, pp. 107-145.

CHEVALIER, Anne, "Le Brabant à l'aube du XVe siècle: fêtes et solennités à la cour des ducs de la branche cadette de Bourgogne-Valois (1406-1430). Le mariage d'Antoine de Bourgogne et d'Elisabeth de Goerlitz" in: *Publications du Centre Européen d'Études Bourguignonnes (XIVe-XVIe s.)*, Dijon, 1994, 34, pp. 174-186.

CHIFFOLEAU, Jacques, *La comptabilité de l'Au-delà. Les hommes, la mort et la religion dans la région d'Avignon à la fin du Moyen Age (vers 1320- vers 1480)*, Rome, École Française de Rome, 1980, 494 p. (Collection de l'École Française de Rome, 47).

CHORLEY, Patrick, "The cloth exports of Flanders and Northern France during the thirteenth century: a luxury trade?" in: *Economic History Review*, Cambridge, 1987, 40, pp. 349-379.

CLOUGH, Cecil H., "Three Gigli of Lucca in England during the Fifteenth and Early Sixteenth Centuries: Diversification in a Family of Mercery Merchants" in: *The Ricardian. Journal of the Richard III Society*, London, 2003, 13, pp. 121-147.

CRAEYBECKX, Jan, *Un grand commerce d'importation: les vins de France aux anciens Pays-Bas (XIIIe-XVIe siècle)*, Paris, S.E.V.P.E.N., 1958, 315 p. (Ports – Routes - Trafics, 9).

DAVID, Henri, "Jeunesse de Jean, second duc de Bourgogne. Le double mariage de Cambrai" in : *Miscellanea Prof. dr. D. Roggen*, Antwerpen, Uitgeverij De Sikkel N.V., 1957, pp. 57-76.

DAVIES, Jonathan, "A 'Paper University'? The Studio lucchese, 1369-1487" in: *History of Universities*, Oxford, 1997-1999, 15, pp. 261-306.

DE BORCHGRAEVE, Christian, *Diplomaten en diplomatie onder hertog Jan zonder Vrees Impact op de Vlaamse politieke situatie*, Kortrijk-Heule, UGA, 1992, 258 p. (Standen en Landen, 115).

DE BORCHGRAEVE, Christian, *Diplomaten en diplomatie onder hertog Jan zonder Vrees Impact op de Vlaamse politieke situatie*, Rijksuniversiteit Gent (onuitgegeven licentiaatsverhandeling), 1988-1989, Volume 3-Annexes II.

DE KEYSER, Raphaël, *Het St. Donaaskapittel te Brugge (1350-1450): bijdrage tot de studie van de hogere geestelijkheid tijdens de Late Middeleeuwen*, Katholieke Universiteit Leuven, unpublished PhD dissertation, 1972, 3 vol.

DELORT, Robert, *Le commerce des fourrures en Occident à la fin du Moyen Age (vers 1300 - vers 1450)*, Rome, Ecole Française de Rome, 1978, 2 vol. (Bibliothèque des Ecoles Françaises d' Athènes et Rome, 236).

DENUCÉ, Jan, *Italiaansche koopmansgeslachten te Antwerpen in de XVIe-XVIIIe eeuwen*, Mechelen, N.V. Het Kompas, 1934, 181 p.

DE ROOVER, Raymond, "La communauté des marchands Lucquois à Bruges de 1377 à 1404" in : *Annales de la Société d'Emulation de Bruges*, Bruges, 1949, 86, pp. 23-89.

DE ROOVER, Raymond, "Les comptes communaux et la comptabilité à Bruges au XIVe siècle" in: *Finances et comptabilité urbaines du XIIIe au XVIe siècle, Colloque international, Blankenberge (1962)*, Bruxelles, Pro Civitate, 1964, pp. 86-107.

DE ROOVER, Raymond, "Le livre de comptes de Guillaume Ruyelle, changeur à Bruges (1369) " in : *Annales de la Société d'Emulation de Bruges*, Bruges, 1934, 77, pp. 15-95.

DE ROOVER, Raymond, *L'Évolution de la Lettre de Change. XIVe-XVIIIe siècles*, Paris, Librairie Armand Colin, 1953, 240 p.

DE ROOVER, Raymond, *Money, Banking and Credit in Medieval Bruges. Italian Merchant-Bankers, Lombards and Money Changers. A Study in the Origins of Banking*, Cambridge (Massachusetts), The Medieval Academy of America, 1948, 420 p.

DE ROOVER, Raymond, "Quelques considérations sur les livres de comptes de Collard de Marke précédées d'un aperçu sur les archives commerciales en Belgique" in: *Bulletin d'Études et d'Informations de l'École Supérieure de Commerce Saint-Ignace*, Anvers, 1930, 7, pp. 445-475.

DE ROOVER, Raymond, "The Bruges money market around 1400" in: *Verhandelingen van de Koninklijke Academie voor Wetenschappen, Letteren en Schone Kunsten van België*, Brussel, 1968, 29, 180 p.

DE ROOVER, Raymond, *The rise and decline of the Medici bank, 1397-1494*, Cambridge (Masachusetts), Harvard University Press, 1963, 500 p.

DE SMET, Claude, *Les emprunts de Philippe le Bon, d'après les comptes de la recette générale de l'État bourguignon*, Université de Lille, unpublished master's thesis, 1956, 215 p.

DE WINTER, Patrick M., *La Bibliothèque de Philippe le Hardi, duc de Bourgogne (1364-1404) Étude sur les manuscrits à peintures d'une collection princière à l'époque du*

« style gothique international », Paris, Centre National de la Recherche Scientifique,1985, 462 p.

DOLLINGER, Philippe, *La Hanse (XIIe-XVIIe siècles)*, Paris, Aubier, 1964, 559 p.

DUMOLYN, Jan, *De Brugse opstand van 1436-1438*, Kortrijk-Heule, U.G.A., 1997, 381 p. (Standen en landen, 101).

DUMOLYN, Jan, *Het hogere personeel van de hertogen van Bourgondië in het graafschap Vlaanderen (1419-1477)*, Universiteit Gent, unpublished PhD dissertation, 2000-2001, 5 vol.

DUMOLYN, Jan, "Population et structures professionnelles à Bruges aux XIVe et XVe siècles" in: *Revue du Nord*, Lille, 1999, 81, 329, pp. 43-64.

DUMOLYN, Jan and **HAEMERS**, Jelle, "Patterns of urban rebellion in medieval Flanders" in: *Journal of Medieval History*, 2005, 31, pp. 369-393.

FAVIER, Jean, *De l'or et des épices. Naissance de l'homme d'affaires au Moyen Âge*, Paris, Librairie Arthème Fayard, 1987, 481 p.

FAVIER, Jean, *Les finances pontificales à l'époque du Grand Schisme d'Occident 1378-1409*, Paris, Editions E. De Boccard, 1966, 853 p. (Bibliothèque des Ecoles Françaises d' Athènes et Rome, 211).

FAVIER, Jean, "Rapondi (Dino)" in: FAVIER, Jean, *Dictionnaire de la France Médiévale*, Paris, Librairie Arthème Fayard, 1993, pp. 805-806.

FAVIER, Jean, "Une ville entre deux vocations : la place d'affaires de Paris au XVe siècle" in : *Annales*, Paris, 1973, 28, pp. 1245-1279.

FERRI, Claudio, "I rapporti fra Lucca, Bruges e le Fiandre dal XV alla metà del XVI secolo, quali emergono dagli atti notarili esistenti nell' Archivio di Stato di Lucca" in : COLE, Herman, COLE, Thomas, FERRI, Claudio, LERA, Guglielmo (eds.), *Lucca e le Fiandre. Brugge 2002. Capitale Europea della Cultura*, Lucca, Istituto Storico Lucchese, 2002, pp. 9-52.

FINOT, Jules M., "Le train de maison d'une grande dame au xive siècle-Étude sur les comptes de l'hotel des sires de Cassel et particulièrement sur ceux d'Yolande de Flandre, comtesse de Bar" in : *Bulletin historique et philologique du comité des travaux historiques et scientifiques*, Paris, 1889, 1-2, pp. 176-202.

FRYDE, E.B. and **FRYDE**, M.M., "Public credit, with special references to North-Western Europe" in: POSTAN, M.M., RICH, E.E. and MILLER, Edward, *The Cambridge Economic History of Europe. Volume III. Economic organization and policies in the Middle Ages*, Cambridge, Cambridge University Press, 1971, pp. 430-553.

GAILLARD, J., *Bruges et le Franc ou leur magistrature et leur noblesse, avec des données historiques et généalogiques sur chaque famille*, Bruges, Gaillard, 1858, 2 vol.

GALOPPINI, Laura, *Mercanti toscani e Bruges nel Tardo Medioevo*, Universiteit Gent, unpublished PhD dissertation, 2002-2003, 397 p.

GEIRNAERT, Noël and **VANDEWALLE**, André (reds.), *Adornes en Jeruzalem. Internationaal leven in het 15de- en 16de-eeuwse Brugge*, Brugge, Gemeentebestuur, 1983, 143 p.

GEIRNAERT, Noël and **VANDEWALLE**, André, "Brugge en Italië" in: VERMEERSCH, Valentin (ed.), *Brugge en Europa*, Antwerpen, Mercatorfonds, 1992, pp. 183-205.

GORIS, J.A., *Étude sur les colonies marchandes méridionales (portugais, espagnols, italiens) à Anvers de 1488 à 1567*, Louvain, Librairie Universitaire, 1925, 702 p.

GREVE, Anke, "De Brugse makelaars" in: RYCKAERT, Marc and VANDEWALLE, André, *Brugge, de geschiedenis van een Europese stad,* Tielt, Lannoo, 1999, p. 73.

GUENEE, Bernard, "Les Grandes Chroniques de France. Le Roman aux roys (1274-1518)" dans: NORA, P., *Les lieux de mémoire. II. La Nation*, Paris, Gallimard, 1986, pp. 189-214.

GUENEE, Bernard, *Un meurtre, une société. L'assassinat du duc d'Orléans 23 novembre 1407*, Paris, Editions Gallimard, 1992, 350 p.

HAEGEMAN, Marc, *De anglofilie in het graafschap Vlaanderen tussen 1379 en 1435*, Kortrijk-Heule, UGA, 1988, 279 p. (Standen en Landen, 90).

HALL, Edwin, *The Arnolfini bethrothal. Medieval marriage and the enigma of van Eyck's double portrait*, Berkeley/Los Angeles (California), University of California Press, 1994, 180 p.

HEERS, Jacques, "L'exil politique, facteur de transferts économiques (Italie centrale. XIIIe-XVe siècle)" in : HEERS, Jacques (ed.), *Exil et civilisation en Italie (XIIe-XVIe siècles)*, Paris, Presses Universitaires de Nancy, 1990, pp. 9-20.

HUGHES, Muriel J., "The library of Philip the Bold and Margaret of Flanders, first Valois duke and duchess of Burgundy" in: *Journal of Medieval History*, Amsterdam, 1978, 4, pp. 145-188.

HUNT, Edwin S. and **MURRAY**, James M., *A history of business in Medieval Europe, 1200-1550*, Cambridge, Cambridge University Press, 1999, 277 p.

JORDAN, William Chester, *The great famine. Northern Europe in the early fourteenth century*, Princeton, Princeton University Press, 1996, 317 p.

KAEUPER, Richard W., *Bankers to the Crown. The Riccardi of Lucca and Edward I*, Princeton (New Jersey), Princeton University Press, 1973, 279 p.

KINTZINGER, Martin, "Sigismond, roi de Hongrie, et la croisade" in: *Annales de Bourgogne*, Dijon, 1996, 68, 3, pp. 23-33.

KUSMAN, David, "Entre noblesse, ville et clergé. Les financiers lombards dans les anciens Pays-Bas aux XIVe-Xve siècles: un état de la question" in: *Publications du Centre Européen d'Études Bourguignonnes (XIVe-XVIe s.)*, Bâle, 1999, 39, pp. 113-132.

KUSMAN, David, "Jean de Mirabello dit van Haelen (ca. 1280-1333). Haute finance et Lombards en Brabant dans le premier tiers du XIVe siècle" in: *Revue Belge de Philologie et d'Histoire*, Bruxelles, 1999, 77, 4, pp. 843-931.

LAZZARESCHI, Eugenio, "Gli statuti dei Lucchesi a Bruges e ad Anversa" in: *Ad Alessandro Luzio Gli Archivi di Stato Italiani Miscellanea di studi storici volume secondo*, Firenze, Felice Le Monnier, 1933, pp. 75-88.

LE GOFF, Jacques, *De woekeraar en de hel. Economie en religie in de middeleeuwen*, Amsterdam, Wereldbibliotheek, 1987, 119 p.

LICHTERVELDE, Pierre de, *Un Grand Commis des Ducs de Bourgogne. Jacques de Lichtervelde. Seigneur de Coolscamp*, Bruxelles, Goemaere, 1943, 340 p.

MANSI, Geraldo, *I Patrizi di Lucca Le antiche famiglie lucchesi ed i loro stemmi*, Lucca, Titania, 1996, 536 p.

MARECHAL, Joseph, *Bijdrage tot de geschiedenis van het bankwezen te Brugge*, Brugge, De Anjelier, 1955, 169 p.

MARECHAL, Joseph, "Duizend jaar Britse aanwezigheid te Brugge" in: MARECHAL, Joseph, *Europese aanwezigheid te Brugge*, Brugge, Genootschap voor Geschiedenis, 1985, pp. 13-40.

MARECHAL, Joseph, "La colonie espagnole de Bruges, du XIVe au XVIe siècle" in: *Revue du Nord*, Lille, 1953, 35, pp. 5-40.

MARECHAL, Joseph, "Le depart de Bruges des marchands étrangers (XVe et XVIe siècles)" in : MARECHAL, Joseph, *Europese aanwezigheid te Brugge. De vreemde kolonies (XIVde-XIXde eeuw)*, Brugge, Genootschap voor Geschiedenis, 1985, pp. 180-210. (Vlaamse Historische Studies, 3).

MCLEAN, P.D. and **PADGETT**, J.F., "Organizational Invention and Elite Transformation: the Birth of Partnership Systems in Renaissance Florence" in: *American Journal of Sociology*, 2006, 111, s.p.

MEEK, Christine E., *The Commune of Lucca under Pisan rule, 1342-1369,* Cambridge (Massachusetts), The Medieval Academy of America, 1980, 127 p.

MEEK, Christine E., *Lucca 1369-1400. Politics and Society in an Early Renaissance City-State*, Oxford, Oxford University Press, 1978, 424 p.

MEEK, Christine E., "Public policy and private profit: tax farming in fourteenth-century Lucca" in: BLOMQUIST, Thomas and MAZZAOUI, Maureen F. (eds.), *The "Other Tuscany" Essays in the history of Lucca, Pisa and Siena during the tirteenth, fourteenth and fifteenth centuries*, Kalamazoo (Michigan), Western Michigan University, 1994, pp. 41-82 (Studies in Medieval Culture, 34).

MERTENS, Jacques, "De woelingen te Brugge tussen 1359 en 1361" in: COPPEJANS, H. en HANSOTTE, G. (reds.), *Album Carlos Wyffels*, Brussel, Algemeen Rijksarchief, 1987, pp. 325-330.

MIROT, Léon, "Forteguerra Forteguerra et sa succession" in: *Bibliothèque de l'Ecole des Chartes*, Paris, 1935, 96, pp. 301-337.

MIROT, Léon, "La colonie lucquoise à Paris du xiiie au xve siècle" in: *Bibliothèque de l'Ecole des Chartes*, Paris, 1927, 88, pp. 50-86.

MIROT, Léon, "La société des Raponde. Dine Raponde" in : *Bibliothèque de l'Ecole des Chartes*, Paris, 1928, 89, pp. 299-389.

MIROT, Léon, "Les Cename" in : *Bibliothèque de l'Ecole des Chartes*, Paris, 1930, 91, pp. 101-160.

MIROT, Léon, "Les Isbarre, monnayeurs royaux, Augustin Isbarre" in: *Bibliothèque de l'Ecole des Chartes*, Paris, 1927, 88, pp. 275-314.

MOLÀ, Lucca, *La communità dei lucchesi a Venezia. Immigrazione e industria della seta nel tardo Medioevo*, Venezia, Istituto veneto di scienze, lettere ed arti, 1994, 354 p.

MOLLAT, Michel, "Recherches sur les finances des ducs Valois de Bourgogne" in: *Revue historique*, Paris, 1958, 219, pp. 285-321.

MOTTU-WEBER, Liliane, "Les activités des marchands-banquiers et des «entrepreneurs» lucquois à Genève aux XVI et XVII siècles" in: FANFANI, T. and MAZZEI, R., *Lucca e l'Europa degli affari. Secoli XV-XVII*, Lucca, Maria Pacini Fazzi editore, 1990, pp. 133- 146.

MUELLER, Reinhold C., *The Venetian money market. Banks, panics, and the public debt, 1200-1500*, Baltimore, Johns Hopkins University Press, 1997, 711 p.

MUND, Stéphane, "Antoine de Bourgogne, prince français et duc de Brabant (1404-1415)" in: *Revue Belge de Philologie et d'Histoire*, Bruxelles, 1998, 76, pp. 319-355.

MUNRO, John H., *Bullion flows and monetary policies in England and the Low Countries, 1350-1500*, Alderschot, Variorum, 1992, 312 p.

MUNRO, John H., "Industrial transformations in the north-west European textile trades, c. 1290-c. 1340: economic progress or economic crisis?" in: CAMPBELL, B.M.S. (ed.), *Before the Black Death. Studies in the 'crisis' of the early fourteenth century*, New York, Manchester University Press, 1991, pp. 110-148.

MUNRO, John H., "The origins of the English 'New Draperies': the resurrection of an old Flemish industry, 1270-1570" in: HARTE N.B. (ed.), *The New Draperies in the Low Countries and England, 1300-1800*, Oxford, Oxford University Press, 1997, pp. 35-127.

MUNRO, John H., *Wool, Cloth and Gold. The Struggle for Bullion in Anglo-Burgundian Trade. 1340-1478*, Bruxelles, Editions de l'Université de Bruxelles, 1973, 241 p.

MURRAY, James M., *Bruges, Cradle of Capitalism, 1280-1390*, Cambridge, Cambridge University Press, 2005, 409 p.

MURRAY, James M., "Family, marriage and moneychanging in Medieval Bruges" in: *Journal of Medieval History*, Amsterdam, 1988, 14, pp. 115-125.

MURRAY, James M., "Handels- en financiële technieken" in: VANDEWALLE, André, *Hanzekooplui en Medicibankiers. Brugge, wisselmarkt van Europese culturen*, Oostkamp, Stichting Kunstboek, 2002, pp. 107-120.

MURRAY, James M., "The Liturgy of the Count's Advent in Bruges, from Galbert to Van Eyck" in: HANAWALT, Barbara A. and REYERSON, Kathryn L. (eds.), *City and Spectacle in Medieval Europe*, Minneapolis, University of Minnesota Press, 1994, pp. 137-152 (Medieval Studies at Minnesota, 6).

MURRAY, James M., *Notaries public in Flanders in the late Middle Ages*, Ann Arbor, Xerox University Microfilms International, 1985, 404 p.

NICHOLAS, David M., "In the Pit of the Burgundian Theater State Urban Traditions and Princely Ambitions in Ghent, 1360-1420" in: HANAWALT, Barbara A. and REYERSON, Kathryn L. (eds.), *City and Spectacle in Medieval Europe*, Minneapolis, University of Minnesota Press, 1994, pp. 271-295 (Medieval Studies at Minnesota, 6).

NICHOLAS, David M., *Town and countryside. Social, economic and political tensions in fourteenth-century Flanders*, Bruges, De Tempel, 1971, 372 p.

NICHOLAS, David M., *The van Arteveldes of Ghent. The varieties of vendetta and the hero in history*, New York, E.J. Brill, 1988, pp. 120-159.

NUYTTENS, Michel and **ZOETE**, Antoine, "De Vier Leden en de Staten van Vlaanderen" in: AUGUSTYN, Beatrijs and PREVENIER, Walter (eds.), *De gewestelijke en lokale overheidsinstellingen in Vlaanderen tot 1795*, Brussel, Algemeen Rijksarchief, 1997, pp. 67-78.

ORIGO, Iris, *The merchant of Prato: Francesco di Marco Datini, 1335-1410*, Boston, David R. Godine Publisher, 1986, 415 p.

PALMER, J.J.N., "England, France, the papacy and the Flemish succession, 1361-9" in: *Journal of Medieval History*, Amsterdam, 1976, 2, pp. 339-364.

PARAVICINI, Werner, "De Hanze als Europees verschijnsel" in: VANDEWALLE, André, *Hanzekooplui en Medicibankiers. Brugge, wisselmarkt van Europese culturen*, Oostkamp, Stichting Kunstboek, 2002, pp. 11-24.

PARAVICINI, Werner, "Die Residenzen der Herzöge von Burgund, 1363-1377" in: PARAVICINI, Werner, *Menschen am Hof der Herzöge von Burgund*, Stuttgart, Jan Thorbecke Verlag, 2002, pp. 445-506.

PAVIOT, Jacques, "Brugge en Frankrijk" in: VANDEWALLE, André, *Hanzekooplui en Medicibankiers. Brugge, wisselmarkt van Europese culturen*, Oostkamp, Stichting Kunstboek, 2002, p. 43.

PAVIOT, Jacques, *La politique navale des ducs de Bourgogne, 1384-1482*, Lille, Presses Universitaires de Lille, 1995, 387 p.

PAVIOT, Jacques, "Le double portrait Arnolfini de Jan van Eyck" in: *Revue Belge d'Archéologie et d'Histoire de l'Art*, Bruxelles, 1997, 66, pp. 19-33.

PAVIOT, Jacques, *Les ducs de Bourgogne, la croisade et l'Orient (fin XIVe siècle-XVe siècle)*, Paris, Presses de l'Université de Paris-Sorbonne, 2003, 394 p.

PAVIOT, Jacques, "Les Portugais à Bruges au XVe siècle" in: *Arquivos do Centro Cultural Calouste Gulbenkian*, Paris, 1999, 38, pp. 1-122.

PAVIOT, Jacques, *Portugal et Bourgogne au XVe siècle (1384-1482) : recueil de documents extraits des archives bourguignonnes*, Paris, Centre culturel Calouste Gulbenkian, 1995, 595 p.

PAVIOT, Jacques and **CHAUNEY-BOUILLOT**, Martine (eds.), "Nicopolis 1396-1996. Actes du colloque international organisé par l'Académie des Sciences, Arts et Belles-Lettres de Dijon et le Centre National de la Recherche Scientifique réuni à Dijon, au Conseil régional de Bourgogne, le 18 octobre 1996" in : *Annales de Bourgogne*, Dijon, 1996, 68, 3, pp. 1-99.

PETTI BALBI, Giovanna, *Mercanti e nationes nelle Fiandre: i genovesi in età bassomedievale*, Pisa, ETS, 1996, 123 p. (Piccola Biblioteca Gisem, 7).

PIRENNE, Henri, *Histoire de Belgique: des origines à nos jours. Tome II*, Bruxelles, La Renaissance du Livre, 1973, 392 p.

POCQUET DU HAUT-JUSSE, B.-A., "Le retour de Nicopolis et la rançon de Jean sans Peur. Compte inédit de maitre Oudart Douay pour le duc de Bourgogne 1397-1398" in: *Annales de Bourgogne*, Dijon, 1937, 9, pp. 296-302.

POCQUET DU HAUT-JUSSE, B.-A., "Les chefs des finances ducales de Bourgogne sous Philippe le Hardi et Jean sans Peur (1363-1419)" in: *Mémoires de la Société pour l'Histoire du Droit et des Institutions des Anciens Pays Bourguignons, Comtois et Romands*, Dijon, 1937, fasc. IV, pp. 5-77.

POCQUET DU HAUT-JUSSE, B.-A., "Les dons du roi aux ducs de Bourgogne Philippe le Hardi et Jean sans Peur (1363-1419)" in: *Mémoires de la Société pour l'Histoire du Droit et des Institutions des Anciens Pays Bourguignons, Comtois et Romands*, Dijon, 1939-1941, fasc. VI et VII, pp. 113-144.

POECK, Dietrich W., "Kontorverlegung als Mittel hansischer Diplomatie" in: JÖRN, Niels, PARAVICINI, Werner and WERNICKE, Horst (eds.), *Hansekaufleute in Brügge. Teil 4: Beiträge der Internationalen Tagung in Brügge April 1996*, Frankfurt am Main, Peter Lang, 2000, pp. 33-53. (Kieler Werkstücke, Reihe D, 13).

PREVENIER, Walter, "Bevolkingscijfers en professionele strukturen der bevolking van Gent en Brugge in de 14de eeuw" in: *Album aangeboden aan Charles Verlinden ter gelegenheid van zijn dertig jaar professoraat*, Wetteren, Universa, 1975, pp. 269-303.

PREVENIER, Walter, "Financiën en boekhouding in de Bourgondische periode: nieuwe bronnen en resultaten" in: *Tijdschrift voor Geschiedenis*, Groningen, 1969, 82, pp. 469-481.

PREVENIER, Walter, "De beden in het graafschap Vlaanderen onder Filips de Stoute (1384-1404)" in: *Belgisch Tijdschrift voor Filologie en Geschiedenis*, Brussel, 1960, 38, pp. 330-365.

PREVENIER, Walter, "Les perturbations dans les relations commerciales anglo-flamandes entre 1379 et 1407. Causes de désaccord et raisons d'une réconciliation" in: *Economies et sociétés au moyen-âge. Mélanges offerts à Edouard Perroy*, Paris, Publications de la Sorbonne, 1973, pp. 471-497.

PREVENIER, Walter, "De verhouding van de Clerus tot de locale en regionale Overheid in het Graafschap Vlaanderen in de Late Middeleeuwen" in: *Bronnen voor de religieuze geschiedenis van België, Middeleeuwen en Moderne Tijden. Verslag Colloquium over Religieuze Geschiedenis*, Brussel 1967, Leuven, s.n., 1968, pp. 9-46. (Bibliothèque de la Revue d'Histoire ecclésiastique, 47).

QUICKE, Fritz, *Les Pays-Bas à la veille de la période bourguignonne (1356-1384) : contribution à l'histoire politique et diplomatique de l'Europe occidentale dans la seconde moitié du XIVe siècle*, Bruxelles, Ed. Universitaires, 1947, 458 p.

RAUZIER, Jean, *Finances et gestion d'une principauté. Le duché de Bourgogne de Philippe le Hardi 1364-1384*, Paris, Ministère de l'économie et des finances, 1996, 766 p.

RAUZIER, Jean, "Les approvisionnements de la cour de Philippe le Hardi, duc de Bourgogne (1371-1384)" in: *Annales de Bourgogne*, Dijon, 1998, 70, pp. 5-29.

RENOUARD, Yves, "Compagnies mercantiles lucquoises au service des papes d'Avignon" in: RENOUARD, Yves, *Études d'histoire médiévale*, Paris, S.E.V.P.E.N., 1968, t. II, pp. 825-831. (Bibliothèque Générale de l'École Pratique des Hautes Études, 6).

RENOUARD, Yves, *Les hommes d'affaires italiens du Moyen Age*, Paris, Librairie Armand Colin, 1968, 336 p.

RENOUARD, Yves, *Les relations des papes d'Avignon et des compagnies commerciales et bancaires de 1316 à 1378*, Paris, Editions E. De Boccard, 1941, 694 p.

ROGGHÉ, Paul, "Gent in de XIVe en XVe eeuw" in: *Appeltjes van het Meetjesland*, Maldegem, 1968, 19, pp. 227-304.

ROGGHÉ, Paul, "Simon de Mirabello in Vlaanderen" in: *Appeltjes van het Meetjesland*, Maldegem, 1958, 9, pp. 5-56.

RYCKAERT, Marc and **VANDEWALLE**, André (eds.), *Brugge. De Geschiedenis van een Europese Stad*, Tielt, Lannoo, 1999, 224 p.

SABBE, Jacques, *Vlaanderen in opstand 1323-1328*, Brugge, Marc Van de Wiele, 1992, 132 p. (Vlaamse Historische Studies, 7).

SABBE, Jacques, "Yolande van Vlaanderen, gravin van Bar en vrouwe van Cassel, en het huis de « Casselberg » in Brugge (1373)" in: *Handelingen van het Genootschap voor Geschiedenis*, Brugge, 2001, 138, 1-2, pp. 33-55.

SARNOWSKY, Jürgen, "Der Fall Thomas Schenkendorf. Rechtliche und diplomatische Probleme um die Königsberger Grosschäfferei des Deutschen Ordens" in: *Jahrbuch für die Geschichte Mittel- und Ostdeutschlands*, München, 1995, 43, pp. 187-275.

SCHNERB, Bertrand, *Les Armagnacs et les Bourguignons. La maudite guerre*, Paris, Librairie Académique Perrin, 1988, 306 p.

SCHNERB, Bertrand, "Un aspect de la politique financière de Jean sans Peur: la question des dépenses de guerre" in: *Publications du Centre Européen d'Études Bourguignonnes (XIVe-XVIe s.)*, Dijon, 1987, 27, pp. 113-128.

SCHNERB, Bertrand, *Jean Sans Peur. Le prince meurtrier*, Paris, Éditions Payot & Rivages, 2005, 824 p.

SCHOUTEET, Albert, "Un emprunt de Louis de Male aux Lombards en 1368" in: *Handelingen van het Genootschap voor Geschiedenis gesticht onder de benaming Société d'Émulation te Brugge*, Bruges, 1954, 91, pp. 160-162.

SLOOTMANS, Cornelius J. F., *Paas- en Koudemarkten te Bergen op Zoom 1365-1565*, Tilburg, Stichting Zuidelijk Historisch Contact, 1985, 3 vol. (Bijdragen tot de geschiedenis van het Zuiden van Nederland, 65).

SMEYERS, Maurits, "Lubert Hautscilt, abt van de Brugse Eeckhoutabdij (1393-1417). Over handschriften, planeten en de toekomst van Vlaanderen" in: *Mededelingen van de Koninklijke Academie voor Wetenschappen, Letteren en Schone Kunsten van België*, Brussel, 1995, 55, nr. 1, pp. 40-104.

SOENS, Tim, *De rentmeesters van de graaf van Vlaanderen Beheer en beheerders van het grafelijk domein in de late middeleeuwen*, Brussel, Paleis der Academiën, 2002, 370 p. (Verhandelingen van de Koninklijke Vlaamse Academie van België voor Wetenschappen en Kunsten, Nieuwe reeks, nr. 9).

SOSSON, Jean-Pierre, *Les travaux publics de la ville de Bruges XIVe-XVe siècles Les matériaux. Les hommes*, Bruxelles, Crédit Communal de Belgique, 1977, 375 p. (Collection Histoire Pro Civitate, série in-8°, n° 48).

SPUFFORD, Peter, *Handbook of medieval exchange*, London, Royal Historical Society, 1986, 376 p.

SPUFFORD, Peter, *Money and its use in Medieval Europe*, Cambridge, Cambridge University Press, 1988, 467 p.

STABEL, Peter, "De gewenste vreemdeling. Italiaanse kooplieden en stedelijke maatschappij in het laat-middeleeuws Brugge" in: *Jaarboek voor Middeleeuwse Geschiedenis*, Hilversum, 2001, 4, pp. 189-221.

STABEL, Peter, "De wisselbrief: een internationaal betaalmiddel" in: VANDEWALLE, André, *Hanzekooplui en Medicibankiers. Brugge, wisselmarkt van Europese culturen*, Oostkamp, Stichting Kunstboek, 2002, p. 121.

STABEL, Peter, "Kooplieden in de Stad" in: VANDEWALLE, André, *Hanzekooplui en Medicibankiers. Brugge, wisselmarkt van Europese culturen*, Oostkamp, Stichting Kunstboek, 2002, pp. 85-96.

STABEL, Peter, "Venice and the Low Countries: commercial contacts and intellectual inspirations" in: AIKEMA, Bernard and BROWN, Beverly Louise (eds.), *Renaissance Venice and the North. Croscurrents in the time of Bellini, Dürer and Titian*, New York, Rizzoli, 1999, pp. 31-43.

STROHM, Reinhard, *Music in Late Medieval Bruges*, Oxford, Clarendon Press, 1985, 273 p.

TEBRAKE, William H., *A Plague of Insurrection. Popular Politics and Peasant Revolt in Flanders, 1323-1328*, Philadelphia, University of Pennsylvania Press, 1993, 170 p.

THIELEMANS, Marie-Rose, *Bourgogne et Angleterre. Relations politiques et économiques entre les Pays-Bas bourguignons et l'Angleterre. 1435-1467*, Bruxelles, Presses Universitaires de Bruxelles, 1966, 641 p.

TREXLER, Richard C., *The Spiritual Power. Republican Florence under Interdict*, Leiden, E.J. Brill, 1974, 208 p.

UYTTEBROUCK, André, *Le gouvernement du duché de Brabant au bas moyen âge (1355-1430)*, Bruxelles, Editions de l'Université de Bruxelles, 1975, 2 vol.

VAN BIERVLIET, Luc, "De Brugse Volto Santo" in: *Handelingen van het Genootschap voor Geschiedenis*, Brugge, 1993, 130, nr. 3, pp. 253-260.

VANDECANDELAERE, Isabel, *De lakennijverheid te Wervik : een prosopografisch overzicht (1382-1470)*, Universiteit Gent, unpublished master's thesis, 2001-2002, 189 p.

VAN DEN ABEELE, Andries, *Het Ridderlijk Gezelschap van de Witte Beer. Steekspelen in Brugge tijdens de late Middeleeuwen*, Brugge, Uitgeverij Walleyn, 2000, 160 p.

VAN DEN BROECK, Peter, *De diplomaten onder de regering van Filips de Stoute als graaf van Vlaanderen (1384-1404): hun bevoegdheid, opleiding en sociale achtergrond.*, Rijksuniversiteit Gent, unpublished master's thesis, 1978-1979, s.p.

VAN DEN NESTE, Evelyne, *Tournois, joutes, pas d'armes dans les villes de Flandre à la fin du Moyen Age (1300-1486)*, Paris, École des Chartes, 1996, 411 p. (Mémoires et Documents de l'École des Chartes, 47).

VANDERMAESEN, Maurice and **VANDEWOUDE**, Katrien, "Het hof der graven van Vlaanderen en hertogen van Bourgondië (11de eeuw-1482)" in: AUGUSTYN, Beatrijs and PREVENIER, Walter (eds.), *De gewestelijke en lokale overheidsinstellingen in Vlaanderen tot 1795*, Brussel, Algemeen Rijksarchief, 1997, pp. 27-43.

VAN DER WEE, Herman, "L'échec de la réforme monétaire de 1407 en Flandre, vu par les marchands italiens de Bruges" in : *Studi in onore de Amintore Fanfani III Medioevo*, Milano, A. Giuffrè, 1962, pp. 578-589.

VAN DER WEE, Herman, *The Growth of the Antwerp Market and the European Economy (fourteenth-sixteenth centuries)*, The Hague, Martinus Nijhoff, 1963, 3 vol.

VAN DER WEE, Herman, "Industrial dynamics and the process of urbanization and de-urbanization from the late middle ages to the eighteenth century" in: VAN DER WEE, Herman (ed.) *The Rise and Decline of Urban Industries in Italy and the Low Countries (late middle ages-early modern times)*, Leuven, Leuven University Press, 1988, pp. 307-381.

VANDEWALLE, André, "De Brugse stadsmagistraat en de deelname van de ambachten aan het bestuur, 14de-15de eeuw" in: PREVENIER, Walter and AUGUSTYN, Beatrijs (reds.), *De Vlaamse instellingen tijdens het Ancien Régime: recent onderzoek in nieuw perspectief. Symposium georganiseerd te Brugge op 18 mei 1998*, Brussel, Algemeen Rijksarchief, 1999, pp. 27-40. (Miscellanea Archivistica Studia, 111).

VANDEWALLE, André, "De vreemde naties in Brugge" in: VANDEWALLE, André, *Hanzekooplui en Medicibankiers. Brugge, wisselmarkt van Europese culturen*, Oostkamp, Stichting Kunstboek, 2002, pp. 27-42.

VANDEWOUDE, Katrien, *De hofhouding van de laatste Vlaamse graaf en de eerste Bourgondische hertog (ca. 1380-1404). Bijdrage tot de kennis van de sociale structuur van het Hotel van Filips de Stoute als centrale instelling*, Rijksuniversiteit Gent (onuitgegeven licentiaatsverhandeling), 1977-1978, s.p.

VAN GERVEN, Jan, "Antwerpen in de veertiende eeuw. Kleine stad zonder toekomst of opkomend handelscentrum?" in: *Belgisch Tijdschrift voor Filologie en Geschiedenis*, Brussel, 1998, 76, pp. 907-938.

VAN HOUTTE, J.A., *De geschiedenis van Brugge*, Tielt, Lannoo, 1982, 606 p.

VAN NIEUWENHUYSEN, Andrée, "La comptabilité d'un receveur de Philippe le Hardi" in: *Hommage au Prof. P. Bonenfant (1899-1965) : études d'histoire médiévale dédiées à sa mémoire par les anciens élèves de son séminaire à l'université libre de Bruxelles*, Wetteren, Universa, 1965, pp. 409-419.

VAN NIEUWENHUYSEN, Andrée, *Les finances du duc de Bourgogne Philippe le Hardi (1384-1404). Economie et Politique*, Bruxelles, ULB, 1984, 551 p.

VAN NIEUWENHUYSEN, Andrée, *Les finances du duc de Bourgogne Philippe le Hardi (1384-1404). Le montant des ressources*, Bruxelles, Académie Royale de Belgique, 1990, 309 p.

VAN NIEUWENHUYSEN, Andrée, "Le transport et le change des espèces dans la recette générale de toutes les finances de Philippe le Hardi" in : *Revue Belge de Philologie et d'Histoire*, Bruxelles, 1957, 35, pp. 55-65.

VAN NIEUWENHUYSEN, Andrée, "L'organisation financière des Etats du duc de Bourgogne Philippe le Hardi" in : *Acta Historica Bruxellensia*, Bruxelles, 1967, 1, pp. 215-247.

VAN ROMPAEY, Jan, "De Bourgondische staatsinstellingen" in: *Algemene Geschiedenis der Nederlanden. 4 Middeleeuwen*, Haarlem, Fibula-Van Dishoeck, pp. 136-155.

VAN ROMPAEY, Jan, "De Grote Raad van de hertogen van Bourgondië en het Parlement van Mechelen" in: *Verhandelingen van de Koninklijke Academie voor Wetenschappen, Letteren en Schone Kunsten van België*, Brussel, 1973, 35, nr. 73, 576 p.

VAN UYTVEN, Raymond, "De overige handelsgoederen te Brugge" in: VANDEWALLE, André, *Hanzekooplui en Medicibankiers. Brugge, wisselmarkt van Europese culturen*, Oostkamp, Stichting Kunstboek, 2002, pp. 73-82.

VAN UYTVEN, Raymond, "Splendour or Wealth: Art and Economy in the Burgundian Netherlands" in: *Transactions of the Cambridge Bibliographical Society*, Cambridge, 1992, vol. 10, part 2, pp. 101-124.

VAN UYTVEN, Raymond, "Stages of economic decline, late medieval Bruges" in: DUVOSQUEL, JEAN-MARIE and THOEN, Erik, *Peasants and townsmen in medieval*

Europe. Studia in honorem Adriaan Verhulst, Gent, Snoeck-Ducaju & Zoon, 1995, pp. 259-269. (Belgisch Centrum voor Landelijke Geschiedenis, 114).

VAN WERVEKE, Hans, "De Vlaamsche munthervorming van 1389-1390" in: *Nederlandsche Historiebladen*, Antwerpen, 1938, 1, pp. 336-347.

VAUGHAN, Richard, *De Bourgondiërs*, Haarlem, Fibula-Van Dishoeck, 1976, 248 p.

VAUGHAN, Richard, *John the Fearless. The growth of Burgundian power*, London, Longmans, 1966, 320 p.

VAUGHAN, Richard, *Philip the Bold. The Formation of the Burgundian State*, London, Longmans, 1962, 278 p.

VAUGHAN, Richard, *Philip the Good. The Apogee of Burgundy*, London, Longmans, 1970, 456 p.

WALSH, R.J., *Charles the Bold and Italy (1467-1477). Politics and Personnel*, Liverpool, Liverpool University Press, 2005, 478 p.

WYFFELS, Carlos, "Nieuwe gegevens betreffende een XIIIde eeuwse «democratische» stedelijke opstand: de Brugse «Moerlemaye» (1280-1281)" in: *Handelingen van de Koninklijke Commissie voor Geschiedenis,* Brussel, 1966, 132, pp. 37-142.

WYFFELS, Carlos, "De Vlaamse hanzen opnieuw belicht" in: *Academiae analecta*, Brussel, 1991, 53, pp. 8-13.

ZOETE, Antoine, "De beden in het graafschap Vlaanderen onder de hertogen Jan zonder Vrees en Filips de Goede (1405-1467)" in: *Verhandelingen van de Koninklijke Academie voor Wetenschappen, Letteren en Schone Kunsten van België*, Brussel, 1995, 56, nr. 149, 275 p.

ZOETE, Antoine, *Organisatie en betekenis van de beden in het graafschap Vlaanderen onder de hertogen Jan zonder Vrees en Filips de Goede (1405-1467)*, Rijksuniversiteit Gent, unpublished PhD dissertation, 1989-1990, 2 vol.

MONETARY NOTE

Equivalencies between late medieval coins were subject to constant change. For the precise rates of exchange at a given time and place, see P. SPUFFORD, *Handbook of medieval exchange*, London, Royal Historical Society, 1986, 376 p. In late medieval Europe, a dichotomy existed in the functions of money. On the one hand, there was the money of account, which was the measure of value used for accounting purposes, on the other hand the actual coins, which were the medium of exchange.

POUND GROOT (lb. gr.): money of account used in Flanders, divided into shillings and pennies. 1 pound equals 20 shillings (s.), 1 shilling equals 12 pennies (p.), 1 pound thus equals 240 pennies.

POUND PARISIS (lb. par.): money of account, divided into shillings and pennies in the same way as the pound groot. A distinction must be made between the Flemish pound parisis, which was often used in the Burgundian administration and which was worth 20 pennies groot, and the royal French pound parisis, which was worth 45 pennies groot.

POUND TOURNOIS (lb. t.): money of account, divided into shillings and pennies in the same way as the pound groot and the pound parisis. 1 pound tournois was worth 36 pennies groot.

FRANC: gold coin, struck by the French kings from 1360 onwards.

ECU: gold coin, struck by the French kings from 1385 onwards. Ecus à la couronne were struck from 1388 to 1475.

NOBLE: gold coin, struck by John the Fearless from 1409 onwards.

FLORIN : gold coin, struck in Florence from 1252 to 1533.

DUCAT : gold coin, struck in Venice from 1284 to 1840.

MOUTON D'OR: gold coin, struck by the French kings from 1311 onwards.

GLOSSARY

AIDE: Subvention of feudal origin imposed by the prince after the approval of his subjects and initially requested on very precize occasions (marriage of the oldest daughter, knighthood of the oldest son, crusade or ransom for the ruler).

ANNUITY: Income from a capital investment paid in a series of regular payments.

ANZIANI: Most important council in Lucchese city politics, dealing with the city's daily governance.

ARMAGNACS: Orleanist party in the French Civil War at the beginning of the fifteenth century, opponents of the Bourguignons.

ASSIGNMENT: Written order received by an officer to pay a certain sum.

BAILIFF: Judicial and police officer charged with the defence of the prince's interests and the prosecution of infractions.

BALÌA: Commission to deal with specific political problems, common in Italian city-politics.

BILL OF EXCHANGE: Draft of one party upon another, by which the first party, the drawer, requests the second party, the drawee or payer, residing in another place to pay to a designated person, or to his order, on a fixed date or on demand, a specified sum of money, the value of which the drawer has received from the remitter or creditor.

BOURGUIGNONS: Burgundian party in the French Civil War at the beginning of the fifteenth century, opponents of the Armagnacs.

BROCADE: Heavy silk fabric, worked with gold or silver wire.

CAHORSINS: Financiers, allowed by the authorities to keep loan tables and granting loans on interest in return for a pledge.

CAMERA APOSTOLICA: Institution in charge of papal finances.

CHAMBRE AUX DENIERS: Office, consisting of the maître d'hôtel, the maître de la chambre aux deniers, a control officer and two clerks, who arranged the hôtel's daily expenses.

CHAMBRE DES COMPTES: Institution charged with the control of all the principality's financial matters

CHAMBERLAIN: Initially one of the domestic functions in the princely household, became a rather honorary title granted to confidants for services rendered.

CHANCELLOR: Head of the ducal administration and the duke's right-hand man, supervising all aspects of ducal government.

CONSERVATORES LIBERTATIS: Balìa to deal with the city's defence, peace and well-being established in Lucca in 1376 and abolished in 1385.

CONSUL: As the yearly elected head of a foreign merchants' nation the official representative of his home town and the nation members vis-à-vis the local authorities, often administering justice in criminal and commercial cases between nation members as well.

CONTADO: countryside surrounding Italian cities

CONTO: account

DAMASK: A fabric of silk, linen, wool or cotton with a reversible pattern woven into it.

DÉCHARGE: Receipt by which a receiver general acknowledged having received a sum from a certain receiver at a given time, owed to a third party (a creditor of the duke or another receiver). The creditor was to hand this document over to the receiver, who was bound to pay the amount.

ESTATES: Representation of the three estates (the nobility, the clergy and the cities). Particularly in Brabant the defendor of the principality's autonomy.

FACTOR: Salaried representative of a merchant company.

GONFALONIERE DI GIUSTIZIA: Highest functionary in Lucchese city politics, presiding the anziani.

HOUSEHOLD: Group of dignitaries, officers or others charged with domestic services to the duke, the duchess or the duke's oldest son.

LOMBARDS: Italian financiers, allowed by the authorities to keep loan tables and granting loans on interest in return for a pledge.

MAÎTRE DE LA CHAMBRE AUX DENIERS: Officer responsible for the revenues and expenses made by the household.

MAÎTRE D'HÔTEL : Initially the officer in charge of the princely household, became a rather honorary title granted to confidants for services rendered.

MEMBERS OF FLANDERS : The cities of Bruges, Ghent, Ypres and the Franc of Bruges, whose representatives represented the whole county of Flanders.

NATION: More or less formal association of merchants originating from the same city or region and trading in the same place. Most of the nations were directed by a consul, held meetings in a nation house and celebrated mass in one of their host city's churches.

OCTROI: Tax to be paid by the Flemish cities to their count for the right to impose excise taxes.

OPERARI: Yearly elected responsibles for financial matters in the Lucchese nation in Bruges.

PACIERI: Yearly elected responsibles for ceremonial matters in the Lucchese nation in Bruges.

PAGATORE: Member of the Lucchese nation in Bruges standing surety for another member.

SENDAL: Light silk fabric similar to a veil.

SOUVEREIGN BAILIFF: Officer charged with the control of the bailiffs' activities and with general police tasks.

TRANSPORT TAX: Annual tax owed by the Flemings to their count, obtained by the latter from the French king in 1312 for the cession of the castellanies of Walloon Flanders.

TREASURER: Officer in charge of the city's financial policy in the urban administration. Officer responsible for the ratification of expenses in the ducal administration. The functions of ducal treasurer and receiver general of all finances have sometimes been entrusted to the same person.

GENEALOGY: GUIDO RAPONDI

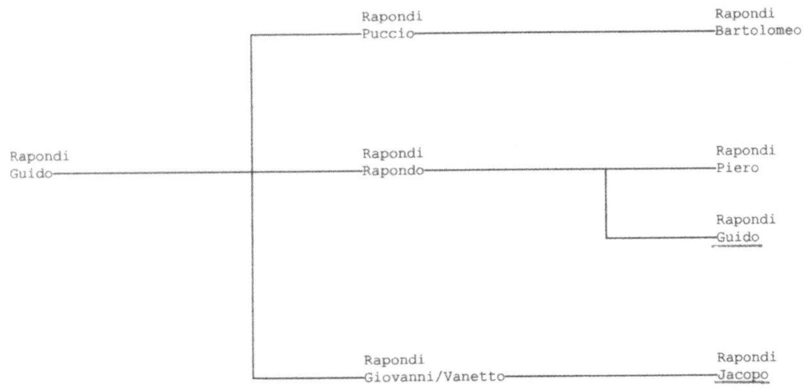

GENEALOGY: JACOPO DI GIOVANNI RAPONDI

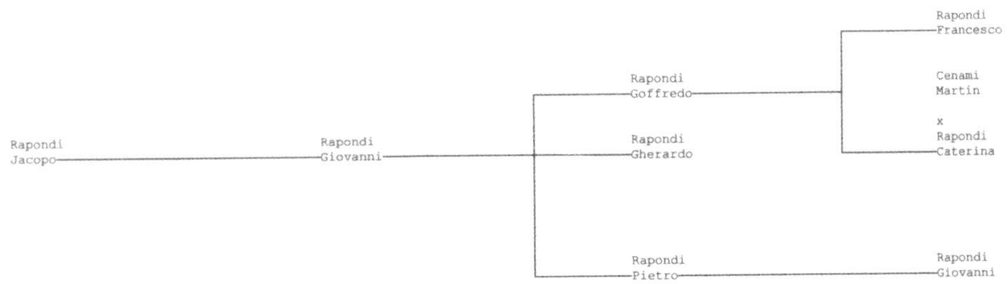

GENEALOGY: GUIDO DI RAPONDO RAPONDI

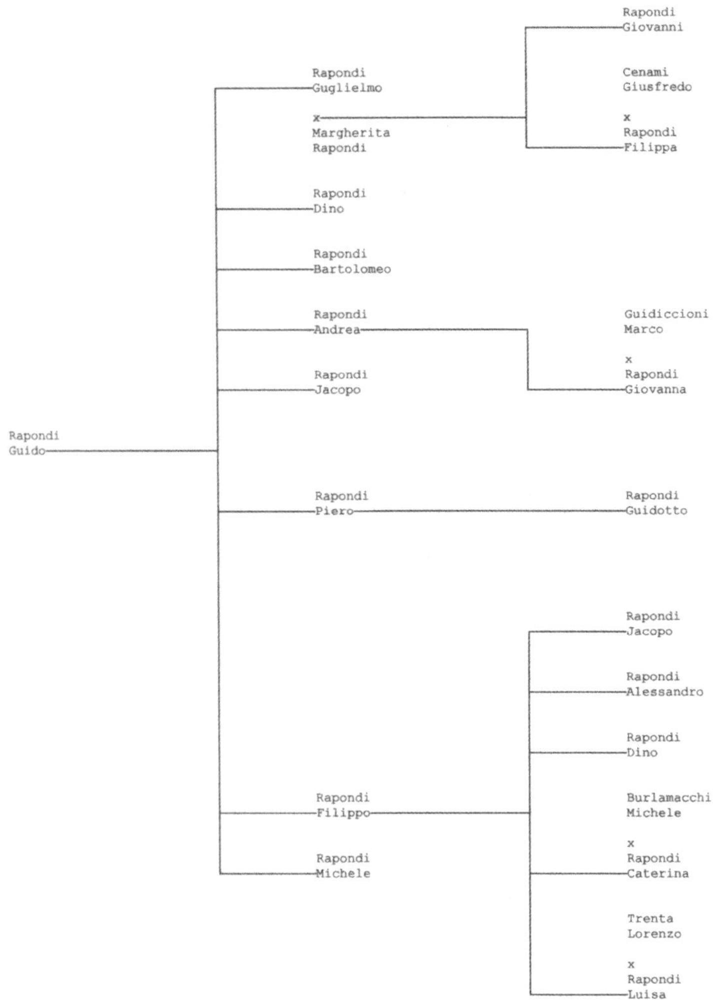

GRAPH 1: PAYMENTS MADE BY BRUGES TRANSFERRED BY THE RAPONDI RECORDED IN THE BRUGES CITY ACCOUNTS

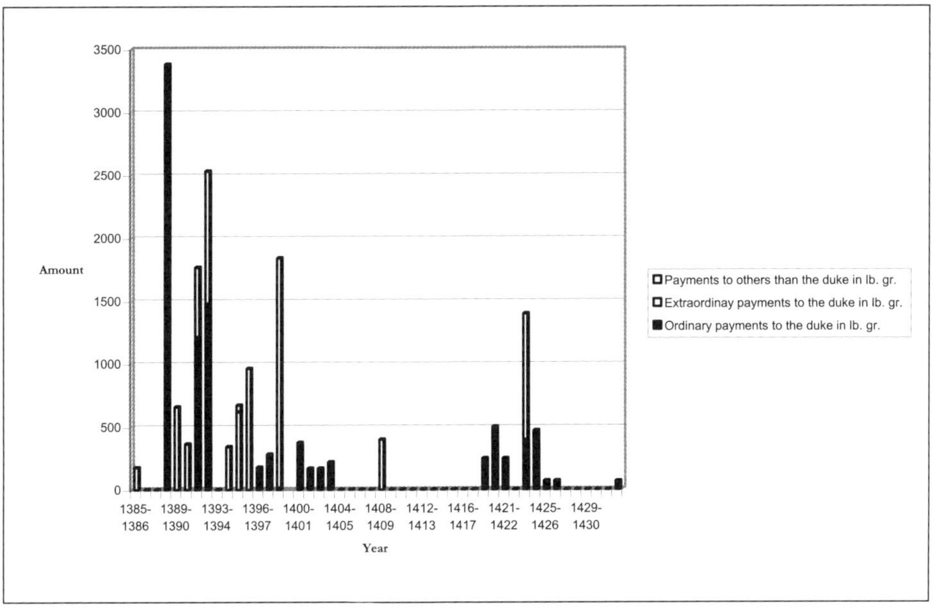

GRAPH 2: LOANS GRANTED BY THE RAPONDI TO BRUGES RECORDED IN THE BRUGES CITY ACCOUNTS

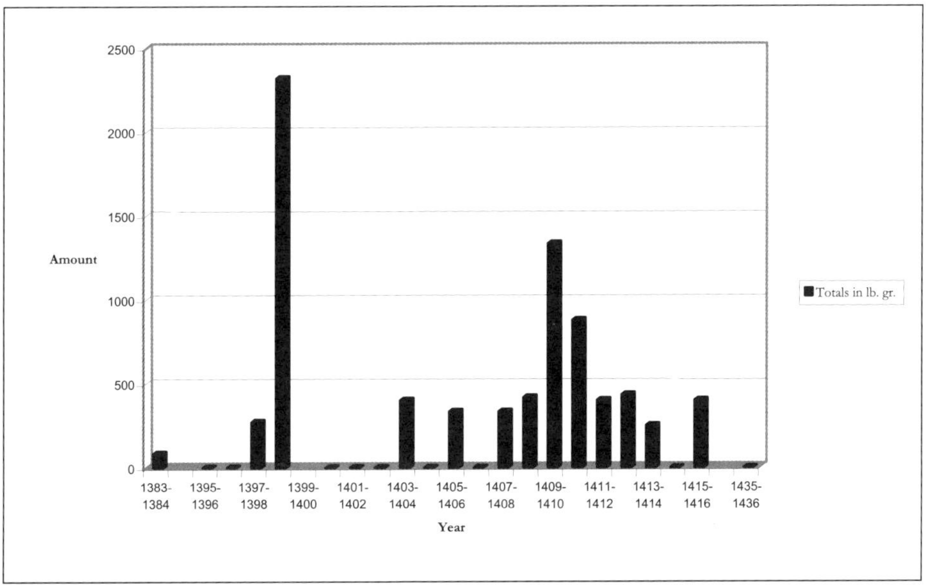

GRAPH 3: REPAYMENTS TO THE RAPONDI BECAUSE OF LOANS RECORDED IN THE DUCAL ACCOUNTS, 1405-1415

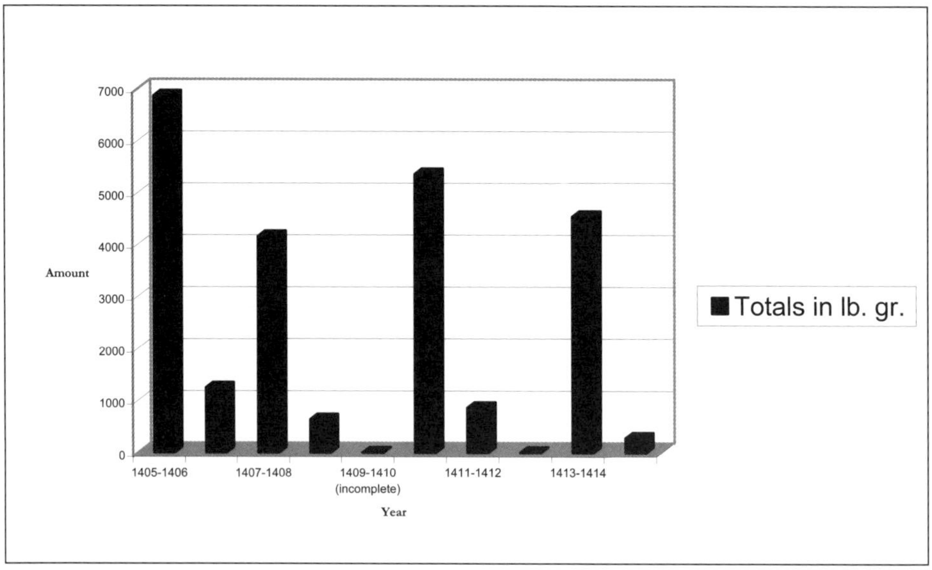

DINO RAPONDI'S TOMB IN THE SAINT DONATIAN'S CHURCH (BRUGES, PUBLIC LIBRARY, MS. 449, I-II, P. 89)

Index